MODEL JURY INSTRUCTIONS

Business Torts Litigation

Third Edition

Business Torts Litigation
Subcommittee on Jury Instructions

SECTION OF LITIGATION
AMERICAN BAR ASSOCIATION

Business Torts Litigation Committee
Paula Boggs, Seattle, Washington, Co-Chair, 1995–1996
Paul H. Dawes, San Francisco, California, Co-Chair, 1995–1996

Subcommittee on Jury Instructions
M. Stanford Blanton, Birmingham, AL, Editor
David B. Hamilton, Baltimore, MD, Editor

Contributing Authors
Chapter One: Benson Everett Legg and Neal C. Baroody, Baltimore, Maryland
Chapter Two: Gary C. Crapster, Dallas, Texas
Chapter Three: Mark E. Saliman, Denver, Colorado
Chapter Four: Michael P. Lynn, Dallas, Texas
Chapter Five: Edward F. Mannino and Marguerite S. Walsh, Philadelphia, Pennsylvania
Chapter Six: M. Stanford Blanton, Birmingham, Alabama and Daniel C. Johnson, Orlando, Florida
Chapter Seven: Robert E. Schaberg, San Francisco, California; Jack N. Sibley, Atlanta, Georgia and Edward Henderson, Jr., Atlanta, Georgia
Chapter Eight: Daniel J. Gleason, Boston, Massachusetts and Michelle J. Lipton, Boston, Massachusetts

Cover design by Emily Friel

Printed in the United States of America.

00 99 98 97 96   5 4 3 2 1

Library of Congress Cataloging-in-Publication Data

Model jury instructions: business torts litigation : a project of the Business Torts Litigation Committee, Subcommittee on Jury Instructions, Section of Litigation, American Bar Association. — 3rd ed.
p. cm.
Includes bibliographical references.
ISBN 1-57073-336-8 (pbk.)
1. Instructions to juries—United States—Forms. 2. Competition, Unfair—United States. 3. Tort liability of corporations—United States. I. American Bar Association. Business Torts Litigation Committee. Subcommittee on Jury Instructions.
KF8984.A65M64 1996
347.73'0758—dc20
[347.307758]   96-19560
CIP

Discounts are available for books ordered in bulk. Special consideration is given to state bars, CLE programs, and other bar-related organizations. Inquire at Publications Planning & Marketing, American Bar Association, 750 North Lake Shore Drive, Chicago, Illinois 60611.

Contents

Chapter One
Inducing Breach of Contract

Chapter Two
Interference with Prospective Advantage

Chapter Three
Injurious Falsehood

Chapter Four
Confusion of Source

Chapter Five
Racketeer Influenced and Corrupt Organizations (RICO) Act

Chapter Six
Fraud, Misrepresentation, Nondisclosure, and Concealment

Chapter Seven
Breach of Fiduciary Duties

Chapter Eight
Misappropriation of Trade Secrets

Foreword

When I began practicing law, there were only a few "how to" books available to the litigator in the business tort area. Learned treatises on tort and contract law existed. None, however, adequately addressed the burgeoning hybrid field of business torts.

When conducting research, the new associate typically canvassed the office to see if any of the more experienced litigators had ever tried a business tort case. The search usually resulted in a trip to the closed files to retrieve dusty pleadings and opinions yellowed with age.

To remedy this situation, the American Bar Association Litigation Section's Business Torts Litigation Committee created, in 1980, a four-chapter volume of model jury instructions for use in trial. The publication of the first edition coincided with the release of the fourth volume of the *Restatement (Second) of Torts,* and was meant to supplement and illuminate the limited treatment of business torts provided in the *Restatement.* To make the project more manageable, the scope of the book was limited to the most common business torts of the time: interference with contract, inducing breach of contract, confusion of source, injurious falsehood, and interference with prospective advantage. Lawyers across the country found the volume to be an invaluable reference work for exploring the fundamentals of business torts.

The eight years following the publication of the first edition brought substantive changes in the law, and it became evident that a second edition to the Model Jury Instructions was necessary. The second edition not only brought current the law underlying the instructions, but detailed the development of new areas of business tort litigation, most notably that under the Racketeer Influenced and Corrupt Organizations (RICO) statute. RICO was enacted in 1970, but the first wave of civil RICO cases did not hit the courts until the 1980s. These cases culminated in the Supreme Court's decision in *Sedima v. Imrex, Co.,* 473 U.S. 479 (1985). The second edition was able to cull the diverse rulings of the courts across the country and provide a concise set of jury instructions.

One of the most useful features of the second edition was the fourteen-page primer of Peter B. Maggs, a professor of law at the University of Illinois at Urbana-Champaign. This easy-to-understand introduction provided a thumbnail sketch of each business tort, and enabled a lawyer to plead a cause of action with the jury instructions in mind.

I had the privilege of updating Chapter One of the second edition, Inducing Breach of Contract. In this endeavor, I was helped by the fellow lawyers in my firm. Special recognition is also due to Gary C. Crapster and Michael P. Lynn, who dedicated countless hours to organizing and editing the second edition.

Work on the current edition of this book, which began nearly six years ago, was motivated by a desire to update the Model Jury Instructions and provide a more comprehensive treatment of the authorities for each instruction.[1] The third edition provides a more global citation base and is, therefore, a more authoritative reference manual. In addition, an effort was made to expand the book to include new "hot" areas of business tort practice. Thus, chapters on fraud, breach of fiduciary duty, and misappropriation of trade secrets have been added.

I believe that business lawyers will find this current edition to be an invaluable library addition. The Business Torts Litigation Committee members are to be commended for their hard work and fine scholarship.

Benson Everett Legg
United States District Court Judge

[1]In 1992, the Business Torts Committee published the Business Torts Committee Desk Book. The third edition of the Model Jury Instructions: Business Torts Litigation provides an excellent companion to the Desk Book.

Preface and Acknowledgments to Third Edition

In the increasingly complex world of business litigation, lawyers, judges, and, ultimately, juries are required to weave difficult concepts together with even more complicated factual situations to arrive at a just result for the litigants. The first two editions of this book were written to assist the reader in framing logical and understandable jury instructions in a wide variety of jurisdictions. This third edition is an effort to continue in the tradition of the first two. This edition not only revises and updates chapters that have appeared before, but expands the scope of the first two editions by adding chapters on misrepresentation and fraud, breach of fiduciary duty, and misappropriation of trade secrets.

As with the two previous editions of this book, every effort has been made to provide current citations of authority for each jury instruction, as well as alternative instructions when the law varies jurisdiction by jurisdiction. The instructions and the supporting citations will provide the reader with an excellent starting place from which to investigate the nuances of a particular jurisdiction, and the instructions themselves should provide an excellent model from which instructions appropriate to a particular issue can be crafted.

No acknowledgments for this edition would be appropriate without first recognizing those who were responsible for the first and second editions of this book. Thus, the preface and acknowledgment pages for the previous editions of this book follow. Because the authors of the previous editions have revised and updated chapters for this book, their contributions to this publication are doubly noted. The authors of the chapters first appearing in the third edition have upheld the standard of excellence established in the earlier editions and share the editor's deep gratitude.

This third edition, including the addition of the new chapters, began at the suggestion of Gary Crapster, Co-Chair of the

Business Torts Committee, and took nearly six years to complete. The editor and chair of the subcommittee responsible for the organization, research, and editing of the book was M. Stanford Blanton, who acknowledges with grateful appreciation the efforts of his co-editor, David B. Hamilton of Baltimore, Maryland, as well as Debra S. Rogers and Lee Ann Pounds, without whose efforts this edition would not have been possible.

M. Stanford Blanton
Birmingham, Alabama

David B. Hamilton
Baltimore, Maryland

Preface and Acknowledgments to Second Edition

The expanding impact of business torts litigation on the relationships of parties conducting business in the United States is readily apparent from the current wave of RICO litigation and major jury verdicts in cases such as *Pennzoil v. Texaco.* The first edition of this book, published in early 1980, was widely recognized as a much-needed reference for litigants and jurists. The first edition was published just after the release of the fourth volume of the *Restatement (Second) of Torts,* and there have been substantial changes in the law during the last eight years. For this reason, the Business Torts Litigation Committee of the Section of Litigation decided to publish this new edition, which both updates the legal citations and revises the jury charges where necessary.

The law varies greatly from state to state on the subjects covered in certain chapters, while in other chapters it is more uniform. For example, significant differences exist from state to state with regard to the elements and proof of interference with contractual relations and interference with prospective business advantage covered in Chapters One and Two. On the other hand, the tort of injurious falsehood has received a more uniform treatment, as reflected in Chapter Three. When the law varies significantly from state to state, the authors have attempted to include citations to major authorities in each regional section of the country. These citations provide an excellent starting point for follow-up research by practitioners seeking the latest cases in any specific state. Although not every instruction in the book is followed by lengthy string citations, the citations discussed in the text of each chapter, along with supplemental research, should facilitate the analysis of the law in any particular state.

Many practitioners have been anxious for the publication of the RICO chapter. It is an important and welcome addition to the book, but the potential for legislation still exists, which may require revisions to the model jury charges. The authors have noted the areas that may be affected by legislation proposed as late as the fall of 1987.

The jury charges on damages vary so greatly from state to state that those charges included with the common law business torts should be treated primarily as a useful guide. Particular care should be taken to follow the law on damages of the applicable state. The most significant changes in the law have involved substantive areas other than damages, and the general instructions on damages as they appeared in the first edition have not been substantially revised.

Acknowledgments for the efforts of lawyers who have made this publication possible must begin with recognition of those who prepared the first edition of the book. Indeed, the book has not been completely rewritten in every respect; rather, it has been updated and revised as necessary. For this reason, the preface and acknowledgment page to the first edition follows.

This revised edition began at the suggestion of George Bramblett of Dallas, Texas, Chair of the Business Torts Committee in 1984. Edward Mannino of Philadelphia, Pennsylvania, became Co-Chair of the Business Torts Committee the next year and devoted significant personal effort and the resources of the committee as a whole to completing the task from 1985 through 1987. The editors and co-chairs of the subcommittee responsible for the organization, research, and rewriting of the book were Gary C. Crapster and Michael P. Lynn, both of Dallas, Texas.

The authors of specific chapters are listed at the front of the book, but many others assisted with research, proofreading, and practical suggestions. Among those making significant contributions were: Patricia L. Agliano, Baltimore, Maryland; C. Philip Campbell, Jr., St. Petersburg, Florida; Douglas S. Carr, Portland, Maine; Joe Connelly, San Francisco, California; C. Phillip Curley, Chicago, Illinois; Eliot Disner, Los Angeles, California; Eugene Z. DuBose, Dallas, Texas; Clement D. Erhardt III, Baltimore, Maryland; Michael J. Essler, Portland, Oregon; Thomas C. Farr, Des Moines, Iowa; William L.

Fouché, Jr., Dallas, Texas; Glenn S. Gitomar, Philadelphia, Pennsylvania; William T. Hangley, Philadelphia, Pennsylvania; Joan Hass, Dallas, Texas; Thomas O. Kloehn, Milwaukee, Wisconsin; Janet Kole, Philadelphia, Pennsylvania; Thomas J. LoSavio, San Francisco, California; Kurt W. Maier, Bowling Green, Kentucky; Ira Marcus, Fort Lauderdale, Florida; Gary Marsh, Atlanta, Georgia; George F. McGunnigle, Minneapolis, Minnesota; Lawrence H. Norton, Baltimore, Maryland; Jennifer M. Nutt, San Francisco, California; John H. Quinn, St. Louis, Missouri; Elizabeth A. Smith, San Diego, California; James A. Smith, Detroit, Michigan; Gloria T. Svanas, Odessa, Texas; Martin Unger, New York, New York; Lawrence M. Watson, Orlando, Florida; David Williams, Baltimore, Maryland.

The committee is greatly indebted to many other members of the Litigation Section who assisted in various stages of this project.

Gary C. Crapster
Michael P. Lynn
Dallas, Texas

Preface and Acknowledgments to First Edition

The four chapters that follow contain suggested model jury instructions for use in trials involving what are frequently called "business torts." That phrase has been applied variously to a number of torts arising in commercial contexts. Although the scope of activity of the Litigation Section's Business Torts Litigation Committee includes such causes of action as civil conspiracy, the so-called "prima facie tort," and others, the committee determined to limit the model instructions to the most commonly encountered business torts: interference with contract, inducing breach of contract, confusion of source, injurious falsehood, and the still-emerging tort often referred to as interference with prospective advantage.

In defining the scope of these instructions, the committee chose to combine concepts in certain instances. Thus, for example, the torts of inducing breach of contract and of interference with contractual relations have been combined because of their common "contract" premises. Similarly, the common law concept of unfair competition has been blended with notions of trademark and trade name infringement to highlight their common heritages. Nevertheless, counsel using these model instructions should not overlook the possibility of structuring separate causes of action to take maximum advantage of the differences involved in those torts that are combined in the following chapters.

In the preparation of these jury instructions, the Business Torts Litigation Committee created a special Subcommittee on Jury Instructions, chaired by Joseph D. Zamore of Cleveland, Ohio, presently the committee's chair. Although a relatively small number of committee members were formally assigned to that subcommittee, dozens of practitioners from all parts of the country were gracious enough to contribute their ideas, instructions used in past instances, and suggestions to the subcommittee. To each of them is due considerable thanks.

Among the authors who contributed to the drafting of the following four chapters, and to whom the subcommittee is indebted, were Rutledge C. Clement, Jr., New Orleans, Louisiana; George H. Connell, Jr., Atlanta, Georgia; Robert L. Hobbins, Minneapolis, Minnesota; Professor Michael J. Hutter, Jr., Albany, New York; Don A. Lynn, Miami, Florida; and Frances Mitchell Schaul, Cleveland, Ohio. In addition, while persons too numerous to list made invaluable contributions, special recognition for their particular contributions of written material to the subcommittee goes to Gerald F. Hempstead, St. Louis, Missouri; James H. Ryan, Chicago, Illinois; Michael C. Schaefer, Denver, Colorado; and Stephen Schnitzer, Newark, New Jersey.

Special acknowledgment must also be given to George H. Connell, Jr., of Atlanta, for his work in reviewing portions of the following material, as well as for his authorship contributions. The supreme gratitude of the subcommittee is reserved to Professor Michael J. Hutter, Jr., of the Albany (N.Y.) Law School, whose writing, editing, and organization skills touched each of the following chapters, and to Neil Peck, of Denver, Colorado, Chair of the Business Torts Litigation Committee when this project was commenced, whose inspiration, assistance, patience, and persistence made the entire project possible.

Joseph D. Zamore
Cleveland, Ohio

Chapter One

Inducing Breach of Contract

1.01 Introduction

Neal C. Baroody

The model jury charges in these first two chapters reflect common law liability for inducing a breach of contract or interfering with contractual relations. The broad tort category of "interference" encompasses not only those situations in which an existing contract is breached or interfered with, but also those situations involving no contract. Examples of such situations include: (a) when a contract is in the formative stages, though incomplete; (b) when there is an ongoing business relationship; and (c) when a business relationship has not yet been established but is reasonably probable.

This chapter covers only the situation in which a third party induces the breach of an existing contract. Chapter Two, "Interference with Prospective Advantage," covers the situation in which no contract exists. This tort also is referred to as "interference with business relations."

Jurisdictions differ on a number of fundamental issues related to the tort of inducing breach of contract. Notwithstanding these differences, the courts of almost all jurisdictions generally require at least the following criteria:

(1) the existence of a valid contract;
(2) knowledge of the contract on the part of the defendant or that it was readily apparent to the defendant;
(3) an intentional interference that causes a breach of the contract; and
(4) economic damages suffered by the plaintiff as a result of the defendant's interference.

The development of the tort has been plagued by doctrinal inconsistency, within and among jurisdictions. *See* Harvey Perlman, *Interference with Contract and Other Economic Expectancies: A Clash of Tort and Contract Doctrine,* 49 U. Chi. L. Rev. 61 (1982) [hereinafter Perlman]. Courts have disagreed on such fundamental matters as the type of contract to be protected, the kind of interference that will be actionable, and the defenses that can be asserted. *See id.;* W. Page Keeton,

Prosser & Keeton on the Law of Torts § 129 (5th ed. 1984) [hereinafter Keeton].

The most significant difference among the courts considering this tort involves the plaintiff's burden of proof. *See* Perlman, *supra* at 65. The traditional view requires the plaintiff to prove that the defendant intentionally interfered with the contract. The defendant has the burden to prove any justification or privilege. An increasing number of courts, however, have applied the test set forth in the *Restatement (Second) of Torts* § 766 (1979). This test requires the plaintiff to prove that the defendant intentionally *and improperly* interfered with the contract. Although the comments to section 766 acknowledge the split of authority and do not purport to determine conclusively the burden-of-proof issue, the addition of the "improper" element has had a significant impact on the development of the law. Most states now require the plaintiff to prove, as an element of the tort, that the defendant's conduct was the result of either an improper motive or improper means.

Sections 766 and 767 of the *Restatement (Second) of Torts* (1979) have heavily influenced the developing law.

> § 766 *Intentional Interference with Performance of Contract by Third Person*
>
> One who intentionally and improperly interferes with the performance of a contract (except a contract to marry) between another and a third person by inducing or otherwise causing the third person not to perform the contract is subject to liability to the other for the pecuniary loss resulting to the other from the failure of the third person to perform the contract.
>
> § 767 *Factors in Determining Whether Interference Is Improper*
>
> In determining whether an actor's conduct in intentionally interfering with a contract or a prospective contractual relation of another is improper or not, consideration is given to the following factors:
>
> (a) the nature of the actor's conduct,
> (b) the actor's motive,
> (c) the interests of the other with which the actor's conduct interferes,

(d) the interests sought to be advanced by the actor,
(e) the social interests in protecting the freedom of action of the actor and the contractual interests of the other,
(f) the proximity or remoteness of the actor's conduct to the interference, and
(g) the relations between the parties.

Today, a majority of jurisdictions have adopted the *Restatement*'s approach and require some showing of intentional wrongful conduct. *See, e.g., Allen & O'Hara, Inc. v. Barrett Wrecking, Inc.,* 898 F.2d 512 (7th Cir. 1990) (applying Wisconsin law); *H.J., Inc. v. Int'l Tel. & Tel. Corp.,* 867 F.2d 1531 (8th Cir. 1989) (applying Connecticut law); *Q.E.R., Inc. v. Hickerson,* 880 F.2d 1178 (10th Cir. 1989) (applying Colorado law); *Brownsville Golden Age Nursing Home, Inc. v. Wells,* 839 F.2d 155 (3d Cir. 1988) (applying Pennsylvania law); *Davis v. West Community Hosp.,* 755 F.2d 455 (5th Cir. 1985) (applying Texas law); *V.C. Video, Inc. v. Nat'l Video, Inc.,* 755 F. Supp. 962 (D. Kan. 1990); *United Truck Leasing Corp. v. Geltman,* 551 N.E.2d 20 (Mass. 1990). *But see City Nat'l Bank of Fort Smith v. Unique Structures, Inc.,* 929 F.2d 1308 (8th Cir. 1991) (Arkansas law requires only showing of intent).

Because not all states have adopted the *Restatement,* the jury issues in this chapter are prepared in the alternative to make them easily adaptable to the legal requirements of the various jurisdictions.

1.02 Inducing Breach of Contract: Generally

The theory underlying the broad tort of interference balances a party's freedom to enter into business relationships with the sometimes competing interests of other parties coexisting in the marketplace. The development of the common law demonstrates the attempts courts have made to delineate the boundaries within which a party may conduct its own affairs without interfering with the business relations of others.

Thus, courts impose liability for inducing a breach of contract when a party, who is a stranger to a contract, induces its breach while acting in a manner other than in the legitimate exercise of the party's own rights. Moreover, the injured party's cause of action extends not only to conduct that results in an actual breach of the contract, but also to conduct that results in substantial interference with the performance or diminution of the value of the contract. *See Arkansas v. Texas,* 346 U.S. 368, 370 (1953). The basic theory is that the right to perform a contract and to reap the profits resulting therefrom, and also the right to performance by the other party, are property rights entitled to protection. *See* M.C. Dransfield, Annotation, *Liability for Procuring Breach of Contract,* 26 A.L.R.2d 1227 § 1 (1952 & Supp. 1992); 8 P.O.F.2d 267 *Interference with Contract* § 1 (1976 & Supp. 1991); 45 Am. Jur. 2d *Interference* § 39 (1969 & Supp. 1992). For an alternative explanation of the intellectual context in which the tort may be understood, see Richard Epstein, *Inducement of Breach of Contract as a Problem of Ostensible Ownership,* 16 J. Legal Stud. 1 (1987).

1.03 Inducing Breach of Contract: Elements of Liability

1.03[1] Generally

For the plaintiff to recover on its claim against the defendant, the plaintiff must prove, by a preponderance of the evidence, each of five [six] things:

(1) that at the time of the acts of the defendant, [name], the plaintiff, [name], was a party to a valid contract with [name of breaching party] to [state purpose of contract];
(2) that the defendant either knew of the existence, or under the circumstances, should have known of the existence, of that contract;
(3) that the acts of the defendant in inducing [name of breaching party] to breach its contract with the plaintiff were intentional within the meaning of the word *intent,* which I will provide you with later in my instructions;
(4) [optional—depending upon law of jurisdiction] that the conduct of the defendant was improper under the factors I will instruct you to consider;
(5) that, as a proximate result of the acts of the defendant, [name of breaching party] was induced to breach its contract with the plaintiff; and
(6) that, as a direct and proximate result of the defendant's conduct, the plaintiff was damaged.

If you find from your consideration of all of the evidence that the plaintiff has proved each of these elements by a preponderance of the evidence, then you will consider the question of the amount of money damages that may be awarded under instructions I will give you.

If you find, however, from your consideration of all of the evidence that the plaintiff has not proved any one or more of these elements by a preponderance of the evidence, then the defendant is not liable, and your verdict should be against the plaintiff and for the defendant.

Comment

This charge reflects the traditional standard for establishing liability and includes the optional element of improper conduct on the part of the defendant. A majority of jurisdictions now require the plaintiff to prove this element. For a more detailed discussion, see § 1.01 and the cases cited therein.

Note that in jurisdictions that do not require the plaintiff to prove that the defendant's conduct was improper (sometimes referred to as requiring the conduct itself or the motive to be malicious, inherently tortious, or unlawful), the charge should not include either optional element 4 above or the instruction in § 1.07, regarding factors used to determine whether interference is improper. Instead, the charge requiring the defendant to prove its conduct was justified or privileged should be submitted. *See* § 1.01, *supra;* § 1.05, *infra.*

1.03[2] Requirement of a Contract

For you to find for the plaintiff on its claim against the defendant, you must find that the plaintiff was a party to a valid contract in full force and effect at the time of the actions complained of and that the contract was breached as a result of the defendant's conduct.

A contract may be defined simply as an oral or written agreement, which the law will enforce, to do or not to do a particular thing in exchange for adequate consideration. If all of the basic elements required by law to exist for there to be a contract are present, a contract is deemed to be valid if it is not illegal, in restraint of trade, or otherwise opposed to public policy. A contract is considered to be in full force and effect if, at the time in question, the agreement was in effect between the parties and not terminated, expired, or otherwise rendered void.

Hence, in order for you to find the existence of a contract sufficient to meet the plaintiff's burden of proof, you must find that there was in effect, at the time of the actions complained of, an agreement between the plaintiff and [name of breaching party] to [state purpose of contract], which agreement was neither illegal nor in restraint of trade nor otherwise opposed to public policy.

[If the jurisdiction is one that does not require that the breached contract be enforceable—and counsel should note the lack of uniformity on this question among the various states—then the following additional paragraph should be added here.]

Should you find that all of the above conditions for a contract have been proved by a preponderance of the evidence, the fact that the contract may have been unenforceable by the plaintiff against [name of breaching party] by virtue of [insert any claimed reason(s)] will not render that contract insufficient to meet the plaintiff's burden of proof as to the existence of a valid contract.

Comment

The last (optional) paragraph of this charge assumes there is no dispute about the existence of basic contractual elements, such as capacity or consideration. The charge speaks only to the immateriality of enforceability. If basic contract law issues are to be decided, a series of paragraphs explaining each of the elements of a contract must be inserted in this charge. Such instructions concerning basic contract principles are omitted here as being beyond the scope of these instructions.

To commit a tort of interference with contractual relations, the defendant must have interfered with a contract existing between two parties. One who interferes with an invalid or void contract will not be held liable in tort. *See Restatement (Second) of Torts* § 774 (1979). Pursuant to section 766, a valid contract is a necessary element of the tort, but comment (f) states that the contract need not be legally *enforceable* as to third persons for a cause of action for tortious interference to lie. *See Restatement (Second) of Torts* § 766 cmt. f (1979). The *Restatement* takes the view that *until* a party to the contract raises a defense that would permit the party to avoid the contract (for example, formal defects, statute of frauds, lack of mutuality, unconscionability, indefiniteness), a defendant may not interfere improperly with the performance of that contract. *See id.* Most courts have adopted the *Restatement*'s approach and allow a party to sue for tortious interference of a contract even though the breached contract was voidable. *See* James O. Pearson, Annotation, *Liability for Interference with Invalid or Unenforceable Contract,* 96 A.L.R.3d 1294 (1979 & Supp. 1992); 8 P.O.F.2d 267 *Interference with Contract* § 2 (1976 & Supp. 1991); 45 Am. Jur. 2d *Interference* § 9 (1952 & Supp. 1992).

For example, courts usually hold that a contract voidable because of the statute of frauds can afford a basis for a tort action when the defendant interferes with the contract's performance. *See Frantz v. Parke,* 729 P.2d 1068 (Idaho Ct. App. 1986); *Winternitz v. Summit Hills,* 532 A.2d 1089 (Md. Ct. Spec. App. 1987), *cert. denied,* 538 A.2d 778 (Md. 1988); *Keenan v.*

Artintype, Inc., 546 N.Y.S.2d 741 (N.Y. Sup. Ct. 1989). *But see Kopp, Inc. v. U.S. Technologies, Inc.*, 539 A.2d 309 (N.J. Super. Ct. App. Div. 1988) (dictum) (other grounds would have precluded action based on interference with contract, when contract apparently had not been agreed to by anyone authorized to bind party, even orally).

Similarly, more courts are following the trend toward allowing recovery for the breach of a contract terminable at will. Although a party to the contract may terminate it at will, courts reason that the interference of another party that induces the wrongful termination is a tort for which recovery may be had. *See Restatement (Second) of Torts* § 766 cmt. g (1979); 45 Am. Jur. 2d *Interference* § 24 (1969 & Supp. 1992); Keeton, *supra* at 995–96; *Nat'l Right to Life Political Action Comm. v. Friends of Bryan*, 741 F. Supp. 807 (D. Nev. 1990); *Leaco Enter., Inc. v. Gen. Elec. Co.*, 737 F. Supp. 605 (D. Or. 1990); *Beyda v. USAir, Inc.*, 697 F. Supp. 1394 (W.D. Pa. 1988); *Sterner v. Marathon Oil Co.*, 767 S.W.2d 686 (Tex. 1989); *Duggin v. Adams*, 360 S.E.2d 832 (Va. 1987).

Courts have remained split, however, when the breached contract was unenforceable for want of consideration, mutuality, or certainty. Although a number of courts have held that a cause of action may lie for the inducement of breach of such contracts, other courts have disagreed. Compare cases where liability was found (*Cook v. MFA Livestock Ass'n*, 700 S.W.2d 526 (Mo. Ct. App. 1985) (indefiniteness); *Carman v. Heber*, 601 P.2d 646 (Colo. Ct. App. 1979) (lack of mutuality); *Allen v. Leybourne*, 190 So. 2d 825 (Fla. Dist. Ct. App. 1966) (lack of consideration)) with cases where no liability was found (*Wedgewood Carpet Mills, Inc. v. Color-Set, Inc.*, 254 S.E.2d 421 (Ga. Ct. App. 1979) (indefiniteness and lack of mutuality); *Grimm v. Baumgart*, 97 N.E.2d 871 (Ind. Ct. App. 1951) (lack of certainty and mutuality)). *See generally* James O. Pearson, Annotation, *Liability for Interference with Invalid or Unenforceable Contract*, 96 A.L.R.3d 1294 (1979 & Supp. 1992).

1.03[3] Requirement of Knowledge

To find for the plaintiff, you must also find that the defendant knew of the existence of the contract between the plaintiff and [name of breaching party]. For this purpose, the defendant need not have had actual knowledge of this specific contract. The requirement of knowledge may be found to exist if, from the facts and circumstances of which defendant had knowledge, the defendant should have known of the existence of the contractual relationship between the plaintiff and [name of breaching party]. This is sometimes referred to as "constructive knowledge."

Comment

This charge represents the generally accepted definition of the extent of knowledge required to meet the burden of proof for this tort. *See Restatement (Second) of Torts* § 766 cmt. i (1979); 8 P.O.F.2d 267 *Interference with Contract* § 2 (1976 & Supp. 1991); 45 Am. Jur. 2d *Interference* § 11 (1969 & Supp. 1992); Keeton, *supra* at 982; *Moloney v. Centner,* 727 F. Supp. 1232 (N.D. Ill. 1989); *Hanley v. Continental Airlines, Inc.,* 687 F. Supp. 533 (D. Colo. 1988); *Kennedy v. William R. Hudson, Inc.,* 659 F. Supp. 900 (D. Colo. 1987); *Yiakas v. Savoy,* 526 N.E.2d 1305 (Mass. App. Ct.), *review denied,* 529 N.E.2d 1346 (Mass. 1988); *DiBasio v. Brown & Sharpe Mfg. Co.,* 525 A.2d 489 (R.I. 1987).

Courts have held that if a party knows the facts that give rise to the plaintiff's contractual rights against another, a party has sufficient knowledge for liability, even though a party is mistaken about the legal significance of the facts and believes there is no contract or the contract means something other than what it is judicially held to mean. *See* 45 Am. Jur. 2d *Interference* § 11 (1969 & Supp. 1992); *Piedmont Cotton Mills, Inc. v. H. W. Ivey Constr. Co.,* 137 S.E.2d 528 (Ga. Ct. App. 1964); *Texaco, Inc. v. Penzoil Co.,* 729 S.W.2d 768 (Tex. Ct. App. 1987), *cert. dismissed,* 485 U.S. 994 (1988); *Calbom v. Knudtzon,* 396 P.2d 148 (Wash. 1964). If the defendant merely enters into an agreement with another knowing that the other cannot perform both the agreement and the contract with the third person, the defendant is not liable for inducing the other to commit a breach of contract with the third person. *See Restatement (Second) of Torts* § 766 cmt. n (1979); 45 Am. Jur. 2d *Interference* § 11 (1969 & Supp. 1992); *Enercomp, Inc. v. McCorhill Pub., Inc.*, 873 F.2d 536 (2d Cir. 1989); *NCC Sunday Inserts, Inc. v. World Color Press, Inc.*, 759 F. Supp. 1004 (S.D.N.Y. 1991); *Seven Star Shoe Co., Inc. v. Strictly Goodies, Inc.*, 657 F. Supp. 917 (S.D.N.Y. 1987). Proof of the defendant's knowledge of the contractual rights at issue may be predicated on circumstantial evidence. *See American Cyanamid Co. v. Elizabeth Arden Sales Corp.*, 331 F. Supp. 597 (S.D.N.Y. 1971); *Texaco, Inc. v. Penzoil Co.*, 729 S.W.2d 768 (Tex. Ct. App. 1987), *cert. dismissed*, 485 U.S. 994 (1988).

1.03[4] Requirement of Intent

1.03[4][a] Generally

The plaintiff also must prove that the defendant intended to induce [name of breaching party] to breach its contract with the plaintiff. Conduct is intentional if done deliberately, with the purpose of inducing [name of breaching party] to breach its contract with the plaintiff. If you find that the defendant's conduct was not intentional, then you must find for the defendant.

Comment

Courts generally have held that inducing breach of contract is an intentional tort. Therefore, there is no liability for interference unless the act or acts in question were committed with the intent to interfere. *See* 45 Am. Jur. 2d *Interference* § 4 (1969 & Supp. 1992). For the cases discussing the general rule, see *Misany v. United States,* 873 F.2d 160 (7th Cir. 1989); *NCC Sunday Inserts, Inc. v. World Color Press, Inc.,* 759 F. Supp. 1004 (S.D.N.Y. 1991); *1301 Connecticut Ave. Assocs.,* 126 B.R. 823 (Bankr. D.D.C. 1991); *Funk v. Sara Lee Corp.,* 699 F. Supp. 1365 (E.D. Wis. 1988); *Liston v. Home Ins. Co.,* 659 F. Supp. 276 (S.D. Miss. 1986).

Generally, negligent interference with an existing contract is not actionable as a tort. *See Restatement (Second) of Torts* § 766C (1979). There is limited authority, however, recognizing liability for negligent interference with contract rights when the resultant damage is physical harm rather than pure economic harm. *See* Keeton, *supra* at 982; *Restatement (Second) of Torts* § 766C (1979); *Getty Refining & Mktg. Co. v. MT Fadi B,* 766 F.2d 829 (3d Cir. 1985).

1.03[4][b] Intent Defined

Intent is defined by the law as that purpose or aim or state of mind with which a person acts or fails to act. Ordinarily, it is reasonable to infer that a person intends the natural and probable consequences of his or her acts.

Comment

The term "intent" is used throughout the *Restatement (Second) of Torts* to denote that the actor desires to cause the consequences of the actor's acts, or that the actor believes the consequences are substantially certain to result from the acts. *Restatement (Second) of Torts* § 8A (1965). This charge reflects the established definition of intent. *See, e.g., City Nat'l Bank of Fort Smith v. Unique Structures, Inc.,* 929 F.2d 1308 (8th Cir. 1991); *Liston v. Home Ins. Co.,* 659 F. Supp. 276 (S.D. Miss. 1986).

1.03[4][c] Proof of Intent

Intent may be proved by indirect or circumstantial evidence. Indeed, it can rarely be established by any other means. Although witnesses may see and hear, and may be able to give direct evidence of what a person does or fails to do, they do not likewise see and hear what a person intends to do or intends to refrain from doing.

Thus, in making your determination about whether the defendant's actions were intentional, you may look at the defendant's objective conduct and, in the absence of contrary evidence, draw an inference that the defendant, by defendant's conduct, intended the natural and probable consequences of defendant's act.

Comment

Cf. Piedmont Cotton Mills, Inc. v. H. W. Ivey Constr. Co., 137 S.E.2d 528 (Ga. Ct. App. 1964). *See generally* M.C. Dransfield, Annotation, *Liability for Procuring Breach of Contract,* 26 A.L.R.2d 1247 § 4 (1952 & Supp. 1992).

1.03[4][d] Requirement of "Malice" [Optional]

To find for the plaintiff, you must find that the defendant acted with malice. Malice, as used in this sense, sometimes known as "legal malice," refers simply to the intentional doing of a harmful act, without justification or excuse—that is, the willful violation of a known right. It is not necessary for the plaintiff to prove malice in the popular sense of hatred, ill will, or spite.

Comment

In jurisdictions that require that "malice" be shown, this charge may be used. It is superfluous in jurisdictions where intent need only be proved as defined in § 1.03[4][b]. This charge includes the traditional distinctions between actual malice and legal malice. *See Restatement (Second) of Torts* § 766 cmts. r, s (1979); 45 Am. Jur. 2d *Interference* § 3 (1969 & Supp. 1992); *see, e.g., Labus v. Navistar Int'l Transp. Corp.*, 740 F. Supp. 1053 (D.N.J. 1990); *Sweeney v. Athens Regional Medical Ctr.*, 709 F. Supp. 1563 (M.D. Ga. 1989); *Roy v. Woonsocket Inst. for Sav.*, 525 A.2d 915 (R.I. 1987).

Due to the confusion engendered by the use of the word "malice," Keeton suggests avoiding the use of this term. *See* Keeton, *supra* at 983–84. The proposed jury instructions can be simplified by replacing this section with the definition of legal malice included in the definition of intent.

Although only legal malice need be established to prove the necessary intent, actual malice in the sense of spite, hostility, or ill will is relevant in all jurisdictions in two senses: (1) proof of legal malice may be made by proof of actual malice; and (2) actual malice must generally be proved to obtain an award of punitive damages. *See* 45 Am. Jur. 2d *Interference* § 3 (1969 & Supp. 1992); *see also* § 1.07[2], *infra.*

Note that it is important to distinguish the concept of actual malice as defined above (spite, hostility, or ill will) from the constitutional doctrine of "actual malice" developed by the United States Supreme Court in *New York Times Co. v. Sullivan*, 376 U.S. 254 (1964), and later defamation cases.

1.03[4][e] Summary of Requirement of Intent

In determining whether the defendant intentionally interfered with the contract between the plaintiff and [name of breaching party], you may look at the defendant's conduct. In the absence of evidence to the contrary, you may infer from the defendant's conduct, or lack of conduct, that the defendant intended those natural and probable consequences that one standing in like circumstances and possessing like knowledge should expect. If you thereby find that the defendant's conduct was in willful violation of a known right of the plaintiff, then the requisite intent was present.

Comment

This charge is recommended to collect and reinforce for the jury the various elements of the requirement that intent be proved as an element of the tort.

1.03[4][f] Unlawful Acts [Optional]

Should you find that the defendant's conduct in interfering with the plaintiff's contractual relationship with [name of breaching party] was itself unlawful, you may find the necessary intent, without anything more.

Comment

In appropriate cases when the conduct complained of may have been unlawful, counsel may include this charge, which incorporates the traditional view that a person must be presumed to intend the consequences of his or her unlawful conduct. *See* 45 Am. Jur. 2d *Interference* § 4 (1969 & Supp. 1992); *H.J., Inc. v. Int'l Tel. & Tel. Corp.*, 867 F.2d 1531 (8th Cir. 1989); *Seven Stars Shoe Co., Inc. v. Strictly Goodies, Inc.*, 657 F. Supp. 917 (S.D.N.Y. 1987).

1.03[5] Requirement That the Breach Be Proximately Caused by the Defendant's Conduct

1.03[5][a] Breach Defined

Breach of contract means the failure of a party to a contract, in the absence of legal excuse or impossibility of performance, to perform any promise that forms the whole or part of the contract. A breach may occur with regard to either an express or implied provision of the contract. An express provision is one that is specifically agreed to by the parties either orally or in writing. An implied provision is one that is recognized by the parties to exist and bind them in their actions despite the fact that it was not specifically spelled out or agreed to by the parties to the contract. An implied provision often arises out of terms that *were* expressly set forth in the contract and agreed to by the parties, and an implied promise constitutes a valid part of the contract.

Comment

This charge is based upon the traditional definition of breach of contract. *See Friedman v. Katzner,* 114 A. 884 (Md. 1921). General contract law, including an analysis of what constitutes breach of contract and the related concepts of materiality and substantial performance, is beyond the scope of these instructions. These definitions are included only because a requisite element of this tort is some form of breach of, or interference with, a contract. State law must be reviewed for peculiarities on this basic instruction.

For a detailed analysis of conduct that constitutes breach of contract, counsel should consult one of the standard texts or treatises in the area of contract law. *E.g.,* John D. Calamari & Joseph M. Perillo, *Law of Contracts* §§ 174–85 (3d ed. 1987); E. Allen Farnsworth, *Contracts* (1982).

1.03[5][b] Breach Required

For the plaintiff to prevail on its claim against the defendant, you must find that the contract in question has been breached. This means you must find that [name of breaching party] failed to perform as agreed under the contract, either by virtue of the express provisions of the contract or as may be implied from the express provisions, in accordance with the definitions of express and implied contractual provisions for which I have already instructed you.

Comment

For the definitions of breach, express provision, and implied provision, see § 1.03[5][a] and the comment thereto, *supra.* It is axiomatic that breach is a requisite element of the tort of inducing breach of contract. *See, e.g., Int'l Union, United Mine Workers of America v. Covenant Coal Group,* 759 F. Supp. 1204 (W.D. Va. 1991); *Price v. Sorrell,* 784 P.2d 614 (Wyo. 1989). For a discussion of the requirement that the contract in question be valid and enforceable (which this instruction implicitly assumes), see § 1.03[2] and comment thereto.

1.03[5][c] Causal Relationship: Generally

You, the jury, must determine whether the defendant was responsible for the refusal of [name of breaching party] to go forward with the contract with the plaintiff. This means that, before you can decide in favor of the plaintiff, you must find, by a preponderance of the evidence, that but for the actions of the defendant, the contract that was not performed would have otherwise been performed.

Comment

This general causation charge, containing the traditional "but for" test, finds wide support among the courts. *See, e.g., Sharma v. Skaarup Ship Management Corp.*, 916 F.2d 820 (2d Cir. 1990), *cert. denied*, 111 S. Ct. 1109 (1991); *Fitzpatrick v. Catholic Bishop of Chicago*, 916 F.2d 1254 (7th Cir. 1990); *Caudill v. Farmland Indus., Inc.*, 919 F.2d 83 (8th Cir. 1990); *Tomson v. Stephan*, 696 F. Supp. 1407 (D. Kan. 1988); *Merrill Lynch Futures, Inc. v. Miller*, 686 F. Supp. 1033 (S.D.N.Y. 1988); *Neterer v. Slabaugh*, 548 N.E.2d 832 (Ind. Ct. App. 1990). *See also* 45 Am. Jur. 2d *Interference* § 5 (1969 & Supp. 1992) ("it must be shown that by reason of defendant's act, a contract which would otherwise have been performed was abandoned").

1.03[5][d] Proximate Cause

If you find that the plaintiff did suffer the losses claimed, you must then determine whether the defendant's conduct was the proximate cause of the plaintiff's loss or damage.

In this regard, the defendant's conduct will be considered to be the proximate cause of the plaintiff's loss or damage if you find that it was a substantial factor in causing that loss or damage. It need not be the *only* cause. The conduct will be a substantial factor in causing the loss or damage if it had such an effect in producing the loss that reasonable men and women would regard it as a cause of the loss or damage, considering a number of other contributing factors, such as whether defendant's conduct created a condition or chain of events that was continuous and active up to the time of the damage to the plaintiff, and the lapse of time between the defendant's conduct and the damage to the plaintiff.

Comment

This charge is based upon *Acme Cigarette Serv., Inc. v. Gallegos*, 577 P.2d 885 (N.M. Ct. App. 1978), and reflects the traditional definition of proximate cause. *See Restatement (Second) of Torts* § 433 (1965). The requirement of causal effect may be stated in somewhat different terms depending upon the jurisdiction. *See generally* Keeton, *supra* at 989.

Although there is some overlap between this instruction and the charge set forth in § 1.03[5][c], instructing the jury with both charges should not lead to confusion or inconsistent verdicts. The first charge is designed to inform the jury that the plaintiff has the burden of proving that, except for the defendant's actions, the plaintiff would have more likely than not received the benefits of its contract with the third party. Instructing the jury with this charge will make it clear to the jury that the defendant's conduct must have been more than merely a contributing cause, it must be a *substantial* factor in inducing the breach. If the latter instruction is not accepted in a certain jurisdiction, the charge set forth in § 1.03[5][c] may be given alone with no adverse impact.

Note that in *Eltolad Music, Inc. v. April Music, Inc.,* 188 Cal. Rptr. 858 (Cal. Ct. App. 1983), the Court of Appeals of California granted the defendant/appellant a new trial based upon the trial court's instruction to the jury that proximate cause constituted "a" moving cause of the breach. The California court held that the correct instruction, as requested by the defendant, was that proximate cause is "the" moving cause of the breach. Such an interpretation, apparently, is not the majority view. *See Fitzpatrick v. Catholic Bishop of Chicago,* 916 F.2d 1254 (7th Cir. 1990).

1.03[5][e] Nonliability of Contractual Parties

Even if you find that the plaintiff's contract was breached and that, but for the defendant's conduct, the contract would otherwise have been performed, then the plaintiff cannot prevail on the claim against the defendant if the defendant was a party to the contract with the plaintiff because the defendant may not be held liable to the plaintiff for inducing defendant's own breach of contract.

Comment

As a general rule, no action for inducing breach of contract may lie against another party to the contract at issue. *See* 45 Am. Jur. 2d *Interference* § 26 (1969 & Supp. 1992); *see, e.g., Farmland Indus., Inc. v. Grain Bd. of Iraq,* 904 F.2d 732 (D.C. Cir. 1990); *Dow Chem. Corp. v. Weevil-Cide Corp., Inc.,* 897 F.2d 481 (10th Cir. 1990); *Knight v. Sharif,* 875 F.2d 516 (5th Cir. 1989); *Northwest Acceptance Corp. v. Lynnwood Equip., Inc.,* 841 F.2d 918 (9th Cir. 1988); *Michelson v. Exxon Research & Eng'g Co.,* 808 F.2d 1005 (3d Cir. 1987); *Powell v. Feroleto Steel Co., Inc.,* 659 F. Supp. 303 (D. Conn. 1986); *Applied Equip. Corp. v. Litton Saudi Arabia Ltd.,* 869 P.2d 454 (Cal. 1994).

1.03[5][f] Nonliability of Corporate Officers, Directors, and Employees

If you find that the defendant was a[n] [officer, director, employee—choose one] of a corporation at the time of the conduct at issue here, and was acting within the scope of defendant's official capacity when doing the acts complained of, then defendant is not *personally* liable to the plaintiff. This is so even though the defendant's conduct may have induced the breach of contract and the corporation itself may be liable to the plaintiff for the defendant's conduct.

Comment

A corporation, albeit a separate and distinct legal entity, can transact business only through its officers, directors, and employees. In many cases, a plaintiff asserting a cause of action for inducing breach of contract will name as defendants the corporate entity *and* various officers, directors, and/or employees. This charge is based on such a scenario and reflects the general rule that such individual defendants are not liable to the aggrieved party. *See, e.g., Piekarski v. Home Owners Sav. Bank, F.S.B.,* 759 F. Supp 542 (D. Minn. 1991); *Litchie v. U.S. Home Corp.,* 655 F. Supp. 1026 (D. Utah 1987); *Energy Constr. v. Georgia Metal Sys. & Eng'g,* 367 S.E.2d 324 (Ga. Ct. App. 1988); *Feaheny v. Caldwell,* 437 N.W.2d 358 (Mich. Ct. App. 1989). *See generally* Thomas G. Fischer, Annotation, *Liability of Corporate Director, Officer, or Employee for Tortious Interference with Corporation's Contract with Another,* 72 A.L.R.4th 492 (1989 & Supp. 1992); 45 Am. Jur. 2d *Interference* § 54 (1969 & Supp. 1992).

Notwithstanding the general rule, personal liability can be imposed for a myriad of reasons. For example, if the actions complained of are detrimental to the corporation and outside the scope of the agent's authority, there is no shield of immunity. *See, e.g., Presto v. Sequoia Sys., Inc.,* 633 F. Supp. 1117 (D. Mass. 1986). Likewise, if the conduct of the individual defendant is otherwise improper or unjustified (that is, based upon personal malice or ill will toward the plaintiff), liability also may be imposed. *See Grosvenor Properties Ltd. v. Southmark Corp.,* 896 F.2d 1149 (9th Cir. 1990); *Piekarski v. Home Owners Sav. Bank, F.S.B.,* 759 F. Supp. 542 (D. Minn. 1991).

1.03[5][g] Joint and Several Liability

Should you find by a preponderance of the evidence that one or more persons other than the defendant [name of the defendant] also induced [name of breaching party] to breach the contract with the plaintiff, that finding will in no way change your finding as to [name of the defendant]. Under the law of this jurisdiction, each person is liable separately, and all persons who are found to have induced a breach of a contract are liable collectively. This means that, if you find the defendant liable for inducing the breach of the contract between the plaintiff and [name of breaching party], in accordance with my instructions, it makes no difference that each of several persons, of whom the defendant is only one, are responsible for but a single breach of that contract. Thus, you must, in that event, still return a finding of liability against the defendant.

Comment

As is the case throughout the law of torts, the general rule is that all persons who unite to induce a breach of contract are jointly and severally liable for the damages inflicted upon the party injured thereby. *See* M.C. Dransfield, Annotation, *Liability for Procuring Breach of Contract,* 26 A.L.R.2d 1227 § 42 (1952 & Supp. 1992); 45 Am. Jur. 2d *Interference* § 54 (1969 & Supp. 1992); *see also Wilson & Co. v. United Packinghouse Workers of America,* 181 F. Supp. 809 (N.D. Iowa 1960); *Hornstein v. Podwitz,* 173 N.E. 674 (N.Y. 1930); *Crowe v. Domestic Loans, Inc.,* 130 S.E.2d 845 (S.C. 1963); *Lien v. Northwestern Eng'g Co.,* 39 N.W.2d 483 (S.D. 1949).

1.04 Inducing Breach of Contract: Factors Affecting Liability

1.04[1] Contracts Terminable at Will

A contract that has no specified term or duration is said to be terminable at will by either party. The liability of a third person for inducing a breach of contract is not affected by the fact that the contract is terminable at will. Therefore, in making your determination about the defendant's liability to the plaintiff, the fact that the contract in question may have been terminable at will by [name of breaching party] may not be a factor in your decision.

Comment

Although there is authority to the contrary, a number of courts have held that a defendant charged with inducing breach of contract is not shielded from liability simply because the contract breached was terminable at will by either party. *See* § 1.03[2], *supra*. *See generally* James O. Pearson, Annotation, *Liability for Interference with at Will Business Relationship,* 5 A.L.R.4th 9 (1981 & Supp. 1992).

Note

Even though the evidence that the contract in question is terminable at will may not affect liability, it may be relevant in assessing damages allegedly suffered by the plaintiff. *See Restatement (Second) of Torts* § 766 cmt. g (1979). It also is relevant when determining the applicability of competition as justification for interference. *See* § 1.05[3], *infra.*

1.04[2] Unlawful Means Employed

Should you find that the means employed by the defendant to induce the breach of contract between the plaintiff and [name of breaching party] were unlawful in and of themselves, then you must find for the plaintiff, regardless of any justification that the defendant may claim.

Comment

The tort of inducing breach of contract, as well as that of interference with prospective economic advantage, has been consistently applied when the means employed by the defendant are independently unlawful. *See Restatement (Second) of Torts* § 767 cmt. c (1979); Perlman, *supra* at 69–78. Stated another way, inducement based upon unlawful means on the part of the defendant destroys any claim of justification. *See* § 1.05[2], *infra.* Examples of such unlawful means are libel, slander, physical violence or threats, intentional infliction of emotional distress, and wrongful discharge. *See, e.g., Pony Express Cab & Bus, Inc. v. Ward,* 841 F.2d 207 (8th Cir. 1988); *Deem v. Lockheed Corp.,* 749 F. Supp. 1230 (S.D.N.Y. 1989); *Duggin v. Adams,* 360 S.E.2d 832 (Va. 1987). The variations and nuances on this subject, however, are numerous and counsel must carefully check the law of the forum jurisdiction to tailor this charge appropriately to the case at bar.

1.04[3] Defendant's Motive

Should you find that the defendant acted *solely* to injure the plaintiff (that is, purely out of a sense of spite and a desire to harm the plaintiff for its own sake, and not to further any legitimate interest of defendant's own that falls within the instructions I will give you later), then you must find for the plaintiff, regardless of any justification the defendant may claim. *Some* ill will on the part of the defendant is permissible, *providing* the defendant acted in substantial part with a proper purpose in mind.

Comment

This instruction is recommended, in appropriate jurisdictions (*see* § 1.05[1], *infra*), to forewarn the jury of the shift of the burden of proof when the defense to be considered is the affirmative defense of justification rather than that consisting solely of denials of matters constituting the plaintiff's case in chief. *See* James O. Pearson, Annotation, *Liability for Interference with at Will Business Relationship*, 5 A.L.R.4th 9 (1981 & Supp. 1992); Keeton, *supra* at 984; § 1.05[2], *infra.*

Note that motive is irrelevant when the defendant is exercising an absolute right. In such a case, the instruction regarding the defendant's motive would not be given. *See, e.g., Caven v. Am. Fed. Sav. & Loan Ass'n*, 837 F.2d 427 (10th Cir. 1988); *Mac Enter., Inc. v. Del E. Webb Dev. Co.*, 645 P.2d 1245 (Ariz. Ct. App. 1982); *Langeland v. Farmers State Bank of Trimont*, 319 N.W.2d 26 (Minn. 1982). The existence of an absolute right is a question of law for the court to decide. *See* M.C. Dransfield, Annotation, *Liability for Procuring Breach of Contract*, 26 A.L.R.2d 1227 § 23 (1952 & Supp. 1992); 45 Am. Jur. 2d *Interference* § 27 (1969 & Supp. 1992).

Note further that absolute rights are to be contrasted with common law and qualified rights. Absolute rights include rights incident to the ownership of property and rights growing out of contractual relationships. *See* 45 Am. Jur. 2d *Interference* § 23 (1969 & Supp. 1992). Such absolute rights may be exercised by the defendant without liability for interference and without reference to the defendant's motive, whereas the defendant's motive *does* play a role in the exercise of ordinary rights. *See id.*

Also note that preliminary Draft No. 1 of *Restatement (Third) of Unfair Competition* would change the present law to provide that if defendant was, in fact, competing with plaintiff, the defendant's motives are irrelevant to the issue of liability.

1.05 Proper or Improper Interference

1.05[1] Burden of Proof

As is the case with the tort of interference with prospective advantage, courts are divided about whether the plaintiff must prove, as an element of the tort, that the defendant's conduct or motive was improper, or whether the burden is upon the defendant to demonstrate that the conduct was privileged and/or justified (that is, an affirmative defense). *See* § 2.09[1], *infra.* Some courts, although including absence of justification or the like as an element of the tort, nevertheless hold that justification is an affirmative defense to be pleaded and proved by the defendant. Practically speaking, "improper conduct" and "justification" are opposite sides of the same coin. In *Gross v. Lowder Realty Better Homes & Gardens,* 494 So. 2d 590, 597 n.3 (Ala. 1986), the Supreme Court of Alabama explained as follows:

> The Restatement utilizes the term 'improper' to describe actionable conduct by a defendant. Non-justification is synonymous with 'improper.' If a defendant's interference is unjustified under the circumstances of the case, it is improper. The converse is also true.

A related issue concerns the burden of proof in a case involving a cause of action for inducing breach of contract. Depending upon the jurisdiction, different instructions are in order concerning the plaintiff's burden of proving improper motive or the defendant's burden of proving justification. *See HPI Health Care v. Mt. Vernon Hosp.,* 545 N.E.2d 679 (Ill. 1989); *see also* § 2.01 and comment thereto, *infra.* The *Restatement (Second) of Torts* does not take a position on the burden-of-proof issue. *See Restatement (Second) of Torts* ch. 37, Introductory Note (1979). By combining the charges on specific conduct set forth in §§ 1.05[2] through [6] with the burden-of-proof instructions set forth below as Options A and B, the model instructions can conceivably fit the law of any jurisdiction.

Option A: Plaintiff's Burden to Show Defendant's Conduct Improper

For the plaintiff to prevail on the claim against the defendant, you must find, by a preponderance of the evidence, that the plaintiff has demonstrated that the defendant's conduct was improper. The law recognizes that certain kinds of conduct under certain circumstances are *not* improper. The following instructions are intended to guide you in deciding whether the plaintiff has satisfied its burden to show that the defendant's conduct was improper.

Option B: Defendant's Burden to Show Conduct Proper

If you find that the plaintiff has met its burden of proof with respect to all of the elements of the tort of inducing breach of contract as to which I have previously instructed you, you must find for the plaintiff and against the defendant, unless you find that the defendant's conduct with respect to the contract in question was proper. The defendant must demonstrate, by a preponderance of the evidence, that the conduct in question was *not* improper.

Comment

The latter option takes into account the affirmative duty of the defendant to prove justification (that is, that defendant's conduct was not improper). This charge reflects that the burden of proof shifts to the defendant once the prima facie tort is demonstrated by the plaintiff. The affirmative defense of proper conduct must automatically fail, though, if the defendant's actions in inducing the breach of contract are inherently unlawful. *See* §§ 1.04[3], *supra,* 2.09[1], *infra.*

1.05[2] Proper or Improper Interference Defined

The determination of whether the defendant's conduct was or was not improper depends upon your consideration of all the facts and circumstances of the case, and a balancing of the following factors:

(1) the nature of the defendant's conduct;
(2) the defendant's motive;
(3) the interests of the plaintiff with which the defendant's conduct interfered;
(4) the interests sought to be advanced by the defendant;
(5) the social interests in protecting the freedom of action of the defendant and the contractual interests of the plaintiff;
(6) the proximity or remoteness of the defendant's conduct to the interference claimed by the plaintiff; and
(7) the relationship among the plaintiff, [name of breaching party], and the defendant.

Comment

This charge is generally based upon *Restatement (Second) of Torts* § 767 (1979). The comments to this *Restatement* section explain the significance of the various factors in depth and should be consulted by counsel. By and large, a majority of jurisdictions are approaching the issue of whether a defendant's interference is proper through an analysis of the seven specific factors set forth by the *Restatement. See, e.g., Allen & O'Hara, Inc. v. Barrett Wrecking, Inc.,* 898 F.2d 512 (7th Cir. 1990); *Q.E.R., Inc. v. Hickerson,* 880 F.2d 1178 (10th Cir. 1989); *Redies v. Nationwide Mut. Ins. Co.,* 711 F. Supp. 570 (D. Colo. 1989); *Reazin v. Blue Cross & Blue Shield of Kansas,* 663 F. Supp. 1360 (D. Kan 1987), *aff'd in part and remanded in part,* 899 F.2d 951 (10th Cir.), *cert. denied,* 110 S. Ct. 3241 (1990). *See also* 45 Am. Jur. 2d *Interference* § 14 (1969 & Supp. 1992).

The lack of improper interference on the part of the defendant—that is, justification for the defendant's conduct (§ 1.05[1])—is by far the most popular defense advanced by defendants in actions for inducing breach of contract. *See* 45 Am.

Jur. 2d *Interference* § 27 (1969 & Supp. 1992) (and cases cited therein).

Regarding the means employed by the defendant in inducing the breach of contract, see § 1.04. Regarding the defendant's motive in inducing the breach, see § 1.04[3].

Although improper interference is a question of fact for the jury to determine in accordance with the several factors set forth in this instruction, the existence and exercise of a superior or an absolute right on the part of the defendant is a question of law for the court. For a discussion on the distinction between absolute and ordinary rights, see § 1.04[3] and the corresponding comment and note.

1.05[3] Self-Interest as Proper or Improper Interference

Should you find that the defendant acted to protect a present, existing economic interest of its own, then you may find that defendant's conduct in inducing the breach of contract between the plaintiff and [name of breaching party] was not improper. Examples of such present economic interests include property interests, contract rights, and financial interests in the affairs of the person induced. Should you find, however, that the defendant acted improperly in pursuit of defendant's own prospective advantage, not yet realized, then you cannot find that defendant's interference was proper.

The fact that the defendant acted only in the pursuit of generalized competition, even if defendant acted solely by lawful means and without an improper purpose, is not alone sufficient to justify conduct which induced a breach of the plaintiff's contract, when the defendant had no present economic rights of defendant's own to protect.

Comment

Regarding the interests of the defendant, see *Restatement (Second) of Torts* § 767, cmts. d, f (1979); 45 Am. Jur. 2d *Interference,* § 30 (1969 & Supp. 1992). Keeton states that

> [t]he defendant is . . . permitted to interfere with another's contractual relations to protect his own present existing economic interests, such as the ownership or condition of property, or a prior contract of his own, or a financial interest in the affairs of the person persuaded. He is not free, under this rule, to induce a contract breach merely to obtain customers or other prospective economic advantage; but he may do so to protect what he perceives to be existing interests. . . . But where the defendant's interest is merely one of prospective economic advantage, not yet realized, he has no such justification.

Keeton, *supra* at 986–87. Thus, Keeton draws a clear distinction between prospective and current interests, and only interference based upon the latter may be considered proper.

Regarding financial interests in the affairs of others, the *Restatement (Second) of Torts,* section 769 and comment (b) thereto provide that a defendant having a financial interest in the business of the person induced to breach defendant's contract with another is automatically shielded from liability, provided that the defendant does not employ wrongful means and acts to protect defendant's own interests. This automatic immunity, though, applies only to the tort of interference with prospective economic advantage, and *not* to inducing breach of contract. Rather, the general provisions of section 767 of the *Restatement (Second) of Torts* apply in such cases when determining whether the defendant's interference is improper. *See* § 1.05[2], *supra.*

Turning to competition, under the approach adopted by the drafters of the *Restatement,* competition (in the absence of unlawful means or acts) fully immunizes a defendant from liability for interference with prospective economic advantage. The same immunity applies when defendant, a competitor, causes the termination of a third party's contract with plaintiff when the contract in question is terminable at will. *See, e.g., Reazin v. Blue Cross & Blue Shield of Kansas, Inc.,* 663 F. Supp. 1360 (D. Kan. 1987), *aff'd in part and remanded in part,* 899 F.2d 951 (10th Cir.), *cert. denied,* 497 U.S. 1005 (1990). When the contract is terminable at will, a defendant is entitled to a jury instruction to the effect that competition justifies the interference, as long as the means and acts of the defendant in bringing about the termination are not improper in and of themselves. *See id.*

The *Restatement,* however, is somewhat ambiguous about whether the privilege of competition extends to interference with existing enforceable contractual relations. Some statements in the *Restatement* indicate that any attempt to interfere with an existing contract for competitive reasons would be tortious. *See Restatement (Second) of Torts* § 767 cmts. e, f. Other statements, however, would seem to permit the following argument: Although competition might not be recognized as a justification, it might be an affirmative defense because only "improper" interference with a contract is tortious under the

Restatement. Cf. Restatement (Second) of Torts § 768 cmt. h (competition not necessarily improper). For a competitor to send its regular advertising or to solicit business with the knowledge that the potential customer is under contract to a competitor might not necessarily constitute an improper inducement of breach. *See Restatement (Second) of Torts* § 766 cmts. m, n; § 768 cmt. a.

Traditionally, courts have held that the mere offer of better terms to a potential customer constitutes liable conduct for interference with a contract without any further showing as to impropriety. Nevertheless, the *Restatement* itself restricts liability to inducements involving improper means. Therefore, fair and legal competition should not support liability for tortious interference with contractual relations. There is some authority for the latter position. *See, e.g., Ocean State Physicians Health Plan v. Blue Cross,* 883 F.2d 1101 (1st Cir. 1989), *cert. denied,* 494 U.S. 1027 (1990); *Reazin v. Blue Cross & Blue Shield of Kansas,* 663 F. Supp. 1360 (D. Kan. 1987), *aff'd in part and remanded in part,* 899 F.2d 951 (10th Cir.), *cert. denied,* 497 U.S. 1005 (1990); *Pino v. Prudential Ins. Co. of America,* 689 F. Supp. 1358 (E.D. Pa. 1988); *E.D. Lacey Mills, Inc. v. Keith,* 359 S.E.2d 148 (Ga. Ct. App. 1987). Even if competition is not considered justification for breaching an existing contract, the defendant may still prevail if defendant is able to justify defendant's conduct based upon the various factors set forth in the *Restatement. See Restatement (Second) of Torts* § 768 (1979).

1.05[4] Defendant Responsible for Welfare of Another

The defendant's conduct was not improper if you find that the defendant was charged with responsibility for the welfare of [name of breaching party] and that the defendant used reasonable means in a good faith attempt to protect the welfare of [name of breaching party].

Comment

This charge is based on section 770 of the *Restatement (Second) of Torts. See* 45 Am. Jur. 2d *Interference* § 33 (1969 & Supp. 1992); *Reazin v. Blue Cross & Blue Shield of Kansas,* 663 F. Supp. 1360 (D. Kan. 1987), *aff'd in part and remanded in part,* 899 F.2d 951 (10th Cir.), *cert. denied,* 497 U.S. 1005 (1990); *Calbom v. Knudtzon,* 396 P.2d 148 (Wash. 1964).

The existence of a confidential relationship between the defendant and the nonplaintiff contracting party is often the key to establishing the propriety of the defendant's conduct. *See Los Angeles Airways, Inc. v. Davis,* 687 F.2d 321 (9th Cir. 1982); *Hopper v. Lennen & Mitchell,* 52 F. Supp. 319 (S.D. Cal. 1943), *aff'd in part and rev'd in part on other grounds,* 146 F.2d 364 (9th Cir. 1944); *Aalgaard v. Merchants Nat'l Bank, Inc.,* 274 Cal. Rptr. 81 (Cal. Ct. App. 1990).

1.05[5] Advice as Proper or Improper Interference

The defendant's conduct was not improper if you find that the defendant provided truthful information to [name of breaching party] or provided honest advice to [name of breaching party] within the scope of a request for the advice.

Comment

This charge is based on section 772 of the *Restatement (Second) of Torts. See* 45 Am. Jur. 2d *Interference* § 34 (1969 & Supp. 1992); *Air Shells, Inc. v. Harrington,* 697 F. Supp. 896 (W.D. Pa. 1988); *C.N.C. Chem. Corp. v. Pennwalt Corp.,* 690 F. Supp. 139 (D.R.I. 1988); *C.R. Bard, Inc. v. Wordtronics Corp.,* 561 A.2d 694 (N.J. Super. Ct. Law Div. 1989); *Four Nines Gold, Inc. v. 71 Const. Inc.,* 809 P.2d 236 (Wyo. 1991); *Prazma v. Kaehne,* 768 P.2d 586 (Wyo. 1989).

1.05[6] Protection of the Public Welfare

The defendant's conduct was not improper if you find that defendant acted in furtherance of the public welfare. To find that the defendant acted in furtherance of the public welfare, you must find that the defendant acted in furtherance of an established public policy that has a greater social value than ensuring the stability of the contract that was breached. An example of such a situation would be when the contract would have injured the public health, safety, or morals.

Comment

Determining whether the defendant's conduct was proper by virtue of having been undertaken in furtherance of the public welfare requires a balancing of the public interest served against the private interest violated. *See, e.g.,* 45 Am. Jur. 2d *Interference* § 29 (1969 & Supp. 1992); *Brownsville Golden Age Nursing Home, Inc. v. Wells,* 839 F.2d 155 (3d Cir. 1988); *Feminist Women's Health Ctr., Inc. v. Mohammed,* 586 F.2d 530 (5th Cir. 1978), *cert. denied,* 444 U.S. 924 (1979); *Stitzell v. York Memorial Osteopathic Hosp.,* 754 F. Supp. 1061 (M.D. Pa. 1991); *W. Technologies v. Sverdrup & Parcel, Inc.,* 739 P.2d 1318 (Ariz. Ct. App. 1986); *Nat'l Collegiate Athletic Ass'n v. Hornung,* 754 S.W.2d 855 (Ky. 1988).

1.06 Compensatory Damages

1.06[1] Generally

Should you find that the defendant is liable for procuring or causing a breach of the plaintiff's contract, and that defendant's actions were neither justified nor privileged, then you may award such damages as will reasonably compensate the plaintiff for the losses plaintiff has sustained from that breach of its contract.

Comment

The general rule regarding damages recoverable for inducing the breach of a contract is that the broad tort principle for damages is applicable: damages are limited to compensation for the actual loss incurred. *See Restatement (Second) of Torts* § 774A (1979); 45 Am. Jur. 2d *Interference* § 57 (1969 & Supp. 1992); M.C. Dransfield, Annotation, *Liability for Procuring Breach of Contract*, 26 A.L.R.2d 1272 § 43 (1952 & Supp. 1992).

Keeton notes that courts have typically taken one of three approaches for awarding damages in interference with contractual relations cases:

(1) contract method: recovery is limited to damages within the contemplation of the parties when the original contract was created;
(2) tort standard: damages are limited to those which are "proximate" to the injury about which the complaint is made (that is, analogous to damages in negligence actions); and
(3) intentional tort standard: recovery is allowed for unforeseen expenses, damage to reputation, and mental suffering, in addition to punitive damages.

Keeton, *supra* at 1002–03.

The *Restatement* has adopted the third standard. Section 744A provides that one can recover the pecuniary loss, consequential losses, and mental distress damages in an action for interference with a contract. *See Restatement (Second) of Torts* § 744A (1979). Numerous courts have likewise adopted the *Re-*

statement's approach. *See Lake Shore Investors v. Rite Aid Corp.*, 461 A.2d 725 (Md. Ct. Spec. App. 1983) (adopting § 774A and citing other jurisdictions that also have done so), *aff'd*, 471 A.2d 735 (Md. 1984). For the recoverable elements of compensatory damages, see § 1.06[3].

1.06[2] Damages: Impossibility of Precise Calculation No Bar to Recovery

If you find that the plaintiff has in fact suffered damage to its business or property, the fact that the precise amount of damage may be difficult to ascertain does not impair plaintiff's right to recover damages. Although you may not render a verdict based upon mere speculation or guesswork, the plaintiff is allowed some reasonable leeway in its method and proof of damage.

Although the law places a burden upon the plaintiff to prove such facts as will enable you, the jury, to arrive at the amount of damages with reasonable certainty, it is not necessary that the plaintiff prove the amount of those damages with mathematical precision. It is required that the plaintiff present only such evidence as might reasonably be expected to be available under the circumstances.

You are permitted to determine the amount of damage by estimation or approximation, as long as a reasonable basis for such estimate or approximation is shown with reasonable certainty. You may use any formula or theory for determining damages that is based upon the evidence in the case and that you believe to be reasonable; you are not bound to reject a formula or theory simply because it does not measure damages to the exact dollar and cent.

Comment

This instruction reflects the established rule that absolute precision is not required for an award of damages, even though total speculation may not be used. Estimation is permitted as long as its method is justified by the record admitted into evidence. *See Restatement (Second) of Torts* § 774A cmt. c (1979); 45 Am. Jur. 2d *Interference* § 57 (1969 & Supp. 1992); *Selby v. Pelletier*, 472 A.2d 1285 (Conn. App. Ct. 1984); *Daly v. Nau*, 339 N.E.2d 71 (Ind. Ct. App. 1975); *Steitz v. Gifford*, 19 N.E.2d 661 (N.Y. 1939). *See also Restatement (Second) of Torts* § 912 (1979). For the rule as applied to other torts, see 22 Am. Jur. 2d *Torts* §§ 819–23 (1988 & Supp. 1992).

1.06[3] Recoverable Elements of Damages

In determining the amount of compensatory damages, you may consider whether the plaintiff suffered any measurable loss of profits by reason of the defendant's conduct. You should be guided by the rule that the plaintiff is entitled to any profits that plaintiff would, with reasonable certainty, have enjoyed, were it not for the breach of plaintiff's contract. In arriving at the amount of profits lost by the plaintiff, you are entitled to consider the plaintiff's past earnings in its business and, in particular, those past earnings resulting from contracts of the nature of the contract in this case. You should also consider all of the other evidence concerning general economic and competitive conditions that you may find to have a bearing on the issue of lost profits.

In addition to lost profits, the plaintiff is entitled to recover any reasonable costs it incurred in an effort to mitigate or reduce plaintiff's damages and to recover business plaintiff lost due to the defendant's wrongful conduct. As a result, you may consider the plaintiff's expenses in determining the amount of compensatory damages.

Comment

Many authorities address the issue of lost profits. *See* 45 Am. Jur. 2d *Interference* §§ 57, 58 (1969 & Supp.1992); *Marcus, Stowell & Beye Gov't Sec., Inc. v. Jefferson Inv. Corp.*, 797 F.2d 227 (5th Cir. 1986); *R.E. Davis Chem. Corp. v. Diasonics, Inc.*, 826 F.2d 678 (7th Cir. 1987); *Central Telecommunications, Inc. v. TCI Cablevision, Inc.*, 800 F.2d 711 (8th Cir. 1986), *cert. denied*, 480 U.S. 910 (1987); *Upjohn Co. v. Riahom Corp.*, 650 F. Supp. 485 (D. Del. 1986); *see also* Charles S. Marvel, Annotation, *Recovery Based on Tortfeasor's Profits in Action for Procuring Breach of Contract*, 5 A.L.R.4th 1296 (1981 & Supp. 1992). Concerning recovery of costs of mitigation or recoupment, see M.C. Dransfield, Annotation, *Liability for Procuring Breach of Contract*, 26 A.L.R.2d 1227 § 43 (1952 & Supp. 1992).

Damages may be recovered in some jurisdictions for mental distress arising out of the interference of contractual relations. *See Restatement (Second) of Torts* § 774A (1979); *Westfield Dev. Co. v. Rifle Inv. Assoc.*, 786 P.2d 1112 (Colo. 1990) (mental distress may be sole element of damages); *Mooney v. Johnson Cattle, Inc.*, 634 P.2d 1333 (Or. 1981).

Although the measure of damages recoverable in an action for inducing a breach of contract varies among jurisdictions, it is generally said that the defendant should be held responsible for all of the quantifiable consequences of defendant's tortious conduct. *E.g.*, 45 Am. Jur. 2d §§ 57–61 *Interference* (1969 & Supp. 1992); *Restatement (Second) of Torts* § 774A (1979). Counsel should examine the case law in each jurisdiction to determine the extent of damages to which the plaintiff may be entitled.

1.06[4] Plaintiff's Burden of Proof

The law distinguishes between the measure of proof necessary to establish the fact that the plaintiff sustained an injury and that which is required to enable you to fix the amount of that damage. As I have instructed you, the fact of injury by reason of the alleged violation must be established by a preponderance of the evidence. This is a higher or more strict degree of proof than is required in proving the amount of damages. In proving the amount of damages, the law requires only that the plaintiff prove such facts as will enable you to arrive at the amount of damages with reasonable certainty. Moreover, the plaintiff is not required to prove the exact amount of damages, but to present only such evidence as might reasonably be expected to be available under the circumstances.

Comment

This instruction represents the general rule imposing a lesser burden of proof on the plaintiff concerning the amount of damage than for the fact of some damage or for establishing the defendant's liability. *See, e.g., H.L. Hayden Co. v. Siemens Medical Sys., Inc.,* 879 F.2d 1005 (2d Cir. 1989); *Franklin Music Co. v. Am. Broadcasting Co.,* 616 F.2d 528 (3d Cir. 1979).

1.07 Punitive Damages

1.07[1] Generally

In addition to actual damages, the law permits you, under certain circumstances, to award the plaintiff what are known as "punitive" or "exemplary" damages. Such damages are awarded in proper and specified instances to punish a wrongdoer for some extraordinary misconduct and to warn others not to engage in similar conduct.

Should you find from a preponderance of the evidence that the plaintiff is entitled to a verdict for actual or compensatory damages, and should you further find that the act or omission of the defendant that proximately caused the actual injury or damage to the plaintiff was malicious, wanton, or oppressive, then you, the jury, may, should you so choose, add to the award of actual damages against the defendant such punitive damages as you shall find to be proper.

Comment

This charge represents the modern view of damages. *See, e.g., Restatement (Second) of Torts* § 908 (1979); 45 Am. Jur. 2d *Interference* § 61 (1969 & Supp. 1992). The *Restatement* makes clear that under appropriate circumstances, punitive damages may be awarded for the tort of contractual interference. *Restatement (Second) of Torts* § 774A cmt. a (1979). *See generally* Sara L. Johnson, Annotation, *Punitive Damages for Interference with Contract or Business Relationship,* 44 A.L.R.4th 1078 (1986 & Supp. 1992). Counsel should note that although generally punitive damages will be awarded upon a showing of malice, wantonness, or oppressiveness, this principle is not universal and may as well be affected by statute in a particular jurisdiction.

For a discussion of the prerequisite of a verdict for actual damages, see the comment to § 1.07[5]. For the requirement of malicious, wanton, or oppressive conduct, see §§ 1.07[2], 1.07[3], and 1.07[4]. *See generally* Lee H. Russ, Annotation, *Standard of Proof As to Conduct Underlying Punitive Damage Awards—Modern Status,* 58 A.L.R.4th 878 (1987 & Supp. 1992).

1.07[2] Requirement of Actual Malice

You may find the defendant's conduct to have been undertaken with actual "malice" sufficient to enable you to award punitive damages if you find it to have been prompted or accompanied by ill will, spite, or a grudge, either toward the plaintiff individually or toward all persons in one or more groups or categories of which the plaintiff is a member.

Comment

Generally, courts require proof of facts tending to establish actual, as opposed to legal, malice to justify an award of punitive damages. *See* 45 Am. Jur. 2d *Interference* § 61 (1969 & Supp. 1992); *Norwood Easthill Assoc. v. Norwood Easthill Watch,* 536 A.2d 1317 (N.J. Super. Ct. App. Div. 1988); *Anthony Pools, Inc. v. Charles & David, Inc.,* 797 S.W.2d 666 (Tex. Ct. App. 1990); *Bellefonte Underwriters Co., Inc. v. Brown,* 663 S.W.2d 562 (Tex. Ct. App. 1984).

Even if not required, actual malice is always an important factor in an award of punitive damages. *See, e.g., Int'l Wood Processors Corp. v. Power Dry, Inc.,* 593 F. Supp. 710 (D.S.C. 1984); *Universal City Studios, Inc. v. Nintendo Co.,* 615 F. Supp. 838 (S.D.N.Y. 1985), *aff'd,* 797 F.2d 70 (2d Cir.), *cert. denied,* 479 U.S. 987 (1986); *Edward Vantine Studios, Inc. v. Fraternal Composite Serv., Inc.,* 373 N.W.2d 512 (Iowa Ct. App. 1985).

1.07[3] Wanton Conduct

You may also award punitive damages if you find that the defendant's act or failure to act was "wantonly" done; that is, that it was undertaken in reckless or callous disregard of, or indifference to, the rights of one or more persons, including the plaintiff.

Comment

See Universal City Studios, Inc. v. Nintendo Co., 615 F. Supp. 838, 863 (S.D.N.Y. 1985), *aff'd,* 797 F.2d 70 (2d Cir.), *cert. denied,* 479 U.S. 987 (1986); *King v. G.D. Van Wagenen Co.,* 717 F. Supp. 667 (D. Minn. 1989); *Liston v. Home Ins. Co.,* 659 F. Supp. 276 (S.D. Miss. 1986); *Ramona Manor Convalescent Hosp. v. Care Enterprises,* 225 Cal. Rptr. 120 (Cal. Ct. App. 1986).

1.07[4] Oppressive Conduct

You also may award punitive damages if, from all of the evidence, you find that the defendant's act or failure to act was "oppressive"; that is, that it was done in a way or manner that injured, damaged, or otherwise violated the rights of the plaintiff with unnecessary harshness or severity, as by misuse or abuse of authority or power, or by taking advantage of some weakness, disability, or misfortune of the plaintiff.

Comment

See Barnes Group, Inc. v. C & C Prod., Inc., 716 F.2d 1023 (4th Cir. 1983); *Rabun v. Kimberly-Clark Corp.*, 678 F.2d 1053 (11th Cir. 1982); *Int'l Wood Processors Corp. v. Power Dry, Inc.*, 593 F. Supp. 710 (D.S.C. 1984), *aff'd*, 792 F.2d 416 (4th Cir. 1986).

1.07[5] Prerequisite of Actual or Nominal Damages

The award of only a nominal sum with respect to the specific losses claimed by the plaintiff will not prevent your awarding punitive damages if you find that the award of punitive damages is justified under these instructions.

Comment

In most states the jury must make a finding of liability and actual, or at least nominal, damages before punitive damages are allowed. *See* Richard C. Tinney, Annotation, *Showing of Actual Damages to Support Award of Punitive Damages,* 40 A.L.R.4th 11 (1985 & Supp. 1992); 45 Am. Jur. 2d *Interference* § 61; *Am. Business Interiors, Inc. v. Haworth, Inc.,* 798 F.2d 1135 (8th Cir. 1986). *But see Platte v. Whitney Realty Co.,* 538 So. 2d 1358 (Fla. Dist. Ct. App. 1989) (punitive damages recoverable although actual damages could not be proved).

In most jurisdictions, an award of nominal damages will suffice for this purpose. *E.g., Taylor v. Sandoval,* 442 F. Supp. 491 (D. Colo. 1977); *Tennant v. Vazquez,* 389 So. 2d 1183 (Fla. Dist. Ct. App. 1980); *Christman v. Voyer,* 595 P.2d 410 (N.M. Ct. App. 1979). *But see Wussow v. Commercial Mechanisms, Inc.,* 279 N.W.2d 503 (Wis. Ct. App. 1979). *See generally* Richard C. Tinney, Annotation, *Showing of Actual Damages to Support Award of Punitive Damages—Modern Cases,* 40 A.L.R.4th 11 (1985 & Supp. 1992).

1.07[6] Decision to Award Punitive Damages: Exclusive Province of the Jury

The decision whether to make any award of punitive damages, in addition to actual damages, is a matter exclusively within the province of you, the jury. To award punitive damages, however, you must find that the defendant's act or omission that proximately caused actual damage to the plaintiff was malicious, wanton, or oppressive, as measured by the instructions I have just given you. You should bear in mind not only the conditions under which, and the purposes for which, the law permits an award of punitive damages to be made, but also the requirement of the law that the amount of such extraordinary damages, when awarded, must be fixed with calm discretion and sound reason and must never be either awarded or affixed in amount because of any sympathy, bias, or prejudice with respect to any party to the case. The award of only a nominal sum for compensatory damages should not, however, prevent you from awarding punitive damages if you find that an award of such damages is justified under these instructions.

Comment

See Restatement (Second) of Torts § 908 cmt. d (1979); 45 Am. Jur. 2d *Torts* § 739 (1988 & Supp. 1992); *Rabun v. Kimberly-Clark Corp.*, 678 F.2d 1053 (11th Cir. 1982); *Christman v. Voyer*, 595 P.2d 410 (N.M. Ct. App. 1979); *Wussow v. Commercial Mechanisms, Inc.*, 279 N.W.2d 503 (Wis. Ct. App. 1979).

1.07[7] Factors the Jury May Consider

Factors you may consider in making an award of punitive damages are as follows:

(1) the character of the defendant's act;
(2) the nature and extent of the harm to the plaintiff that the defendant caused or intended to cause; and
(3) the defendant's wealth.

As I instructed you earlier, the character of the defendant's conduct may suffice for an award of punitive damages when the defendant acted with personal ill will, spite, or hatred; when the defendant acted with conscious disregard of the rights of the plaintiff; or when the defendant acted in an oppressive fashion.

The nature and extent of the harm done to the plaintiff is an important factor in your determination of the amount of any award of punitive damages, as the law generally requires that the amount of punitive damages awarded bear some reasonable relationship to the amount of actual damage and harm inflicted.

Finally, because punishment and discouragement are the fundamental purposes of punitive damages, you may consider the wealth of the defendant to determine what amount of damages will constitute true punishment.

Comment

See Hollins v. Powell, 773 F.2d 191 (8th Cir.), *cert. denied*, 475 U.S. 1119 (1985); *Miller v. Rukoff-Sexton, Inc.*, 845 F.2d 209 (9th Cir. 1988); *Rupert v. Sellers*, 368 N.Y.S.2d 904 (N.Y. App. Div. 1975). *See generally* Annotation, *Punitive Damages: Relationship to Defendant's Wealth As a Factor in Determining Propriety of Award*, 87 A.L.R.4th 141 (1991 & Supp. 1992). Some states, such as Hawaii, have statutes making the financial condition of the defendant relevant to the amount of punitive damages awardable. Others, like New York, protect the defendant from possible prejudice at trial through the use of a bifurcated trial procedure. *See Aldrich v. Thomson McKinnon Sec., Inc.,* 589 F. Supp. 683 (S.D.N.Y. 1984).

Chapter Two

Interference with Prospective Advantage

2.01 Introduction

Gary C. Crapster

The model jury charges in this section address the conditions of liability at common law of one who unjustifiably interferes with another's reasonable expectations of economic advantage. Denominated as interference with prospective advantage or interference with business relations, this business tort continues to expand. Because its boundaries are flexible and vague, this business tort may provide recourse for a person in business who has been aggrieved by conduct that does not fit other, better-defined business torts.

This chapter focuses on tortious interference with economic relationships that fall short of consummated contracts. The business torts discussed in Chapters One and Two (inducing breach of contract and interference with prospective advantage) are generally recognized as subcategories of the broader concept of interference with advantageous economic relations. Both torts have long been recognized at common law, but the developing jurisprudence continues to be heavily influenced by the *Restatement (Second) of Torts* (1977), which places both torts under the broader category of interference with advantageous economic relations. After discussing the tort of interference with contractual relations in sections 766 and 766A, the *Restatement (Second)* in section 766B sets forth the elements of tortious interference with prospective contractual relations. The *Restatement (Second)* then discusses legal principles related to both torts in sections 767–774A. Although there are many similarities between the two torts, liability against the defendant is frequently easier to prove when there is an existing contract, rather than only a prospective relationship. This is because there is a stronger public policy to protect relations that have reached the point of enforceable rights for both sides. *Pac. Gas & Elec. v. Bear Stearns & Co., et al.*, 791 P.2d 587 (Cal. 1990).

The central inquiry surrounding the tort of interference with prospective economic advantage involves an issue it shares with the related business tort discussed in Chapter One: whether, under all of the circumstances, the interference with the prospective advantage is "improper." The test for impropriety is necessarily vague because of the myriad of fact patterns in which such conduct can arise. According to the *Restatement (Second) of Torts* (1977), the "real question is whether the actor's conduct was fair and reasonable under the circumstances. Recognized standards of business ethics, business customs and practices are pertinent, and consideration is given to concepts of fair play and whether the defendant's interference is not sanctioned by the 'rules of the game.'" *Restatement (Second) of Torts* § 767(g) cmt. (1977).

The courts in almost all jurisdictions will protect reasonable expectations of future economic advantage—not just those evidenced by contract—from improper interference. Thus, liability may be imposed for "interfering with an existing noncontractual relationship, with relations, generally." 17 P.O.F.2d 517, 524–25 *Tortious Interference with At Will Business Relationship* (1978); 45 Am. Jur. 2d *Interference* § 49 (1969). Some examples are interference with the prospect of acquiring employment or employees, the opportunity of purchasing or selling goods or services, the opportunity for brokerage commissions, leasing opportunities, lending relationships, and practically any other commercial relationship imaginable that would probably lead to economic benefits. *See generally* Note, *Tortious Interference with Conduct of a Business*, 56 Yale L.J. 885 (1947); William L. Prosser, *The Law of Torts* § 130 (4th ed. 1971).

The specific elements of this tort listed by the courts of most jurisdictions are similar but not identical. In substance, the courts of almost all jurisdictions have generally required at least the following:

(1) the existence of a valid business relationship or expectancy, with the reasonable probability of future economic benefit to the plaintiff;
(2) knowledge of the relationship or expectancy on the part of the defendant or that it was readily apparent to the defendant;
(3) a reasonable certainty that, except for the conduct of the defendant, the plaintiff would have entered into or continued the relationship;

(4) interference of the defendant that was intentional, as opposed to negligent; and
(5) economic damage to the plaintiff as a result of the defendant's interference.

The most significant difference noted among the various states involves the procedural treatment given by the courts to the issue of whether the defendant's conduct under the particular circumstances is the type of conduct that society should discourage. Although there is consensus that only "improper" or "tortious" conduct should be compensable, courts in different jurisdictions disagree about the burden of proof on this issue. From a defense perspective, the issue may take the form of whether the defendant's conduct was justified or privileged. From the plaintiff's perspective, however, the issue may be whether the law requires proof that the defendant's interference was truly tortious or "improper."

The various states are not in accord on whether the plaintiff must plead and prove that the conduct itself was improper as an additional element to those listed above, or whether the defendant has the burden to prove any particular justification or privilege that may apply. The majority of the cases that followed the original *Restatement of Torts* (1939) held that once the plaintiff showed an intentional interference, the defendant had the burden to prove any justification or privilege. The *Restatement (Second) of Torts* (1977), however, requires as an element of the tort that the defendant intentionally *and improperly* interfere with the plaintiff's prospective advantage. Although the comments to the *Restatement (Second) of Torts* (1977) acknowledge the split of authority and do not purport to determine the burden-of-proof issue conclusively, the addition of the "improper" element in the *Restatement (Second)* has significantly affected the development of the law. The majority of states now require that the plaintiff show as an element of the tort that the defendant's conduct was based upon either an improper motive or an improper means.

The two sections of the *Restatement (Second) of Torts* (1977) that have heavily influenced the development of the law are sections 766B and 767:

§ 766B *Intentional Interference with Prospective Contractual Relation*

One who intentionally and improperly interferes with another's prospective contractual relation (except a contract to marry) is subject to liability to the other for the pecuniary harm resulting from loss of the benefits of the relation, whether the interference consists of

(a) inducing or otherwise causing a third person not to enter into or continue the prospective relation or
(b) preventing the other from acquiring or continuing the prospective relation.

§ 767 *Factors in Determining Whether Interference Is Improper*

In determining whether an actor's conduct in intentionally interfering with a contract or a prospective contractual relation of another is improper or not, consideration is given to the following factors:

(a) the nature of the actor's conduct,
(b) the actor's motive,
(c) the interests of the other with which the actor's conduct interferes,
(d) the interests sought to be advanced by the actor,
(e) the social interests in protecting the freedom of action of the actor and the contractual interests of the other,
(f) the proximity or remoteness of the actor's conduct to the interference, and
(g) the relations between the parties.

Examples of cases that define the tort without requiring proof of malicious, inherently tortious, or otherwise improper conduct are: *Cherry, Bekaert & Holland v. Brown*, 582 So.2d 502 (Ala. 1991); *Alyeska Pipeline Serv. Co. v. Aurora Air Serv., Inc.*, 604 P.2d 1090 (Alaska 1979), *but see Geolar, Inc. v. Gilbert/Commonwealth, Inc. of Michigan*, 874 P.2d 937 (Alaska 1994) (suggesting improper conduct usually issue for jury); *Antwerp Diamond Exch. of Am., Inc. v. Better Business Bureau of Maricopa County, Inc.*, 637 P.2d 733 (Ariz. 1981); *United Bilt Homes, Inc. v. Sampson*, 832 S.W.2d 502 (Ark. 1992) (but noting conduct unjustified); *Blank v. Kirwan*, 703 P.2d 58 (Cal. 1985); *Seaman's Direct Buying Serv., Inc. v. Standard Oil Co. of California*, 686 P.2d 1158 (Cal. 1984); *Buckaloo v. Johnson*, 537 P.2d 865 (Cal. 1975); *Aalgaard v. Merchants Nat'l Bank, Inc.*, 274 Cal. Rptr. 81

(Cal. Ct. App. 1990); *Fellhauer v. City of Geneva*, 568 N.E.2d 870 (Ill. 1991); *Eisenbach v. Esformes*, 582 N.E.2d 196 (Ill. 1991); *Macke Laundry Serv. Ltd. Partnership v. Mission Assocs., Ltd.*, 873 P.2d 219 (Kan. 1994); *Owen v. Williams*, 77 N.E.2d 318 (Mass. 1948); *Joba Constr. Co. v. Burns & Roe, Inc., 329* N.W.2d 760 (Mich. Ct. App. 1982); *Rusk Farms, Inc. v. Ralston Purina Co.*, 689 S.W.2d 671, 679 (Mo. Ct. App. 1985); *Mike Pratt & Sons, Inc. v. Metalcraft, Inc.*, 383 N.W.2d 758 (Neb. 1986); *Victoria Bank & Trust Co. v. Brady*, 811 S.W.2d 931 (Tex. 1991) (involving interference with contract rights, but specifically removing lack of justification as element of plaintiff's claim); *Mitchell v. Aldrich*, 163 A.2d 833 (Vt. 1960); *Catercorp., Inc. v. Catering Concepts, Inc.*, 431 S.E.2d 277 (Va. 1993); *Sea-Pac Co., Inc. v. United Food and Commercial Workers Local Union*, 699 P.2d 217 (Wash. 1985); *Cherberg v. Peoples Nat'l Bank of Washington*, 564 P.2d 1137 (Wash. 1977); *King v. City of Seattle*, 525 P.2d 228 (Wash. 1974); *Calbom v. Knudtzon*, 396 P.2d 148 (Wash. 1964); *C. W. Dev., Inc. v. Structures, Inc. of West Virginia*, 408 S.E.2d 41 (W. Va. 1991); *Bd. of Trustees of Weston County Sch. Dist. No. 1, Weston County v. Holso*, 584 P.2d 1009 (Wyo. 1978); *Daniels v. Dean*, 833 P.2d 1078 (Mont. 1992).

Examples of cases that require the plaintiff to show more specifically as part of its prima facie case that the defendant's conduct was tortious in itself or "improper" as labeled by section 766B of the *Restatement (Second) of Torts* (1977) are: *Geolar, Inc. v. Gilbert/Commonwealth, Inc. of Michigan*, 874 P.2d 937 (Alaska, 1994); *Fantaco Enter., Inc. v. Iavarone*, 555 N.Y.S.2d 921 (N.Y. App. Div. 1990); *Int'l Mining Co. v. Allen & Co., Inc.*, 567 F. Supp. 777 (S.D.N.Y. 1983) (citing New York law); *Ellis v. City of Valdez*, 686 P.2d 700 (Alaska 1984); *Envtl. Plan. v. Superior Court (Detmold Pub.)*, 680 P.2d 1086 (Cal. 1984); *Rickel v. Schwinn Bicycle Co.*, 192 Cal. Rptr. 732 (Cal. Ct. App. 1983); *Solomon v. Aberman*, 493 A.2d 193 (Conn. 1985); *Blake v. Levy*, 464 A.2d 52 (Conn. 1983); *Sportsmen's Boating Corp. v. Hensley*, 474 A.2d 780 (Conn. 1983); *Green v. Johnston Realty*, 442 S.E.2d 843 (Ga. 1994); *Lykins v. Nationwide Mut. Inc. Co.*, 448 S.E.2d 716 (Ga. Ct. App. 1994); *Harsha v. State Sav. Bank*, 346 N.W.2d 791 (Iowa 1984); *Nesler v. Fisher & Co.*, 452 N.W.2d 191, 199

(Iowa 1990); *Fischer v. Unipac Serv. Corp.*, 519 N.W.2d 793 (Iowa 1994); *Travelers Indem. v. Merling*, 605 A.2d 83 (Md. 1992); *United Wild Rice, Inc. v. Nelson*, 313 N.W.2d 628 (Minn. 1982); *Buller v. Pulitzer Publishing Co.*, 684 S.W.2d 473 (Mo. Ct. App. 1984); *Am. Business Interiors v. Haworth, Inc.*, 798 F.2d 1135 (8th Cir. 1986) (Missouri law required plaintiff to show no justification, but noted that innocent conduct might suffice); *Killian Constr. Co. v. Jack D. Ball & Assoc.*, 865 S.W.2d 889 (Mo. Ct. App. 1993); *Bolz v. Myers*, 651 P.2d 606 (Mont. 1982); *M&M Rental Tools, Inc. v. Milchem, Inc.*, 612 P.2d 241 (N.M. Ct. App. 1980); *Embree Constr. Group, Inc. v. Rafcor, Inc.*, 411 S.E.2d 916 (N.C. 1992); *Cameron v. New Hanover Memorial Hosp., Inc.*, 293 S.E.2d 901 (N.C. Ct. App. 1982); *Spartan Equip. Co. v. Air Placement Equip. Co.*, 140 S.E.2d 3 (N.C. 1965); *Top Serv. Body Shop v. Allstate Ins. Co.*, 582 P.2d 1365 (Or. 1978); *Willamette Dental Group, P.C. v. Oregon Dental Serv. Corp.*, 882 P.2d 637 (Or. Ct. App. 1994); *Thompson v. Tel. & Data Sys., Inc.*, 881 P.2d 819 (Or. Ct. App. 1994); *Yaindl v. Ingersoll-Rand Co.*, 422 A.2d 611 (Pa. 1980); *Triffin v. Janssen*, 626 A.2d 571 (Pa. Super. Ct. 1993); *Schulman v. J.P. Morgan Inv. Management, Inc.*, 35 F.3d 799 (3d Cir. 1994) (applying Pennsylvania law); *Adler, Barish, Daniels, Levin and Creskoff v. Epstein*, 393 A.2d 1175 (Pa. 1978); *Glenn v. Point Park College*, 272 A.2d 895 (Pa. 1971); *Cloverleaf Dev., Inc. v. Horizon Fin., F.A.*, 500 A.2d 163 (Pa. Super. Ct. 1985); *State Nat'l Bank of El Paso v. Farah Mfg. Co., Inc.*, 678 S.W.2d 661, 688 (Tex. Ct. App. 1984); *Deauville Corp. v. Federated Dep't Stores*, 756 F.2d 1183, 1196 (5th Cir. 1985); *Leigh Furniture and Carpet Co. v. Isom*, 657 P.2d 293 (Utah 1982); *Quadra Enter., Inc. v. R.A. Hanson Co., Inc.*, 667 P.2d 1120 (Wash. Ct. App. 1983); *Torbett v. Wheeling Dollar Sav. & Trust Co.*, 314 S.E.2d 166 (W. Va. 1983); *Liebe v. City Fin. Co.*, 295 N.W.2d 16 (Wis. Ct. App. 1980); *Four Nines Gold, Inc. v. 71 Constr., Inc.*, 809 P.2d 236 (Wyo. 1991).

Note that many of the decisions, particularly those published before the *Restatement (Second) of Torts* (1977), do not focus on the specific differences in approach among the various jurisdictions. Opinions with specific discussions of the split of authority are: *Seaman's Direct Buying Serv. Inc. v. Standard Oil*

Co. of California, 686 P.2d 1158, 1165 (Cal. 1984); *Aalgaard v. Merchants Nat'l Bank, Inc.,* 274 Cal. Rptr. 81 (Cal. Ct. App. 1990); *Ramona Manor Convalescent Hosp. v. Care Enter.,* 225 Cal. Rptr. 120 (Cal. Ct. App. 1986); *Harsha v. State Sav. Bank,* 346 N.W.2d 791, 799–800 (Iowa 1984); *United Wild Rice, Inc. v. Nelson,* 313 N.W.2d 628, 632–33 (Minn. 1982); *Yaindl v. Ingersoll-Rand Co.,* 422 A.2d 611, 622 (Pa. 1980); *Adler, Barish, Daniels, Levin and Creskoff v. Epstein,* 393 A.2d 1175 (Pa. 1978); *Victoria Bank & Trust v. Brady,* 811 S.W.2d 931 (Tex. 1991); *Leigh Furniture and Carpet Co. v. Isom,* 657 P.2d 293, 302–05 (Utah 1982).

The jury issues in this chapter are prepared in the alternative to make them more easily adaptable to the legal requirements of the various jurisdictions.

2.02 General Instructions

2.02[1] Theory of Interference with Prospective Advantage

In this case the plaintiff, [name], seeks to recover money damages from the defendant, [name], for alleged interference with plaintiff's prospective advantage. That is, the plaintiff contends that, because of the defendant's conduct, plaintiff was prevented from [state what plaintiff would have acquired], and as a result plaintiff suffered monetary loss.

The law recognizes that everyone has a right to establish and conduct a lawful business, free from unjustified interference, and is entitled to the protection of organized society, through its courts, whenever that right is unlawfully invaded. Generally speaking, the question for you to decide is whether the plaintiff's right to such an expectancy has in fact been invaded, and whether, under all of the factors I will instruct you to consider, any such invasion was improper.

In these charges, I will give you the applicable legal principles upon which you are to determine this question.

Comment

This charge is based upon language from *Buxbom v. Smith,* 145 P.2d 305, 310 (Cal. 1944). *See also* Fowler v. Harper, *Law of Torts* § 6.11 (2d ed. 1986).

2.02[2] Elements of Liability

To find liability for interference with prospective advantage, you, the jury, must find from a preponderance of evidence:

(1) that there existed a [business relationship or expectancy—choose one] with the probability of future economic benefit for the plaintiff;

(2) that the defendant, at the time the acts complained of were committed, knew of this relationship or expectancy, or should have known of it;

(3) that, except for the conduct of the defendant, the plaintiff was reasonably certain to have continued the business relationship or to have entered into [state nature of expectancy];

(4) that the conduct of the defendant was intentional;

(5) [optional—depending upon law of jurisdiction] that the conduct of the defendant was improper under the factors I will instruct you to consider; and

(6) that as a direct and proximate result, the plaintiff suffered damage.

If you find that the plaintiff has proved each of these elements by a preponderance of the evidence, then you will consider the question of the amount of money damages under instructions I will give you.

Comment

This charge reflects the traditional standard for establishing liability, and includes the optional element of improper conduct on the part of the defendant. This element, included in the *Restatement (Second) of Torts* (1977), is required by an increasing number of jurisdictions. For a more detailed discussion, see § 2.01 and the cases cited there. In some jurisdictions this issue must be raised by the defendant as part of defendant's justification or privilege defense. In jurisdictions of this latter variety, item (5) listed above should be omitted, and the propriety of the defendant's conduct should be framed defensively with the burden of proof on the defendant. *See* § 2.09, *infra.*

2.03 Existence of Relationship

2.03[1] Generally

The plaintiff contends that at the time of the defendant's conduct, there existed a [state business relationship or expectancy, whichever is applicable]. You must first determine whether there existed such a [business relationship or expectancy—choose one].

In determining this question, the [business relationship or expectancy—choose one] need not be evidenced by a contract. It is sufficient if you find from the evidence that there were either prior dealings or a prior course of conduct between plaintiff and [name of third party] from which there would be a reasonable expectation of future economic benefit. The plaintiff must show this expected benefit with some degree of specificity, such that it is a realistic expectation, but it need not be shown with certainty, because prospective things in nature are necessarily uncertain. The law requires more than a mere hope or optimism; what is required is a reasonable likelihood or probability.

Comment

The relationship itself must be between the plaintiff and some entity other than the defendant. However, courts may reach differing conclusions on whether interference among parties to a triangular relationship may apply. For a discussion involving insurer/agent/insured, see *Travelers Indemnity v. Merling*, 605 A.2d 80, 83 (Md. 1992).

There must have been a reasonable likelihood of an economic benefit to the plaintiff before any liability should be found. Sometimes, the fact that a contract once existed, but expired, may demonstrate no relationship remains. *See, e.g., Ice Bros., Inc. v. Bannowsky*, 840 S.W.2d 57 (Tex. Civ. App. 1992); *Macke Laundry Serv. Ltd. Partnership v. Mission Assoc., Ltd.*, 873 P.2d 219 (Kan. 1994); *Ontap Premium Quality Waters, Inc. v. Bank of N. Illinois, N.A.*, 634 N.E.2d 425 (Ill. App. Ct. 1994); *Am. Business Interiors v. Haworth, Inc.*, 798 F.2d 1135 (8th Cir. 1986); *see also Verkin v. Melroy*, 699 F.2d 729 (5th Cir. 1983); *Youst v. Longo*, 729 P.2d 728 (Cal. 1987); *Buckaloo v. Johnson*, 537 P.2d 865 (Cal. 1975); *North v. State*, 400 N.W.2d 566 (Iowa 1987); *Joba Constr. Co. v. Burns & Roe, Inc.*, 329 N.W.2d 760 (Mich. Ct. App. 1982); *Schipani v. Ford Motor Co.*, 302 N.W.2d 307 (Mich. Ct. App. 1981); *Thompson Coal Co. v. Pike Coal Co.*, 412 A.2d 466, 471 (Pa. 1979); *Behrend v. Bell Tel. Co.*, 363 A.2d 1152 (Pa. Super. Ct. 1976); *Mobil Oil Corp. v. Cook*, 494 S.W.2d 926 (Tex. Civ. App. 1973); *Sea-Pac Co., Inc. v. United Food and Commercial Workers Local Union*, 699 P.2d 217 (Wash. 1985); *Broten v. May*, 735 P.2d 86 (Wash. Ct. App. 1987). The plaintiff should be able to articulate the existence of a specific relationship with a specific party rather than speculate by, or based on, inconclusory terms that some relationship might have existed absent the defendant's conduct. *DuPage Aviation Corp. v. DuPage Airport Authority*, 594 N.E.2d 1334 (Ill. App. Ct. 1993); *Continental Mobile Tel. Co., Inc. v. Chicago SMSA Ltd. Partnership*, 587 N.E.2d 1169 (Ill. App. Ct. 1992); *Eisenbach v. Esformes*, 582 N.E.2d 196 (Ill. 1991).

This charge assumes that the business relationship or expectancy is a "valid" one. *See* 45 Am. Jur. 2d *Interference* §§ 7, 50 (1969). If the facts of specific cases raise questions about whether the relationship or expectancy is illegal under the applicable law, the charge should be drafted to reflect this question. Relationships terminable at will that involve unenforceable covenants not to compete, for example, cannot form the basis for an action for tortious interference. *Travel Masters, Inc. v. Star Tours, Inc.*, 827 S.W.2d 830 (Tex. 1992). An opinion excluding all competitive contests or sporting contests is found in *Youst v. Longo*, 729 P.2d 728 (Cal. 1987).

2.04 Knowledge

2.04[1] Generally

To find for the plaintiff, you must also find that the defendant knew of the existence of this [business relationship or expectancy—choose one]. To have knowledge means that the defendant has information concerning the [business relationship or expectancy—choose one], which was discovered by the defendant or was brought to defendant's attention by others.

In this regard, knowledge may be found to exist if, from the facts and circumstances of which the defendant had knowledge, the defendant should have known of the existence of such [business relationship or expectancy—choose one].

Comment

Almost all cases require that the defendant knew of the existence of the relationship, because the action is an intentional tort. *See Southwestern Bell Tel. Co. v. John Carlo Texas, Inc.*, 843 S.W.2d 470 (Tex. 1992); *Macke Laundry Serv. Ltd. Partnership v. Mission Assoc., Ltd.*, 873 P.2d 219 (Kan. 1994); *Blank v. Kirwan*, 703 P.2d 58 (Cal. 1985); *Seaman's Direct Buying Serv., Inc. v. Standard Oil Co. of California*, 686 P.2d 1158, 1165 (Cal. 1984); *O'Fallon Dev. Co., Inc. v. City of O'Fallon*, 356 N.E.2d 1293 (Ill. App. Ct. 1976); *Witte Transp. Co. v. Murphy Motor Freight Lines, Inc.*, 193 N.W.2d 148 (Minn. 1971); *Chaves v. Johnson*, 335 S.E.2d 97 (Va. 1985); *King v. Seattle*, 525 P.2d 228 (Wash. 1974); *Bd. of Trustees of Weston County Sch. Dist. No. 1, Weston County v. Holso*, 584 P.2d 1009 (Wyo. 1978).

Note that disputes may arise when the claim is that a defendant corporation had knowledge because one of its employees was aware of the relationship. The dispute would be whether that employee's knowledge can be attributed to the employer. This charge does not address that issue, and the law of the applicable jurisdiction should be applied.

2.05 Causation

2.05[1] Generally

You, the jury, must determine whether the defendant was responsible for preventing the plaintiff from entering into the relationship with [name of third party]. In other words, you must decide whether, except for the interference of the defendant, the plaintiff was reasonably certain to have entered into the relationship or fulfilled the expectancy with [name of third party].

Comment

This issue has some conceptual similarity to the instruction in § 2.03[1] regarding whether the plaintiff had a reasonable expectancy before the alleged interference. However, the two questions are distinct and should be submitted separately. It must first be shown that the plaintiff had a reasonable expectancy and then be shown that the defendant interfered in a way that caused the expectancy to fail or otherwise damaged it. The causation requirement may be stated somewhat differently in various jurisdictions. *See* 17 P.O.F.2d 517, 529 *Tortious Interference with At Will Business Relationship* (1978); § 2.08[1] cmt., *infra.*

2.05[2] Substantial Factor

The defendant's conduct will be deemed to be responsible for the plaintiff's failure to enter into the relationship if it was a substantial factor in causing the third party not to enter into the relationship or to fulfill the expectancy with the plaintiff.

Comment

This instruction is intended to be used in conjunction with the definition of the phrase "substantial factor" at § 2.08[3]. *See Restatement (Second) of Torts* § 433 (1965). The instruction should be used only if it is consistent with the causation requirement of the applicable jurisdiction. The instruction in § 2.05[1] essentially explains to the jury that the plaintiff's burden is to show that, except for the defendant's conduct, the plaintiff was reasonably certain to have obtained the prospective benefit.

There is an important difference between the two instructions, and if the substantial-factor instruction and definition in this section and in § 2.08[3] are not recognized by the courts of the forum, they should not be submitted. A defendant's conduct that satisfies the "but for" causation requirement in § 2.05[1] would undoubtedly also constitute a substantial factor. However, conduct that might be found a substantial factor in § 2.05[2] might not necessarily pass the "but for" causation requirement in § 2.05[1], because circumstances other than the defendant's conduct might have caused the plaintiff's loss, regardless of the defendant's conduct. Therefore, the substantial-factor instruction may present a much less rigorous causation requirement for a plaintiff. *See Cipollone v. Liggett Group, Inc.*, 893 F.2d 541, 561–62 n.17 (3d Cir. 1990); *Doupnik v. General Motors Corp.*, 275 Cal. Rptr. 715, 721–22 (Cal. Ct. App. 1990).

2.06 Intentional Interference

2.06[1] Generally

You, the jury, must determine whether the defendant intended to prevent the plaintiff from continuing or acquiring this [business relationship or expectancy—choose one]. Conduct is intentional if done deliberately, with the purpose of interfering with plaintiff's [business relationship or expectancy—choose one]. If you find that the defendant's conduct was not intentional, then you must find for the defendant.

Comment

This charge reflects the well-established view that interference with prospective economic advantage requires intentional conduct on the part of the defendant, calculated to disrupt or destroy the business relationship or expectancy. In some cases there may be a similarity in the requirement of intent and the need to specifically define a relationship with a third party. For example, in *J. Eck & Sons, Inc. v. Reuben H. Donnelley Corp.*, 572 N.E.2d 1090 (Ill. App. Ct. 1991), the court found that an intentional refusal by the defendant to sell an advertisement to plaintiff did not involve the intent to harm a particular relationship with a third party. *See Ellis v. City of Valdez,* 686 P.2d 700 (Alaska 1984); *Seaman's Direct Buying Serv., Inc. v. Standard Oil Co. of California,* 686 P.2d 1158 (Cal. 1984); *Buckaloo v. Johnson,* 537 P.2d 865 (Cal. 1975); *Ramona Manor Convalescent Hosp. v. Care Enter.,* 225 Cal. Rptr. 120 (Cal. Ct. App. 1986); *O'Fallon Dev. Co., Inc. v. City of O'Fallon,* 356 N.E.2d 1293 (Ill. App. Ct. 1976); *Witte Transp. Co. v. Murphy Motor Freight Lines, Inc.,* 193 N.W.2d 148 (Minn. 1971); *Ice Bros., Inc. v. Bannowsky,* 840 S.W.2d 57 (Tex. Civ. App. 1992); *C. W. Dev., Inc. v. Structures, Inc. of West Virginia,* 408 S.E.2d 41 (W. Va. 1991); 45 Am. Jur. 2d *Interference* § 50 (1969).

An interesting discussion of the difference between intent to do the act that allegedly caused the interference and the actual intent to interfere is found in *Southwestern Bell Telephone Co. v. John Carlo Texas, Inc.,* 843 S.W.2d 470 (Tex. 1992). In this case, the Texas Supreme Court reversed because the jury instructions did not specifically require the jury to find an intent to interfere with plaintiff's contract.

Note that some courts have additionally required that the intentional act be tortious itself. *E.g., Kecko Piping Co., Inc. v. Town of Monroe,* 374 A.2d 179 (Conn. 1977). Others require that the defendant be guilty of fraud, misrepresentation, intimidation, or other malicious conduct. *See Verkin v. Melroy,* 699 F.2d 729 (5th Cir. 1983); *Lash v. State,* 14 So. 2d 229 (Ala. 1943); *Blake v. Levy,* 464 A.2d 52 (Conn. 1983); *Jones v. O'Connell,* 458 A.2d 355 (Conn. 1983); *Spartan Equip. Co. v. Air Placement Equip. Co.,* 140 S.E.2d 3 (N.C. 1965); *Bray v. Squires,* 702 S.W.2d 266 (Tex. Ct. App. 1985); *State Nat'l Bank of El Paso v. Farah Mfg. Co., Inc.,* 678 S.W.2d 661, 688 (Tex. Ct. App. 1984); *Exxon Corp. v. Allsup,* 808 S.W.2d 648 (Tex. Civ. App. 1991); *Deauville Corp. v. Federated Dep't Stores,* 756 F.2d 1183, 1186 (5th Cir. 1985). Others require the plaintiff to prove that the defendant's objective was to bring financial injury or destruction on the plaintiff. *Page County Appliance Ctr., Inc. v. Honeywell, Inc.,* 347 N.W.2d 171 (Iowa 1984); *Fischer v. Unipac Serv. Corp.,* 519 N.W.2d 793 (Iowa 1994).

Some courts, however, have specifically held that a showing of malice is not required. *Chaves v. Johnson,* 335 S.E.2d 97 (Va. 1985); *Martin v. Wing,* 667 P.2d 1159 (Wyo. 1983). In many jurisdictions, particularly in cases decided before the *Restatement (Second) of Torts* (1977), issues concerning the nature and means of the defendant's interference and motivation come into the case only when the defendant raises the defense of justification or privilege. In such cases, the showing of actual malice may be required to overcome a privilege otherwise recognized. *Ray Dancer, Inc. v. DMC Corp.,* 594 N.E.2d 1344 (Ill. App. Ct. 1992).

The instructions found in optional item (5) of § 2.02[2] and in § 2.07 should also be used in jurisdictions that require the plaintiff to prove more than that the defendant intended the conduct. See the comments at §§ 2.01, 2.02[2], and 2.07 for lists of authorities that will assist in researching the law of various states. *See Restatement (Second) of Torts* § 767 (1977). Possible additional support for actual malice to overcome privilege: *King v. Levin,* 540 N.E.2d 492, 494 (Ill. App. Ct. 1989) (deals with prospective advantage); *Arlington Heights Nat'l Bank v. Arlington Heights Fed. Sav. & Loan Ass'n,* 229 N.E.2d 514, 518 (Ill. 1967); *Huskie v. Griffin,* 74 A. 595, 596 (N.H. 1909).

2.06[2] Proof of Intentional Interference

Intent ordinarily may not be proved directly, because there is no way of scrutinizing the operations of the human mind. You may infer a person's intent from conduct substantially certain to interfere with the plaintiff's business expectation, but you are not required to infer it and should consider all of the circumstances. You may consider any statement made or act done or omitted by a party whose intent is an issue, and all of the facts and circumstances that indicate the party's state of mind. Furthermore, in determining the defendant's intention, the law assumes that every person intends the natural consequences of one's knowingly done acts. Thus, if you find that the defendant's conduct was knowingly done or knowingly omitted, you may draw the inference and find, unless the contrary appears from the evidence, that the defendant intended all the natural and probable consequences of defendant's conduct.

Comment

See Fischer v. Unipac Serv. Corp., 519 N.W.2d 793 (Iowa 1994); *Southwestern Bell Tel. Co. v. John Carlo Texas, Inc.*, 843 S.W.2d 470 (Tex. 1992); *DeVoto v. Pac. Fidelity Life Ins. Co.*, 618 F.2d 1340, 1347 (9th Cir. 1980); *Baker v. United States*, 310 F.2d 924 (9th Cir. 1962) (criminal case), *cert. denied*, 372 U.S. 954 (1963); *Golden v. Sommers*, 56 F.R.D. 3 (M.D. Pa. 1972), *aff'd*, 481 F.2d 1398 (3d Cir. 1973); *Seaman's Direct Buying Serv., Inc. v. Standard Oil Co. of California*, 686 P.2d 1158, 1165 (Cal. 1984); *Ramona Manor Convalescent Hosp. v. Care Enter.*, 225 Cal. Rptr. 120 (Cal. Ct. App. 1986); *Martin v. Wing*, 667 P.2d 1159 (Wyo. 1983); 3 Devitt, Blackmar & Wolff, *Federal Jury Practice and Instructions* § 81.03 (4th ed. 1992).

2.06[3] Conduct Knowingly Done

An act (or omission) is done knowingly if done purposefully and voluntarily, and not because of mistake, inadvertence, or other innocent reason.

Comment

See § 2.06[2]; *Hayes v. Irwin,* 541 F. Supp. 397, 429 (N.D. Ga. 1982); *Am. Sanitary Serv., Inc. v. Walker,* 554 P.2d 1010, 1013 (Or. 1976).

2.07 Factors Determining Whether Interference Is Improper

In your deliberations, you should consider the following factors in determining whether the conduct of the defendant was improper:

(1) the nature of the defendant's conduct;

(2) the defendant's motive;

(3) the interests of the plaintiff with which the conduct interfered;

(4) the interests sought to be advanced by the defendant;

(5) the interest of our society in balancing the need to protect the freedom of the defendant to engage in such conduct with the need to protect prospective advantages such as sought by the plaintiff;

(6) the proximity or remoteness of the defendant's conduct to the interference about which the plaintiff complains; and

(7) the nature of the relationship between the plaintiff and defendant.

Comment

The preceding instruction should be used only in jurisdictions that follow section 766B of the *Restatement (Second) of Torts* (1977), which requires that the defendant's interference be improper. See the comments and lists of authorities in various states in §§ 2.01 and 2.02[2]. There is a split of authority about whether the plaintiff must prove either improper motives or means on the part of the defendant as part of a prima facie case, or whether such matters are relevant only if the defendant attempts to prove a justification or privilege for defendant's intentional conduct.

This instruction should be given if item (5) of the general instructions in § 2.02[2] is used. If it is not given, the propriety of the defendant's conduct may be submitted as an affirmative defense as discussed in § 2.09.

The language follows section 767 of the *Restatement (Second) of Torts* (1977). A great many jurisdictions have essentially adopted the *Restatement (Second) of Torts* factors for determining if conduct is improper. *See Green v. Interstate United Management Serv. Corp.*, 748 F.2d 827 (3d Cir. 1984); *Int'l Mining Co. v. Allen & Co., Inc.* 567 F. Supp. 777 (S.D.N.Y. 1983); *Harsha v. State Sav. Bank*, 346 N.W.2d 791 (Iowa 1984); *Adler, Barish, Daniels, Levin and Creskoff v. Epstein*, 393 A.2d 1175 (Pa. 1978); *Leigh Furniture and Carpet Co. v. Isom*, 657 P.2d 293 (Utah 1982); *Glass v. Glass*, 321 S.E.2d 69 (Va. 1984); *Liebe v. City Fin. Co.*, 295 N.W.2d 16 (Wis. Ct. App. 1980); *C. W. Dev., Inc. v. Structures, Inc. of West Virginia*, 408 S.E.2d 41 (W. Va. 1991). *See also Employer's Fire Ins. Co. v. Love It Ice Cream Co.*, 670 P.2d 160 (Or. 1983); *Hughes v. Houston Northwest Medical Ctr., Inc.*, 680 S.W.2d 838 (Tex. Civ. App. 1984) (suggesting unfounded litigation, knowingly brought, can constitute improper interference). *But cf. Pac. Gas & Elec. v. Bear Stearns*, 791 P.2d 587 (Cal. 1990); *Village Supermarket, Inc. v. Mayfair Supermarkets, Inc.*, 634 A.2d 1381 (N.J. Super. Ct. Law Div. 1993) (holding that merely inducing party to seek judicial determination of its rights is privileged as matter of law).

2.08 Damage to Plaintiff Proximately Resulting from Conduct

2.08[1] Generally

You must also consider whether the defendant's conduct was the proximate cause of damage to the plaintiff. If you find that the defendant's conduct was not the proximate cause of damage to the plaintiff, your verdict will be for the defendant.

Comment

Most appellate courts that have listed the elements of the tort of interference with prospective advantage have included the requirement that the plaintiff be damaged as a result of the interference. *Buckaloo v. Johnson,* 537 P.2d 865 (Cal. 1975). This instruction would satisfy the requirement for a showing of damage, but it duplicates the issue of causation found in § 2.05. Depending upon the law of the jurisdiction, either the charge in this action or the one in § 2.05 may be used.

2.08[2] Monetary Loss

The plaintiff claims to have suffered monetary loss in the following respects: [set forth plaintiff's claims].

If you find that the plaintiff did not suffer such a loss, your verdict will be for the defendant.

Comment

This charge reflects the well-established rule that the plaintiff must in fact suffer some damage to establish a prima facie case in tort. *Buckaloo v. Johnson,* 537 P.2d 865 (Cal. 1975).

2.08[3] Substantial Factor

If you find that the plaintiff did suffer the losses it claims, you must then determine whether the defendant's conduct was the proximate cause of the plaintiff's loss or damage.

In this regard, the defendant's conduct will be deemed to be the proximate cause of the plaintiff's loss or damage if you find that it was a substantial factor in causing that loss or damage. It need not be the *only* cause. The conduct will be a substantial factor in causing the loss or damage if it had such an effect in producing the loss that reasonable people would regard it as a cause of the loss or damage. In resolving this issue, you may consider the number of other contributing factors, whether the defendant's conduct created a condition or chain of events that was continuous and active up to the time of the damage to plaintiff, and the lapse of time between the defendant's conduct and the damage to the plaintiff.

Comment

See § 2.05[2], *supra.*

This charge reflects the traditional definition of proximate cause, which uses the substantial-factor element. It is adapted from section 433 of the *Restatement (Second) of Torts* (1965). Regarding conflict between the "but for" and substantial-factor tests, see the comment accompanying § 2.05[2]. *See also* 1 James A. Dooley, *Modern Tort Law* § 8.03 (1977).

2.09 Defenses: Justifications/Privileges

2.09[1] Generally

As discussed in §§ 2.01, 2.02[2], and 2.07, the procedural treatment of defenses of justification and privilege varies in the different states. As stated by the California Supreme Court in 1984:

> The factors enumerated by this court in *Herron* were patterned closely after those listed in the original Restatement of Torts (1939) section 767. The Restatement (Second) of the Law of Torts (1977) abandons use of the term "privilege" or "justification" in favor of the term "improperly interferes," so as to avoid questions of burden of pleading or proof (*id.*, at p. 5), but the factors to be used in determining whether interference is "improper" (§ 767) are essentially the same.

Envtl. Plan. v. Superior Court (Detmold Pub.), 680 P.2d 1086, 1090 (Cal. 1984).

Some states have either abandoned or are diminishing emphasis on such affirmative defenses in favor of considering whether, under various factors, the defendant's conduct was improper. However, some states have moved in the other direction, removing the "improper" element from the plaintiff's burden and shifting it to the defendant's burden as an affirmative defense. *See Victoria Bank & Trust v. Brady,* 811 S.W.2d 931 (Tex. 1991); *Gonzalez v. San Jacinto Methodist Hosp.,* 880 S.W.2d 436 (Tex. Civ. App. 1994). In *Southwestern Bell Tel. Co. v. John Carlo Texas, Inc.,* 843 S.W.2d 470 (Tex. 1992), the court reversed a plaintiff's verdict because the trial court failed to define "justification" for the jury as follows: Interference is privileged when it results from the exercise of a party's own bona fide rights or when the party possesses an equal or superior interest to that of the plaintiff. For a more specific discussion and list of cases from various states on the burden-of-proof issue, see §§ 2.01, 2.02[2], and 2.07.

The following two charges are optional, depending upon the rule regarding burden of proof in the particular forum. Option A is for use in states where the plaintiff must show the defendant's conduct or motive was improper. Option B places the burden of proof on the defendant to establish a specific affirmative defense.

The *Restatement (Second) of Torts* (1977), in sections 768–74, discusses conduct traditionally recognized as "privileged." The instructions in §§ 2.09[2] through [5] reflect those principles but do not include a position on burden of proof. Therefore, a combination of any of the instructions on specific conduct in §§ 2.09[2] through [5], with the burden-of-proof instruction in either choice A or B in the following section, could be used to fit the appropriate law of any jurisdiction.

Option A: Plaintiff's Burden to Show Defendant's Conduct Improper

You have been instructed that to recover, the plaintiff has the burden to prove various facts by a preponderance of the evidence. One of those facts was that the defendant's conduct was improper. The law recognizes that certain kinds of conduct under certain circumstances are not improper. The following instructions are intended to guide you in deciding whether the plaintiff has satisfied its burden to show the defendant's conduct was improper under the facts as you find them.

Option B: Defendant's Burden to Show Conduct Proper Because It Was Justified or Privileged

The defendant claims [state basis of claimed justification and/or privilege]. The plaintiff denies [state disputed fact or facts]. If you find that the defendant has not sustained its burden of proving that [state disputed fact or facts], then the conduct was not justified or privileged, and your verdict will be for the plaintiff, provided you find that the plaintiff has met its burden of proof on what plaintiff must establish to prove liability. If you find that the defendant has sustained its burden of proving that [state disputed fact or facts], your verdict will be for the defendant.

Comment

Note that the defense of justification/privilege will be present in the case only if conduct constituting the interference is not "unlawful." *See, e.g.,* William L. Prosser, *The Law of Torts* § 130 (4th ed. 1971); 1 Fowler V. Harper, et al., *Law of Torts* § 6.11 (2d ed. 1986). *Cf. Lowell v. Mother's Cake & Cookie Co.* 144 Cal. Rptr. 664 (Cal. Ct. App. 1978). Whether the defendant's conduct is "unlawful" appears to be a question of law for the court. *Tuttle v. Buck,* 119 N.W. 946 (Minn. 1909). Thus, in a case in which the defendant asserts a justification or privilege, the court must initially determine whether the defendant's conduct is unlawful. If the court determines that it is lawful, and the other circumstances surrounding the invoking of the justification or privilege, if proved, are such to make the conduct justified or privileged, the existence of the circumstances on which the justification or privilege is based becomes a question of fact for the jury. *Restatement (Second) of Torts* § 767 cmt. l (1977); *Gianelli Distrib. Co. v. Beck & Co.,* 219 Cal. Rptr. 203, 222 (Cal. Ct. App. 1985).

2.09[2] Competition as Proper or Improper Interference

The defendant asserts that its conduct was proper because it occurred during the course of competition between the defendant and the plaintiff. The law recognizes that one is justified or privileged to cause a third party not to enter into or continue a business relationship or expectancy with one's competition as long as the conduct relates to competition between the two competitors and the party is acting, at least in part, to advance its own interests in such competition, and as long as the party does not use wrongful means to compete.

You must first determine, then, whether the conduct of the defendant relates to competition between the defendant and the plaintiff for the business of [name of third party]. If you find that it does, then you will determine whether the defendant's purpose was, at least in part, to advance defendant's interest in competing with the plaintiff. For example, if you should find that the defendant was seeking to acquire the business diverted from the plaintiff for itself, then as long as the defendant's conduct was at least in part directed to that end, the fact that you may find it was also motivated by other reasons will not render it improper in the eyes of the law. But if you find that the defendant's conduct was motivated solely by bad faith or ill will, and not at all for the advancement of competitive interests, you must find that the conduct was not justified and that it was improper.

Comment

Competition is one of the most frequently applied defenses. Note that competition is widely recognized as an even stronger defense in cases involving interference with only prospective advantage, as contrasted with contracts. The elements are set out in section 768 of the *Restatement (Second) of Torts* (1977). The facts of each case may require some modification to the instruction. See discussions of the defense in *C. E. Servs., Inc. v. Control Data Corp.*, 759 F.2d 1241 (5th Cir. 1985); *Northwest Airlines v. Am. Airlines*, 853 F. Supp. 1110 (D.

Minn. 1994); *DEFCO, Inc. v. Decatur Cylinder, Inc.*, 595 So. 2d 1329 (Ala. 1992); *Public Sys., Inc. v. Towry*, 587 So. 2d 969 (Ala. 1991); *Edwards v. Anaconda Co.*, 565 P.2d 190 (Ariz. Ct. App. 1977); *Buckaloo v. Johnson*, 537 P.2d 865 (Cal. 1975); *A-Mark Coin Co. v. Gen. Mills, Inc.*, 195 Cal. Rptr. 859 (Cal. Ct. App. 1983); *Rickel v. Schwinn Bicycle Co.*, 192 Cal. Rptr. 732 (Cal. Ct. App. 1983); *Bowl-Mor Co., Inc. v. Brunswick Corp.*, 297 A.2d 61 (Del. Ch. 1972); *Doliner v. Brown*, 489 N.E.2d 1036 (Mass. App. Ct. 1986); *United Wild Rice, Inc. v. Nelson*, 313 N.W.2d 628 (Minn. 1982); *Embree Constr. Group, Inc. v. Rafcor, Inc.*, 411 S.E.2d 916 (N.C. 1992); *Crockett v. Sahara Realty Corp.*, 591 P.2d 1135 (Nev. 1979); *Fantaco Enter., Inc. v. Iavarone*, 555 N.Y.S.2d 921 (N.Y. App. Div. 1990); *Consol. Petroleum Indus., Inc. v. Jacobs*, 648 S.W.2d 363–67 (Tex. Ct. App. 1983); *Light v. Transp. Ins. Co.*, 469 S.W.2d 433 (Tex. Ct. App. 1971); *Quadra Enter., Inc. v. R.A. Hanson Co.*, 667 P.2d 1120 (Wash. Ct. App. 1983).

Several of the courts have adopted Prosser's statement:

> So long as the plaintiff's contractual relations are merely contemplated or potential, it is considered to be in the interest of the public that any competitor should be free to divert them to himself by all fair and reasonable means.

William L. Prosser, *Law of Torts* § 130 at 954 (4th ed. 1971).

Whether the defendant has utilized "wrongful means" may be an issue for the court or for the jury. As noted above, unlawful conduct would defeat any privilege. However, a fact question may exist about whether unlawful or wrongful conduct occurred. The comments to section 767(a) of the *Restatement* list various circumstances that may be adapted to particular cases for instructions on conduct or means used by a party. *Restatement (Second) of Torts* § 767(a) cmts. at 29–32 (1977). Most "unlawful" conduct in the cases falls into tortious or even criminal categories. However, a garden variety breach of contract, if done for improper purposes, may be found actionable in tort under certain circumstances. In *American National Petroleum Co. v. Transcontinental Gas Pipe Line Corp.*, 798 S.W.2d 274 (Tex. 1990), the court rejected the defense that standard contract remedies were exclusively applicable when the only action taken was to breach the defendant's own contract.

The California Supreme Court noted that because it is actionable to interfere with a relationship that is purely prospective, it would be illogical not to protect a contractual relationship, even if it were terminable at will, or unenforceable. However, the court drew the line and found it not actionable for an interloper merely to induce or cause another to file suit for the purpose of seeking a declaration of the parties' rights. *Pac. Gas & Elec. Co. v. Bear Stearns & Co.*, 791 P.2d 587 (Cal. 1990).

2.09[3] Financial Interest

Interference with a prospective business relationship of another is not improper if the person interfering has a financial interest in the prospective relationship and acts in a reasonable way to protect that person's financial interest from being prejudiced by the prospective contract or business relation.

If you find that, before the defendant's conduct, defendant had a financial interest connected to [state the prospective relationship alleged by the plaintiff], and that defendant's conduct was a reasonable attempt exercised in good faith to protect that interest, then the defendant's conduct is not improper even if it did interfere with [state the prospective relationship].

Comment

The instruction is based on sections 769, 771, and 773 of the *Restatement (Second) of Torts* (1977). *See also Geolar, Inc. v. Gilbert/Commonwealth, Inc. of Michigan,* 874 P.2d 937 (Cal. 1994); *Alyeska Pipeline Serv. Co. v. Aurora Air Serv., Inc.,* 604 P.2d 1090 (Alaska 1979); *Envtl. Plan. v. Superior Court (Detmold Pub.),* 680 P.2d 1086 (Cal. 1984); *Asia Inv. Co., Ltd. v. Borowski,* 184 Cal. Rptr. 317 (Cal. Ct. App. 1982); *Travelers Indem. v. Merling,* 605 A.2d 83 (Md. 1992); *Doliner v. Brown,* 489 N.E.2d 1036 (Mass. App. Ct. 1986); *Schulman v. J.P. Morgan Inv. Management, Inc.,* 35 F.3d 799 (3d Cir. 1994) (applying Pennsylvania law); *Victoria Bank & Trust Co. v. Brady,* 811 S.W.2d 931 (Tex. 1991) (recognizing equal interest only if exercised in good faith); *Lone Star Ford, Inc. v. McCormick,* 838 S.W.2d 734 (Tex. Civ. App. 1992); *Brown v. Safeway Stores, Inc.,* 617 P.2d 704 (Wash. 1980); *Roy v. Cunningham,* 731 P.2d 526 (Wash. Ct. App. 1986); *Quadra Enter., Inc. v. R.A. Hanson Co., Inc.,* 667 P.2d 1120 (Wash. Ct. App. 1983).

Sometimes it may appear obvious that the defendant has its own legitimate financial interest in the matter such that a summary judgment appears proper on this point. However, care should be taken to decide whether fact questions exist about whether the financial interest was exercised properly and in good faith. In *Hopkins v. Highlands Insurance Co.,* 838 S.W.2d 819 (Tex. Civ. App. 1992), the court reversed a summary judgment in favor of an insurance company that claimed it had a proper financial interest in refusing to insure a particular driver employed by the insured. Although the insurer clearly asserted a valid financial interest, the court found factual questions regarding whether the driving record requirements were uniformly applied in good faith to all other drivers. For a discussion of the application of governmental immunity to this tort, see *North v. State,* 400 N.W.2d 566 (Iowa 1987).

Generally, there should be a presumption that corporate officers, directors, and shareholders have a qualified privilege to interfere with prospective economic relations between the corporation and a third party. *Lone Star Ford v. McCormick,* 838 S.W.2d 734 (Tex. Civ. App. 1992). However, that presumption may be overcome when the means used or motives are found to be improper. *Ray Dancer, Inc. v. DMC Corp.,* 594 N.E.2d 1344 (Ill. App. Ct. 1992). *See also Embree Constr. Group, Inc. v. Rafcor,* 411 S.E.2d 916 (N.C. 1992); *Sammon v. Watchung Hills Bank for Sav.,* 611 A.2d 674 (N.J. Super. Ct. Law Div. 1992). Even partners may face liability if it is found that a relationship terminable at will is harmed by one using improper means or motives. *Wilensky v. Blalock,* 414 S.E.2d 1 (Ga. 1992).

The interest of a manager or agent in recommending against the continuation of a relationship between a third party and the principal is similar. A number of cases have debated whether a privilege for such a manager is absolute or qualified, but in the absence of clear evidence of improper motives or self-dealing, it is difficult for a plaintiff to overcome. *See Aalgaard v. Merchants Nat'l Bank, Inc.,* 274 Cal. Rptr. 81 (Cal. Ct. App. 1990); *Geick v. Kay,* 603 N.E.2d 121 (Ill. App. Ct.

1992); *Am. Medical Int'l v. Giurintano,* 821 S.W.2d 331 (Tex. Civ. App. 1991). A bankruptcy trustee has been held to be immune from a tortious interference suit. *Clements v. Barnes,* 834 S.W.2d 45 (Tex. 1992). A franchisor's right to select its franchisees has been held sufficient to preclude an action for interference. *Roberts v. Gen. Motors Corp.,* 643 A.2d 956 (N.H. 1994).

2.09[4] Defendant Responsible for Welfare of Another

Interference with [state prospective business relationship] is not improper if you find that the defendant is charged with the responsibility for the welfare of [state the third person with whom the plaintiff intended to enter into the relationship] and the defendant used reasonable means in a good-faith attempt to protect the welfare of [the third person with whom the plaintiff intended to enter into the relationship].

Comment

The charge is based on section 770 of the *Restatement (Second) of Torts* (1977). For support: *Gott v. Berea College,* 161 S.W. 204 (Ky. Ct. App. 1913); *Dehnert v. Arrow Sprinklers, Inc.,* 705 P.2d 846, 850 (Wyo. 1985) (dealing with defense in interference with contractual relations action).

2.09[5] Truthful Information or Advice

Interference with [state the prospective business relationship] is not improper when the only conduct of the party interfering is to provide truthful information or to provide honest advice in good faith within the scope of a request for the advice.

If you find that the defendant's only conduct interfering with [state the prospective advantage] was to provide truthful information, then the defendant's conduct was not improper. Likewise, if you find that the defendant's only conduct was to provide honest advice that was within the scope of advice requested by [state the third party with whom the plaintiff desired to have a business relationship], then the defendant's conduct was not improper.

Comment

The charge is based on section 772 of the *Restatement (Second) of Torts* (1977). The question of whether the advice is given in good faith or for other motives may be a jury question. See *Welter v. Seton Hall University*, 579 A.2d 332 (N.J. Super. Ct. App. Div. 1990) for an interesting discussion about whether the employment rights of certain nuns were violated or harmed due to "honestly held . . . [and] truly religiously motivated" beliefs, or were the subject of other nonreligious goals.

2.10 Damages

2.10[1] Generally

I am turning now to the question of damages and what can be considered in determining an award of money in this case. By including damages in these instructions, I do not wish to suggest or imply anything about the issue of liability or about whether any damages have been proved in this case.

Two kinds of damages can be considered in this case. They are compensatory damages and punitive damages.

Compensatory damages will consist of the plaintiff's direct economic losses and out-of-pocket expenses resulting from the defendant's conduct. In other words, the defendant is liable for all damages suffered by the plaintiff that were caused by the defendant's conduct.

Punitive damages will consist of the amount awarded by you, not as compensation to the plaintiff for wrong done, but as punishment to the defendant and as a deterrent to others.

Comment

In an action for interference with prospective advantage, the plaintiff generally may be awarded compensatory damages as well as punitive damages. *See, e.g., Elsbach v. Mulligan,* 136 P.2d 651 (Cal. Ct. App. 1943); 45 Am. Jur. 2d *Interference* §§ 58, 61 (1969). Some states, however, do prohibit or restrict the award of punitive damages.

2.10[2] Compensatory Damages

If, after considering the evidence in this case and the instructions of the Court, you should find the issues in favor of the plaintiff, then it is my duty to tell you what damages the plaintiff would be entitled to recover. It would be such a sum as you believe, from the evidence, will fairly and reasonably compensate the plaintiff for any damage the plaintiff has suffered by reason of the defendant's acts complained of and for the anticipated profits of which the plaintiff was deprived, provided they are of such a nature to be beyond the speculative stage.

In determining compensatory damages, you may consider whether the plaintiff suffered any measurable loss of profits as a result of the defendant's conduct. In this case, the plaintiff claims that its business was affected because of loss of profits plaintiff might have earned but for the defendant's conduct.

For lost profits to be recovered, there must be a reasonable basis for computing them. Ordinarily, it is sufficient for this purpose to show actual past profits and losses; that is, past receipts and expenses in the plaintiff's business. Although they cannot be taken as an exact measure of future or anticipated profits, you, the jury, should consider those past profits and losses together with the uncertainties and contingencies by which they probably would have been affected. It would be proper for you to consider any normal increase in business that might have been reasonably expected in the light of past developments and existing conditions in the plaintiff's business. You may also take into consideration future uncertainties, such as increased competition, increased operating costs, and changes in economic trends. Losses and profits that are mere guesses, speculative, remote, or uncertain, or unwarranted estimates of witnesses should not be considered.

Damages, if any, should be restricted to such losses, if any, as are proved by facts from which their existence is logically and legally inferable. The general rule on the subject of damages is that all damages resulting necessarily, immediately, and directly from the wrong are recoverable, and not those that are contingent and uncertain or mere speculation.

Although a qualified person may make estimates concerning probable profits or losses of a going business, you should, in weighing all such evidence, take into consideration, among other things, the truth or falsity of the basis of such estimates; the knowledge or lack of knowledge of the witnesses of all of the conditions on which the estimate is based; whether the facts assumed as a basis for an estimate rest upon actual accounts and records kept in the ordinary course of business rather than in uncertain recollections; and knowledge of the witness in the particular line of business about which the witness testifies. From all of the evidence in this case bearing on the subject, you should determine for yourselves the probability or improbability, and the amount, of profits anticipated by the plaintiff.

The difficulty or uncertainty in ascertaining or measuring the precise amount of any damages does not preclude recovery, and you, the jury, should use your best judgment in determining the amount of such damages, if any, based upon the evidence.

In determining compensatory damages, you may consider whether the plaintiff suffered any measurable loss to its goodwill. The goodwill of a company is an intangible business asset that reflects the basic human tendency to do business with a merchant who offers products of the type and quality the customer desires and expects. Service to the customer, and a willingness to stand behind a warranty and other representations about the quality of the products sold by a merchant, are factors in the goodwill of that business.

The goodwill attached to a product is a part of the overall business value that is the goodwill of the company. It is possible, therefore, that the general goodwill of a corporation may be damaged by the loss of goodwill to a particular

product. Whether this has occurred is a question of fact for you to determine.

If you find that the plaintiff's goodwill has been damaged either by injury to the goodwill associated with a particular product or by injury to the plaintiff's general business reputation, you may assess such compensatory damages as you may find shown by the evidence. The measure of the plaintiff's damage is the difference between the value of such goodwill before and after the acts of the defendant.

[Other losses for which the plaintiff seeks recovery can be inserted here.]

That the defendant did not actually anticipate or contemplate that these losses would occur is not a relevant factor for you to consider.

If you find that the plaintiff is entitled to a verdict in accordance with these instructions, but you do not find that the evidence before you is sufficient to show that the plaintiff has sustained any substantial damages, then you may return a verdict for the plaintiff on one or more of the theories of liability and fix the amount of the compensatory damages in a nominal sum such as one dollar. Such a verdict would determine the rights of the parties, and the Court can then issue orders directing their future conduct.

Comment

The plaintiff can recover for "all losses legally caused by the defendant's interference, if they are reasonably ascertainable." 17 P.O.F.2d 517, 545 *Tortious Interference with At Will Business Relationship* (1978). For support: *Wheeler v. Woods,* 723 P.2d 1224, 1229 (Wyo. 1986).

Among losses that the plaintiff can recover are lost profits, general loss to its business, and harm to goodwill. *See, e.g., Buxbom v. Smith,* 145 P.2d 305 (Cal. 1944); *Elsbach v. Mulligan,* 136 P.2d 651 (Cal. Ct. App. 1943). These losses are simply illustrative and should not be interpreted as excluding other kinds of losses.

The lost-profits part of the charge is from *F. L. Mendez & Co. v. Gen. Motors Corp.*, 161 F.2d 695 (7th Cir. 1947), an antitrust case. The goodwill part is from *Big O Tire Dealers, Inc. v. Goodyear Tire & Rubber Co.*, 408 F. Supp. 1219 (D. Colo. 1976), *modified on other grounds*, 561 F.2d 1365 (10th Cir. 1977).

2.10[3] Punitive Damages

The purpose of awarding punitive or exemplary damages is to punish a wrongdoer for some extraordinary conduct and to serve as an example or warning to others not to engage in such conduct.

If you find [applicable legal standard for circumstances under which an award of punitive damages is appropriate], then, in addition to compensatory damages, you may also award the plaintiff a reasonable sum as punitive damages.

Whether to make any award of punitive or exemplary damages, in addition to actual damages, is a matter exclusively within the province of the jury. I instruct you to bear in mind not only the conditions under which, and the purposes for which, the law permits an award of punitive or exemplary damages. Also bear in mind that the law requires that the amount of such extraordinary damages, when awarded, must be fixed by you with calm discretion and sound reason, and must never be awarded or fixed in amount because of any sympathy, bias, or prejudice you may feel toward any party in this case.

The award of a nominal sum of compensatory damages would not prevent your awarding punitive damages, if you find that the award of punitive damages is justified under these instructions.

Comment

As noted in § 2.09[1], in jurisdictions where punitive damages are allowable, they are also permitted in actions for interference with prospective advantage. Because the standard for the award of punitive damages varies from state to state, counsel should insert the appropriate standard in the charge. For some examples of factors and criteria, see the various subsections of § 1.07.

Chapter Three

Injurious Falsehood

3.01 Introduction

Mark E. Saliman

The model jury charges in this section address the conditions for the imposition of liability at common law upon one who makes false statements of fact that disparage the quality of another's goods or services. These damages pertain to only one aspect of the tort of injurious falsehood, which embraces any nondefamatory false statement that causes financial injury. A similar tort, for example, is the tort of slander of title, in which a defendant can incur liability for making malicious statements about the title to the plaintiff's property, resulting in special damages to the plaintiff. *Childers v. Commerce Mortgage Inv.*, 579 N.E.2d 219 (Ohio Ct. App. 1989); *Kensington Dev. Corp. v. Israel*, 407 N.W.2d 269 (Wis. Ct. App. 1987), *aff'd*, 419 N.W.2d 241 (Wis. 1988). *See generally* W. Page Keeton, *Prosser & Keeton on the Law of Torts* § 128 (5th ed. 1984) [hereinafter Keeton]; Prosser *Restatement (Second) of Torts* § 623A (1976).

A plaintiff in such cases must prove publication or communication to a third person of a false derogatory statement of fact concerning its goods or services. *Art Metal-U.S.A., Inc. v. United States*, 753 F.2d 1151, 1155 (D.C. Cir. 1985); *Sys. Operations, Inc. v. Scientific Games Dev. Corp.*, 555 F.2d 1131 (3d Cir. 1977); *Womack v. McDonald*, 121 So. 57 (Ala. 1929); *New England Oil & Pipeline Co. v. Rogers*, 7 P.2d 638 (Okla. 1931); 1 F. Harper & F. James, *Law of Torts* § 6.3 (1956); Note, *The Law of Commercial Disparagement: Business Defamation's Impotent Ally*, 63 Yale L.J. 75 n.58 (1953).

The plaintiff must also show that the defendant's statement was understood to refer to the plaintiff's goods or services and to disparage their quality. *Art Metal-U.S.A., Inc. v. United States*, 753 F.2d 1151, 1155 (D.C. Cir. 1985); *Nat'l Ref. Co. v. Benzo Gas Motor Fuel Co.*, 20 F.2d 763 (8th Cir.), *cert. denied*, 275 U.S. 570 (1927); *Caron Corp. v. R.K.O. Pictures, Inc.*, 28 N.Y.S.2d 1020 (N.Y. App. Div. 1941), *aff'd*, 35 N.Y.S.2d 715 (N.Y. App. Div. 1942), *cert. denied*, 318 U.S. 757 (1943).

In addition, the plaintiff must prove that the statement was made maliciously. *Dale Sys. v. Gen. Teleradio*, 105 F. Supp. 745

(S.D.N.Y. 1952); *Taggart v. Savannah Gas Co.*, 175 S.E. 491 (Ga. 1934); William L. Prosser, *Injurious Falsehood: The Basis of Liability*, 59 Colum. L. Rev. 425 (1959). In some jurisdictions, this element may be satisfied by establishing that the defendant acted with knowledge or reckless disregard of the falsity of the statement (*Art Metal-U.S.A., Inc. v. United States*, 753 F.2d 1151, 1155 (D.C. Cir. 1985)), or with specific intent to cause harm to the plaintiff or plaintiff's pecuniary interest. *Williams v. Burns*, 540 F. Supp. 1243 (D. Colo. 1982); Cal. Civ. Code, § 3294(c)(1) (1995). In some instances, malice may be implied if the other elements of the tort are present. *Gudger v. Manton*, 1934 P.2d 217 (Cal. 1943).

Finally, the plaintiff must prove that the statements were a substantial factor in causing plaintiff's actual monetary loss (special damages). *E.g., Landstrom v. Thorpe*, 189 F.2d 46 (8th Cir.) *cert. denied*, 342 U.S. 819 (1951); *Eversharp, Inc. v. Pal Blade Co.*, 182 F.2d 779 (2d Cir. 1950); *Polygram Records, Inc. v. Superior Court*, 216 Cal. Rptr. 252 (Cal. Ct. App. 1985); *Rite Aid Corp. v. Lake Shore Inv.*, 471 A.2d 735 (Md. 1984); *Julie Research Lab., Inc. v. Gen. Resistance, Inc.*, 25 A.D.2d 634, 268 N.Y.S.2d 187 (N.Y. App. Div. 1966), *aff'd*, 227 N.E.2d 892 (N.Y. 1967); *Restatement (Second) of Torts* § 633 (1976).

In this regard, when the damage claimed is loss of customers, courts have held that the proof must identify the persons who ceased to be or refused to become customers. *E.g., Forum Publications, Inc. v. P.T. Publishers, Inc.*, 700 F. Supp. 236 (E.D. Pa. 1988); *Drug Research Corp. v. Curtis Publishing Co.*, 166 N.E.2d 319 (N.Y. 1960); Comment, 18 U. Chi. L. Rev. 114, 116 n.15 (1950) (collecting cases). Other courts have allowed more general proof of lost sales; that is, the plaintiff has not been required to identify specific lost customers when lost sales could be proved by other evidence. *Charles Atlas, Ltd. v. Time-Life Books, Inc.*, 570 F. Supp. 150 (S.D.N.Y. 1983); *Marr v. Putnam*, 246 P.2d 509 (Or. 1952); *Restatement (Second) of Torts* § 633 cmt. h (1976). In *Charles Atlas*, the courts strongly disapproved of a rule requiring the specific identity of lost customers; however, other courts continue to favor a policy of identification. *Forum Publications, Inc. v. P.T. Publishers, Inc.*, 700 F. Supp. 236 (E.D. Pa. 1988).

Counsel should be cognizant of the fact that, when applicable, the requirement of "special damages" may limit the utility of the action, as documenting the loss of specific customers—which would probably be the most common type of damage suffered as a result of the publication of a false statement—will often be difficult. As one commentator has observed:

> The result of this requirement is that the more sophisticated the business, the more difficult it is to satisfy the damage proof requirements. As the business increases in size and complexity, and if the plaintiff is a national or regional seller, it becomes more and more difficult for him to compile a list of lost customers. In contrast to the small storekeeper, he often does not note the loss of customers immediately, nor recall their names or their reasons for terminating their business with him.

Edward L. Graf, *Disparaging the Product—Are the Remedies Reliable?* 9 Duq. L. Rev. 163, 176 (1971).

In view of the special-damages requirement in some jurisdictions, counsel should explore the possibility of a defamation action that does not require the proof of special damages. If the attack on one's goods or services implies that the plaintiff is dishonest, lacks integrity, or has acted reprehensibly, an action in defamation may lie. *See, e.g., Harwood Pharmacal Co. v. Nat'l Broadcasting Co.*, 174 N.E.2d 602 (N.Y. 1961); *Larsen v. Brooklyn Daily Eagle*, 150 N.Y.S. 464 (N.Y. App. Div. 1914), *aff'd*, 108 N.E. 1098 (N.Y. 1915); Harry Hibschman, *Defamation or Disparagement*, 24 Minn. L. Rev. 625 (1940). In any event, as previously noted, the trend may be away from the requirement of identifying specific lost customers.

Injurious falsehood is "subject to all of the privileges recognized both in cases of personal defamation and in those of other types of interference with economic advantage." *Gen. Elec. Co. v. Sargent & Lundy*, 916 F.2d 1119 (6th Cir. 1990), *appeal after remand*, 954 F.2d 724 (6th Cir. 1992); *B. C. Morton Int'l Corp. v. FDIC*, 199 F. Supp. 702 (D. Mass. 1961); Keeton, *supra* § 128 at 924. Thus, the generally accepted rules regarding absolute privilege to publish defamatory matter apply to the publication of injurious falsehood as well as conditional privileges. *E.g., Gen. Elec. Co. v. Sargent & Lundy,* 916 F.2d 1119 (6th Cir. 1990), *appeal after remand,* 954 F.2d 724 (6th Cir. 1992); *B. C. Morton, Int'l Corp. v. FDIC,* 199 F. Supp. 702 (D. Mass. 1961); *Restatement (Second) of Torts* § 623 (1976). *E.g., Restatement (Second) of Torts* §§ 646A, 647, 649 (1976).

Whether the circumstances make the statement privileged is a question of law for the court. *Gen. Elec. Co. v. Sargent & Lundy,* 916 F.2d 1119 (6th Cir. 1990), *appeal after remand,* 954 F.2d 724 (6th Cir. 1992); *Redco Corp. v. CBS, Inc.,* 758 F.2d 970 (3d Cir.), *cert. denied,* 474 U.S. 843 (1985); *Restatement (Second) of Torts* § 652 (1976). The existence of the circumstances on which the privilege is based and the determination, in the case of a conditional privilege, regarding whether it has been abused are, however, questions of fact for the jury. *Gen. Elec. Co. v. Sargent & Lundy,* 916 F.2d 1119 (6th Cir. 1990). In this respect, the defendant bears the burden of proving the facts establishing the existence of an absolute or conditional privilege. *Redco Corp. v. CBS, Inc.,* 758 F.2d 970 (3d Cir.), *cert. denied,* 474 U.S. 843 (1985); *Restatement (Second) of Torts* § 651B (1976).

When a conditional privilege is found to exist, the plaintiff may then refute it. This may be done by showing actual malice. *Olivieri v. McDonald's Corp.,* 678 F. Supp. 996 (E.D.N.Y. 1988). Most courts hold that actual malice is established by proof that the person making the statement knew it was false or, even if the person making it did not know it was false, that it was made with a deliberate desire to do another person harm or was made recklessly, without regard to the consequences and under circumstances from which the defendant, as a reasonably prudent person, should have anticipated that injury to another would follow. *See, e.g., Redco Corp. v. CBS, Inc.,* 758 F.2d 970 (3d Cir.), *cert. denied,* 474 U.S. 843 (1985); *Modern Prods., Inc. v. Schwartz,* 734 F. Supp. 362 (E.D. Wis. 1990); *Long v. Rucker,* 149 S.W. 1051 (Mo. Ct. App. 1912); *John W. Lovell Co. v. Houghton,* 22 N.E. 1066 (N.Y. 1889); *Morrison v. Nat'l Broadcasting Co.*, 266 N.Y.S.2d 406 (N.Y. App. Div. 1965), *rev'd on other grounds*, 227 N.E.2d 572 (N.Y. 1967).

However, the U.S. Supreme Court permitted a judgment for recovery of "presumed and punitive" damages to stand absent a showing of actual malice when the action was between two private parties and did not involve a public concern. *Dun & Bradstreet, Inc. v. Greenmoss Builders, Inc.*, 472 U.S. 749 (1985). In *Dun & Bradstreet*, a credit-reporting agency sent to five of its subscribers a report falsely indicating that Greenmoss Builders had filed a voluntary petition for bankruptcy and misstating Greenmoss's assets and liabilities. The Court reasoned that the private nature of the wrong and the limited distribution of the report, coupled with the state's interest in compensating private individuals for injury to their reputations, adequately supported the award. Under these circumstances, there was no First Amendment violation.

Notwithstanding *Dun & Bradstreet*, the issue of whether constitutional limitations on the action for defamation should be carried over to the tort of injurious falsehood has not been finally and fully resolved. *Gertz v. Robert Welch, Inc.*, 418 U.S. 323 (1974); *New York Times Co. v. Sullivan*, 376 U.S. 254 (1964); *Restatement (Second) of Torts* § 623A cmt. c (1976); *Unelko Corp. v. Rooney*, 912 F.2d 1049 (9th Cir. 1990), *cert. denied*, 111 S. Ct. 1586 (1991) (holding injurious falsehood actions subject to same First Amendment requirements as defamation actions).

In *Bose Corp. v. Consumers Union of the United States, Inc.*, 508 F. Supp. 1249, 1269–76 (D. Mass. 1981), a product disparagement case, the district court considered whether the *New York Times v. Sullivan* rule prohibiting a public official from recovering damages for a defamatory falsehood relating to official conduct in the absence of actual malice applies as well to a product disparagement case and, if so, whether a corporation can become a public figure. The district court answered both questions affirmatively.

The court of appeals reversed the district court on other grounds, noting that the *New York Times v. Sullivan* public-figure issue had not been disputed in the court of appeals and accepting the lower court's conclusion on this subject. *Bose Corp. v. Consumers Union of the United States, Inc.*, 692 F.2d 189, 195–96 (1st Cir. 1982), *aff'd*, 466 U.S. 485 (1984). The U.S. Supreme Court upheld the court of appeals and discussed at length standards of review under the First Amendment. In doing so, it acknowledged the court of appeals' acceptance of the district court's public-figure conclusions.

The *Dun & Bradstreet* and *Bose* opinions, although informative, leave unclear the extent, if any, of constitutional limitations on business defamation actions. The charges set forth in this chapter do not include charges related to these complex constitutional issues, as they are beyond the scope of the chapter and tend to be fact specific. However, counsel should be aware that such considerations may apply.

Finally, counsel should also be aware that Preliminary Draft No. 1 of the *Restatement (Third) of the Law, Unfair Competition* may differ from these charges in some respects. Although the Preliminary Draft is presently of limited authority and subject to revision before being approved by the American Law Institute, the propensity of courts to follow Restatements may, in the future, affect these instructions.

3.02 General Instructions

3.02[1] Theory of Injurious Falsehood

In this case the plaintiff, [name], seeks to recover money damages from the defendant, [name], for what the plaintiff claims to be an injurious falsehood published by the defendant. That is, the plaintiff contends that the defendant said of plaintiff's [specify goods and/or services involved] that it [set forth statement claimed to be disparaging or derogatory], and that as a result plaintiff suffered certain losses. The law recognizes that, in certain circumstances, a person who makes a statement about another person's goods or services, which is reasonably understood to cast doubt upon or disparage the quality of those goods or services for those who hear the statement, may be liable for the monetary loss that results directly and naturally from the statement involved.

In these charges, I will give to you the applicable legal principles upon which you are to determine whether the plaintiff should receive a verdict in its favor.

Comment

This charge is based on the one recommended in section 3:55 of *New York Pattern Jury Instructions* (1968), and the one used in *Big O Tire Dealers, Inc. v. Goodyear Tire & Rubber Co.*, 408 F. Supp. 1219 (D. Colo. 1976), *modified on other grounds*, 561 F.2d 1365 (10th Cir. 1977), *dismissed*, 434 U.S. 1052 (1978). *See also Art Metal-U.S.A., Inc. v. United States*, 753 F.2d 1151, 1155 (D.C. Cir. 1985).

3.02[2] Elements of Liability

To find liability for injurious falsehood, you, the jury, must find from a preponderance of the evidence that

(1) the defendant published a statement, and the statement was reasonably understood by those who heard it to cast doubt upon the quality of plaintiff's [identify goods and/or services];
(2) the statement was false;
(3) the statement was maliciously made by the defendant; and
(4) the statement was a substantial factor in causing the plaintiff monetary loss.

If you find that the plaintiff has proved these elements by a preponderance of the evidence, then you will consider the question of damages under instructions to be given.

Comment

This charge reflects the traditional standard for establishing liability for injurious falsehood concerning one's goods or services. *See, e.g., Art Metal-U.S.A., Inc. v. United States,* 753 F.2d 1151, 1155 (D.C. Cir. 1985); *Williams v. Burns,* 540 F. Supp. 1243 (D. Colo. 1982); *Neville v. Higbie,* 20 P.2d 348 (Cal. Ct. App. 1933); *Teilhaber Mfg. Co. v. Unasco Materials Storage,* 791 P.2d 1164 (Colo. Ct. App. 1989), *cert. denied,* 803 P.2d 517 (Colo. 1991); *Drug Research Corp. v. Curtis Publishing Co.,* 166 N.E.2d 319 (N.Y. 1957); Keeton, *supra* § 128; Note, *Corporate Defamation and Product Disparagement: Narrowing the Analogy to Personal Defamation,* 75 Colum. L. Rev. 963, 968–72 (1975); Note, *The Law of Commercial Disparagement: Business Defamation's Impotent Ally,* 63 Yale L.J. 65 (1953).

Note that there will also be liability if the statement is intended to convey a disparaging meaning and is so understood, although reasonable people would not have so understood it. *Kollenberg v. Ramirez,* 339 N.W.2d 176 (Mich. Ct. App. 1983); *Restatement (Second) of Torts* § 629 cmt. f (1976). In such a case, the charge should be amended to read "that it was intended to be and was in fact understood to cast doubt."

Implicit in this charge is that the court has already made some initial determinations. *See Restatement (Second) of Torts* § 652 (1976). For example, whether the statement is capable of a disparaging meaning is a question of law for the court, but whether the statement was reasonably so understood is a question of fact for the jury. *Redco Corp. v. CBS, Inc.,* 758 F.2d 970, 971 (3d Cir. 1985). Similarly, because the disparaging statement must be one of fact and not opinion, the court will resolve this question. *E.g., Stores, Inc. v. Sentinel Publishing Co., Inc.,* 516 A.2d 220 (N.J. 1986); Note, *The Law of Commercial Disparagement: Business Defamation's Impotent Ally,* 63 Yale L.J. 65, 75–76 (1953). *Cf. Testing Sys., Inc. v. Magnaflux,* 251 F. Supp. 286 (E.D. Pa. 1966). The court will also determine whether any loss the plaintiff has proved is sufficient to create a cause of action (that is, constitutes special damages). *Id.*

3.02[3] Jury's Reliance on Improper Fact

To establish the claim against the defendant, the plaintiff must prove by a preponderance of the evidence each of the four elements I just mentioned to you. Only then may you find for the plaintiff.

Comment

This charge follows from the authority cited in the comment to § 3.02[2]. It is recommended to remind the jury that liability will be established only upon a finding that all four elements have been proved.

3.03 Publication

3.03[1] Generally

The plaintiff contends that the defendant published to the plaintiff's customers and potential customers a statement that could reasonably be understood by those who heard it to cast doubt on the quality of the plaintiff's [goods and/or services]. The defendant denies that such a statement was published, according to the meaning of the word "published," which I will give you. If you find that the statement was not published, your verdict will be for the defendant.

Comment

Injurious falsehood, as defamation, requires publication. *Art Metal-U.S.A., Inc. v. United States,* 753 F.2d 1151, 1155 (D.C. Cir. 1985); Keeton, *supra* § 128. Note that this charge assumes the defendant is not denying that the statement was made, but is only denying publication. If the making of the statement is denied, then, of course, an additional charge will be required to reflect this issue.

3.03[2] Definition of Publication

Words are published when, either intentionally or negligently, they are communicated in any manner or circulated in any manner to any person other than the [plaintiff, or, if plaintiff is a corporation, the officers of the plaintiff]. For you to find that the words were published, you must feel that the defendant knew, or had reason to know, the contents of the statement.

[State basis here of claimed publication.] Defendant denies [state disputed facts].

If you find that the plaintiff has not sustained plaintiff's burden of proving that [state disputed facts], your verdict must be for the defendant.

Comment

This charge is based on the charge used in *Big O Tire Dealers, Inc. v. Goodyear Tire & Rubber Co.*, 408 F. Supp. 1219 (D. Colo. 1976), *modified on other grounds*, 561 F.2d 1365 (10th Cir. 1977), *cert. dismissed*, 434 U.S. 1052 (1978). *See Gen. Elec. Co. v. Sargent & Lundy*, 916 F.2d 1119 (6th Cir. 1990); *Cubby, Inc. v. CompuServe, Inc.*, 776 F. Supp. 135 (S.D.N.Y. 1991); *Hawaiian Ins. & Guar. Co., Ltd. v. Blair, Ltd.*, 726 P.2d 1310 (Haw. Ct. App. 1986).

3.04 Disparaging Statement

3.04[1] Generally

In this action, the plaintiff contends that the defendant said of plaintiff's [goods and/or services] that it [set forth statement claimed to be disparaging]. Defendant denies that the statement was understood to [insert "refer to the plaintiff's goods and/or services" or "cast doubt on the quality of the plaintiff's goods and/or services," depending upon defense used]. You must first determine whether the statement was reasonably understood to [insert "refer to the plaintiff's goods and/or services" or "cast doubt on the quality of the plaintiff's goods and/or services"]. If you find that the statement was not reasonably understood to [insert "refer to the plaintiff's goods and/or services" or "cast doubt on the quality of the plaintiff's goods and/or services"], your verdict will be for the defendant.

Comment

Whether an allegedly disparaging statement refers to the plaintiff's goods or services or is understood to cast doubt upon the quantity or the quality of the plaintiff's goods or services are questions that may arise in cases concerning injurious falsehood. Resolution of these questions of fact is a matter for the jury. *See, e.g., Nat'l Ref. Co. v. Benzo Gas Motor Fuel Co.,* 20 F.2d 763 (8th Cir.), *cert. denied,* 275 U.S. 570 (1927); *Caron Corp. v. R.K.O. Pictures, Inc.,* 28 N.Y.S.2d 1020 (N.Y. App. Div. 1941), *aff'd,* 35 N.Y.S.2d 715 (N.Y. App. Div. 1942), *cert. denied,* 318 U.S. 757 (1943).

This charge is based on the charge used in *Kern v. News Syndicate Co.,* 244 N.Y.S.2d 665 (N.Y. App. Div. 1963). Although *Kern* involved a defamation cause of action, the charge is equally applicable to injurious falsehood actions.

Authorities in accord include *Art Metal-U.S.A., Inc. v. United States,* 753 F.2d 1151, 1155 (D.C. Cir. 1985); *Crinkley v. Dow Jones & Co.,* 385 N.E.2d 714 (Ill. App. Ct. 1978); *Ruder & Finn, Inc. v. Seaboard Surety Co.,* 422 N.E.2d 518 (N.Y. 1981). Also note that section 629, comment (f) of the *Restatement (Second) of Torts* (1976), provides authority for the argument that liability will also be found if the statement is intended to convey a disparaging meaning and is so understood, although reasonable people would not have so understood it. *See Kollenberg v. Ramirez,* 339 N.W.2d 176 (Mich. Ct. App. 1983).

3.04[2] Reference to Plaintiff

The statement does not mention the plaintiff's [goods and/or services] by name, but the plaintiff contends that it was reasonably understood by those who [heard or read—choose one] the statement from [set forth references in the statement and extrinsic facts in the case that the plaintiff contends relate the statement to plaintiff] that the statement referred to plaintiff's [goods and/or services]. If you find that those who [heard or read—choose one] the statement reasonably understood that it referred to the plaintiff, based on the content of the statement and from facts about the plaintiff's [goods and/or services] known to such people, then you will consider [state next disputed issue in the action].

Comment

This charge is based on the one recommended in section 3.23 of *New York Pattern Jury Instructions* (1968). Although the charge is for use in a defamation cause of action, the charge is equally applicable to injurious falsehood actions. The authorities referenced in the comment to § 3.04[1] and *Blatty v. New York Times Co.,* 728 P.2d 1177 (Cal. 1986), *cert. denied,* 485 U.S. 934 (1988), also support this charge.

3.04[3] Disparaging Quality

The plaintiff contends that the defendant's statement was reasonably understood by those who [heard or read—choose one] it to cast doubt upon the quality of its [goods and/or services] in that [set forth plaintiff's argument on this point]. If you find that such meaning could reasonably be attached to it, you will then consider [set forth next disputed issue in the action].

Comment

This charge is based upon *Denis v. R.J. Reynolds Tobacco Co.,* 107 N.Y.S.2d 877 (N.Y. App. Div. 1951), *aff'd,* 106 N.E.2d 64 (N.Y. 1952); *Restatement (Second) of Torts* § 629, comment (f) (1976). As noted in § 3.02[2], if the statement is intended to convey a disparaging meaning and is in fact so understood, although reasonable people would not have so understood it, the suggested charge in § 3.02[2] should be used.

3.04[4] Plain Meaning

In determining whether the statement was reasonably understood to [insert "refer to the plaintiff's goods and/or services" or "cast doubt on the quality of the plaintiff's goods and/or services," depending on the allegation], you should consider the plain and natural meaning of the words used in the plain and popular sense in which the public would understand them. You should also consider the words used in their complete context and not dwell upon isolated parts of phrases. Thus, you must interpret the words used in connection with and as a related part of the complete communication and give them such meaning as would naturally be given by persons of ordinary understanding and intelligence.

Comment

This charge is one that was used in *Big O Tire Dealers v. Goodyear Tire & Rubber Co.*, 408 F. Supp. 1219 (D. Colo. 1976), *modified on other grounds*, 561 F.2d 1365 (10th Cir. 1977), *cert. dismissed*, 434 U.S. 1052 (1978). *See Flotech, Inc. v. E.I. DuPont de Nemours Co.*, 627 F. Supp. 358 (D. Mass. 1985), *aff'd*, 814 F.2d 775 (1st Cir. 1987).

3.05 Falsity

3.05[1] Generally

If you find that the statement made by the defendant was reasonably understood by those who read it to cast doubt on the quality of the plaintiff's [goods and/or services], you must then determine whether the statement was false. If you find that it was not, your verdict will be for the defendant. If you find that it was false, you will then consider whether the statement was made maliciously.

Comment

In injurious falsehood cases, the burden is upon the plaintiff to prove the statement is false, rather than, as in defamation, upon the defendant to establish its truth as a defense. *Aldabbagh v. Arizona Dep't of Liquor Licenses and Control,* 783 P.2d 1207 (Ariz. Ct. App. 1989); *Hurlbut v. Gulf Atl. Life Ins. Co.,* 749 S.W.2d 762 (Tex. 1987); Keeton, *supra* § 128.

3.05[2] Puffing

If you find that the defendant's statement was merely "puffing," according to the meaning of the word "puffing" that I will give you, you will find for the defendant. A general statement of comparison by the defendant stating that [his/her] [goods and/or services] are of better quality than those of the plaintiff, when the statement does not include specific facts relating to the plaintiff's [goods and/or services], is puffing.

Comment

This instruction should be given when the defendant asserts that his/her statement was not false, but was merely a statement of comparison or opinion. This charge is based on *Brignoli v. Balch Hardy and Scheinman, Inc.,* 645 F. Supp. 1201 (S.D.N.Y. 1986).

3.05[3] Determining Falsity

The plaintiff contends that the statement made by the defendant was false because [set forth plaintiff's argument]. You will determine from the evidence presented whether the plaintiff has established what plaintiff claims to be the actual situation, and then compare that with the statement made by the defendant. The motivation of the defendant is unimportant if you find that there is no substantial difference between the statement and the actual situation as determined by you. If you find that there was no substantial difference between the statement and the actual situation as determined by you, your verdict will be for the defendant. If you find that the statement differed in some substantial respect from the actual situation as determined by you, your finding will be for the plaintiff on this issue.

Comment

This charge is based on section 634 of the *Restatement (Second) of Torts* (1976). As for the truth of the facts stated, see generally *Brinson v. Carter*, 113 S.E. 820 (Ga. Ct. App. 1922); *Felt v. Germania Life Ins. Co.*, 133 N.Y.S. 519 (N.Y. App. Div. 1912). Truthfulness, and not motivation, is the decisive factor of this instruction. Thus, even if defendant's goal in publishing the statement is to harm the plaintiff, there is no injurious falsehood if the statement is true. *C.R. Bard, Inc. v. Wordtronics Corp.*, 561 A.2d 694 (N.J. Super. Ct. Law Div. 1989).

3.06 Malice

3.06[1] Generally

The burden of proving malice is upon the plaintiff. [Use as much of the remainder of this paragraph as the evidence in the case warrants.] A false statement is made maliciously if the person making it knows that the statement is false. A false statement is made maliciously even though the person making it did not know that it was false if (1) it is made with [(use only when defendant has no privilege) intent to interfere with another person's interest or] a deliberate desire to do another person harm, or (2) it is made recklessly, without regard to the consequences, and under circumstances from which the defendant as a reasonably prudent person would have anticipated that injury to another would follow. If you find that the defendant had serious doubts about the truth of the statement, you will conclude that it was made recklessly. Ill will alone, however, does not constitute malice.

If you find that the statement was not made maliciously, your verdict will be for the defendant.

Comment

This charge is based on section 3.55 of *New York Pattern Jury Instructions* (1968). It reflects the accepted view concerning how malice may be established. *See, e.g., Ezmirlian v. Otto,* 34 P.2d 774 (Cal. Ct. App. 1934); *Morrison v. Nat'l Broadcasting Co.,* 266 N.Y.S.2d 406 (N.Y. App. Div. 1965), *rev'd on other grounds,* 227 N.E.2d 572 (N.Y. 1967); *John W. Lovell Co. v. Houghton,* 22 N.E. 1066 (N.Y. 1889); *Restatement (Second) of Torts* § 623A (1976). Recent authorities in accord include *Bacchus Industries, Inc. v. Arvin Industries, Inc.,* 939 F.2d 887 (10th Cir. 1991); *Art Metal-U.S.A., Inc. v. United States,* 753 F.2d 1151 (D.C. Cir. 1985); *Modern Products, Inc. v. Schwartz,* 734 F. Supp. 362 (E.D. Wis. 1990); and *Williams v. Burns,* 540 F. Supp. 1243 (D. Colo. 1982). *See also* Cal. Civ. Code § 3294(c)(1) (West or Deering 1995). In a slander of title action, the mere filing of an interest in the land records that is later determined to be false does not show malice. Rather, it must be shown that the claim was false, that the defendant knew it was false when the defendant filed it, and/or that defendant filed it intending to harm the plaintiff. *Peckham v. Hirschfeld*, 570 A.2d 663 (R.I. 1990).

For a discussion of problems in proving malice, see Note, *The Law of Commercial Disparagement: Business Defamation's Impotent Ally*, 63 Yale L.J. 65, 78–82 (1953).

3.06[2] Proof of Malice: No Privilege

From the making of a false statement the law presumes malice. Therefore, if you find that the statement was false, you must find malice unless on all the evidence you find the presumption overcome.

In determining whether the statement was made maliciously, you may consider [set forth factors for which there is evidence, such as the language in which the statement was cast; whether at the time the defendant made the statement defendant knew that the statement was false or believed that it was true; whether it was recklessly made with intent to interfere; and all of the other facts and circumstances surrounding the making of the statement]. If you find that the statement was not made maliciously, your verdict will be for the defendant.

Comment

This charge reflects the presumption that most courts recognize when the defendant does not claim a privilege, or the court rules as a matter of law that the statement is not privileged, or the jury determines that the facts do not establish a privilege. See the discussion in § 3.01. Some courts, however, do not presume malice even in the absence of a privilege. *L.L. Bean, Inc. v. Drake Publishing, Inc.*, 625 F. Supp. 1531 (D. Me. 1986), *rev'd on other grounds*, 811 F.2d 26 (1st Cir.), *appeal dismissed and cert. denied*, 483 U.S. 1013 (1987).

3.06[3] Proof of Malice: Claim of Conditional Privilege

A statement concerning another's [goods and/or services] made by one who [state basis of claim of conditional privilege] is said to be privileged if [state elements of privilege]. Even if a privileged statement is in fact false and disparaging of the quality of plaintiff's [goods and/or services], the person making the statements may not be held liable in damages unless, in making the statement, [state conditions when conditional privilege will be defeated].

In this action, you must determine whether the defendant's statement was one that was privileged. The defendant claims [state basis of claimed privilege]. The plaintiff denies [state disputed fact or facts]. If you find that the defendant has not sustained the burden of proving that [state disputed fact or facts], then the statement was not privileged. You then need not consider further the question of privilege, and you may then presume malice in accordance with the previous charge. If you find that the defendant has sustained the burden of proving that fact, I charge you that the occasion was privileged.

If the statement is privileged, the law will not presume malice, and you must then consider whether the plaintiff has established that the statement was in fact maliciously made, in accordance with my earlier charge to you. If you find that the plaintiff has not proved malice, your verdict will be for the defendant. If you find that the plaintiff has proved malice, you will then consider whether the statement was a substantial factor in causing monetary loss to the plaintiff.

Comment

This charge should be used when there is a claim of conditional privilege and the court rules that if the facts claimed are proved, a conditional privilege will exist. It reflects how claims of privilege are raised and how conditional privilege relates to the issue of malice. *Redco Corp. v. CBS, Inc.,* 758 F.2d 970 (3d Cir.), *cert. denied,* 474 U.S. 843 (1985). *Cf. Restatement*

(Second) of Torts § 651 cmt. e (1976). A showing of actual malice or abuse of privilege will defeat the affirmative defense of conditional privilege. *Olivieri v. McDonald's Corp.*, 678 F. Supp. 996 (S.D.N.Y. 1988); *Binkewitz v. Allstate Ins. Co.*, 537 A.2d 723 (N.J. Super. Ct. App. Div. 1988).

3.06[4] Proof of Malice: Absolute Privilege

The defendant claims that the defendant's statement is absolutely privileged. The law recognizes that a person has the right to make a statement, even though the statement is disparaging or maliciously made, when [state basis of the claimed absolute privilege].

In this action, you must determine whether the defendant's statement was made on an absolutely privileged occasion. Defendant claims [state basis of claimed privilege]. Plaintiff denies [state disputed fact or facts]. If you find that the defendant has not sustained its burden of proving [state disputed fact or facts], then the occasion was not privileged and your verdict will be for the plaintiff, provided you find that plaintiff has met the burden of proof on what plaintiff must establish to prove liability. If you find that the defendant has sustained the burden of proving [state disputed fact or facts], your verdict will be for the defendant.

Comment

It is a question of law for the court whether an absolute privilege exists. *E.g., Gen. Elec. Co. v. Sargent & Lundy,* 916 F.2d 1119 (6th Cir. 1990); *Dairy Stores, Inc. v. Sentinel Publishing Co., Inc.,* 516 A.2d 220 (N.J. 1986); *Cheatum v. Wehle,* 159 N.E.2d 166 (N.Y. 1959); *Restatement (Second) of Torts* § 52 (1976). Only when there is a question of fact concerning when and where the statement in issue was made will there be a question for the jury. *E.g., Douglas v. Collins,* 196 N.E. 577 (N.Y. 1935); *Restatement (Second) of Torts* § 656 (1976). Absolute privilege arises in many situations; for example, statements made in judicial proceedings and statements made preceding a judicial proceeding if made in contemplation of litigation. *Gen. Elec. Co. v. Sargent & Lundy,* 916 F.2d 1119 (6th Cir. 1990); *Dairy Stores, Inc. v. Sentinel Publishing Co., Inc.,* 516 A.2d 220 (N.J. 1986) (statement of opinion is absolutely privileged).

3.07 Special Damages

3.07[1] Generally

If you find that the statement was made maliciously, you will next consider whether the statement was a substantial factor in causing monetary loss to plaintiff.

Comment

This charge reflects the essential element of special damages, which plaintiff must prove as an essential part of plaintiff's cause of action. *See* §§ 3.01, 3.02[3], *supra*. *See also, e.g., Golden Palace, Inc. v. Nat'l Broadcasting Co., Inc.*, 386 F. Supp. 107 (D.D.C. 1974), *aff'd mem.*, 530 F.2d 1094 (1976); *Morrison v. Nat'l Broadcasting Co.*, 266 N.Y.S.2d 406 (N.Y. App. Div. 1965), *rev'd on other grounds*, 227 N.E.2d 572 (N.Y. 1967); *Penn-Ohio Steel Corp. v. Allis-Chalmers Mfg. Co.*, 184 N.Y.S.2d 58 (N.Y. App. Div. 1959).

3.07[2] Monetary Loss

The plaintiff claims to have suffered monetary loss in the following respects: [set forth plaintiff's claims].

If you find that the plaintiff did not suffer such a loss, your verdict will be for the defendant.

Comment

The special damages the plaintiff must prove as an essential part of its cause of action means monetary loss. Examples of monetary loss that are recoverable include lost sales (*e.g., Hunt Oil Co. v. Berry,* 86 So. 2d 7 (Miss. 1956), *corrected,* 86 So. 2d 854 (Miss. 1956); *but see Marr v. Putnam,* 246 P.2d 509 (Or. 1952)), and expenses of legal proceedings, as well as other expenses necessary to counteract the publication. *E.g., Maytag Co. v. Meadows Mfg. Co.,* 45 F.2d 299 (7th Cir. 1930), *cert. denied,* 283 U.S. 843 (1931); *Womack v. McDonald,* 121 So. 57 (Ala. 1929); *Dowse v. Doris Trust Co.,* 208 P.2d 956 (Utah 1949).

Additional authorities in accord include *Falls v. Sporting News Publishing Company,* 714 F. Supp. 843 (E.D. Mich. 1989), *on remand from* 834 F.2d 611 (6th Cir. 1987), *aff'd* 899 F.2d 1221 (6th Cir. 1990); *Paulson v. Kustom Enterprises, Inc.,* 483 P.2d 708 (Mont. 1971); *Summa Corp. v. Greenspun,* 655 P.2d 513 (Nev. 1982); and *Den Norske Ameriekalinje Actiesselskabet v. Sun Printing and Publishing Association,* 122 N.E. 463 (N.Y. 1919).

Pecuniary loss must be shown. *Zerpol Corp. v. DMP Corp.,* 561 F. Supp. 404 (E.D. Pa. 1983); *Polygram Records, Inc. v. Superior Court,* 216 Cal. Rptr. 252 (Cal. Ct. App. 1985). Generally, for plaintiff to recover damages for lost sales it must show an established business, the amount of sales from a substantial time period preceding the publication, the amount of sales following the publication, facts showing that the decrease was caused by the publication (see § 3.07[3]), and either the identity of specific lost customers or facts showing that it would not be possible to identify specific customers. *Forum Publications, Inc. v. P.T. Publishers, Inc.,* 700 F. Supp. 36 (E.D. Pa. 1988). *See also Charles Atlas, Ltd. v. Time-Life Books, Inc.,* 570

F. Supp. 150 (S.D.N.Y. 1983); *Teilhaber Mfg. Co. v. Unasco Materials Storage,* 791 P.2d 1164 (Colo. Ct. App. 1989), *cert. denied,* 803 P.2d 517 (Colo. 1991).

The losses claimed to have been suffered will initially be ruled on by the court to determine whether they constitute special damages. *See* § 3.02[2] cmt., *supra.*

3.07[3] Substantial Factor

If you find that the plaintiff did suffer the claimed losses, you must then determine whether the defendant's statement was the proximate cause of the plaintiff's loss or damage.

In this regard, the defendant's statement will be determined to be the proximate cause of the plaintiff's loss or damage if you find that it was a substantial factor in causing that loss or damage, but it need not be the only factor. The statement is a substantial factor in causing the loss or damage if it had such an effect in producing the loss that reasonable persons regard it as a cause of the loss or damage, considering the number of other contributing factors, whether defendant's conduct created a condition or chain of events that was continuous and active up to the time of the damage to the plaintiff, and the lapse of time between the defendant's conduct and the damage to the plaintiff. A mere possibility that the statement caused the damage, however, is insufficient because it is too speculative. If you find that the effect of the statement is too speculative, your verdict will be for the defendant.

Comment

Injurious falsehood is actionable only if it is a substantial factor in causing monetary loss. *E.g., Erick Bowman Remedy Co. v. Jensen Salsbery Lab.,* 17 F.2d 255 (8th Cir. 1926); *Polygram Records, Inc. v. Superior Court,* 216 Cal. Rptr. 252 (Cal. Ct. App. 1985); *Am. Ins. Co. v. France,* 111 Ill. App. 382 (Ill. App. Ct. 1903); *Waste Distillation Technology, Inc. v. Blasland & Bouck Eng'rs, P.C.,* 523 N.Y.S.2d 875 (N.Y. App. Div. 1988); *SRW Assoc. v. BellPort Beach Property Owners,* 517 N.Y.S.2d 741 (N.Y. App. Div. 1987); *Raeder v. New York Times,* 149 N.E.2d 526 (N.Y. 1957), *aff'g* 165 N.Y.2d 619 (N.Y. App. Div. 1957). The charge is based upon these cases and other sources. *See*

Bernard S. Meyer, chairman, *New York Pattern Jury Instructions* §§ 3.55, 2.70 (1968); *Restatement (Second) of Torts* § 433 (1965); 1 J. Dooley, *Modern Tort Law* § 8.03 (1977).

For further discussion on establishing causation, see Note, *The Law of Commercial Disparagement: Business Defamation's Impotent Ally*, 63 Yale L.J. 65, 88–90 (1953).

3.07[4] Award of Damages

If you find that even though the plaintiff suffered a loss, the statement was not a substantial factor in causing that loss, your verdict will be for the defendant. If you find the statement was a substantial factor in causing the plaintiff pecuniary loss, your verdict will be for the plaintiff in the amount of such monetary loss as you find resulted directly and naturally from the making of the statement.

Comment

See § 3.07[3] cmt., *supra.* In most jurisdictions an award of only nominal damages will not satisfy the requirement of special damages and, therefore, will result in a verdict for the defendant. *Rite Aid Corp. v. Lake Shore Investors,* 471 A.2d 735 (Md. 1984).

In many jurisdictions the torts of injurious falsehood and defamation overlap; however, although plaintiff can sue under both theories, plaintiff may recover damages under only one. *Falls v. Sporting News Publishing Co.,* 834 F.2d 611 (6th Cir. 1987).

3.08 Punitive Damages

3.08[1] Generally

The purpose of awarding punitive or exemplary damages is to punish a wrongdoer for some extraordinary conduct and to serve as an example or warning to others not to engage in such conduct.

If you find [state the applicable legal standard for the circumstances under which an award of punitive damages is appropriate], then, in addition to awarding the plaintiff damages for the special losses that were suffered, you may also award the plaintiff a reasonable sum as punitive damages.

Whether to make any award of punitive or exemplary damages in addition to actual damages is a matter exclusively within the province of the jury. You should bear in mind the conditions under which, and the purposes for which, the law permits an award of punitive or exemplary damages to be made, but you must also bear in mind that the amount of such extraordinary damages, when awarded, must be fixed with calm discretion and sound reason, and must never be awarded or fixed in amount because of any sympathy, bias, or prejudice you may feel toward any party in this case.

Comment

In jurisdictions where punitive damages are allowable, they are also permitted in injurious falsehood actions. *E.g., Kendall v. Stone,* 4 N.Y. Sup. Ct. (2 Sanf.) 269, *rev'd on other grounds,* 5 N.Y. 14 (1851). *See also Big O Tire Dealers, Inc. v. Goodyear Tire & Rubber Co.,* 408 F. Supp. 1219 (D. Colo. 1976), *modified on other grounds,* 561 F.2d 1365 (10th Cir. 1977), *cert. dismissed,* 434 U.S. 1052 (1978); *Rite Aid Corp. v. Lake Shore Investors,* 471 A.2d 735 (Md. 1984); *Brooks v. Harrison,* 91 N.Y. 83 (N.Y. 1883).

Chapter Four

Confusion of Source

4.01 Introduction

Michael P. Lynn

The model jury charges in this section deal with the conditions of liability at common law for one who attempts to sell one's goods or services as the goods or services of another. Although no uniform terminology has been generally accepted, the courts are in agreement that relief may be predicated upon theories commonly known as trademark infringement, trade name infringement, and unfair competition. *See* 1 J. McCarthy, *Trademarks & Unfair Competition* § 2.2 (3d ed. 1992); *Developments in the Law—Competitive Torts,* 77 Harv. L. Rev. 888, 908–09 (1964).

The touchstone of liability for trademark and trade name infringement and for unfair competition is the likelihood of customer confusion about the source of products or services. Some modern courts, however, have drawn a distinction between "trademark" (or trade name) law and "unfair competition" law by stating that the former focuses on the narrow question of the use of a word, device, or symbol to distinguish one's goods, services, or business, while the latter relates to a broader issue of the total effect of a product and package on the consumer. As one court has observed: "The essential element of a trademark [or trade name] is the exclusive right of its owner to use a word or device to distinguish [the owner's] product [or business]. On the other hand, a claim of unfair competition considers the total physical image given by the product and its name together. Thus, unfair competition exists if the total impression of package, size, shape, color, design and name upon the consumer will lead the consumer to confuse the origin of the product." *Jean Patou, Inc. v. Jacqueline Cochran, Inc.,* 201 F. Supp. 861, 863 (S.D.N.Y. 1962), *aff'd,* 312 F.2d 125 (2d Cir. 1963). 1 J. McCarthy, *Trademarks & Unfair Competition* § 2.02 at 2–13 (3d ed. 1992). *See also Corning Glass Works v. Jeannette Glass Co.,* 308 F. Supp. 1321 (S.D.N.Y.) *aff'd,* 432 F.2d 784 (2d Cir. 1970). Accordingly, counsel will have to make an initial decision whether to seek relief for trademark and/or trade name infringement, for unfair competition, or both.

4.01[1] Trademark Infringement

The term "trademark" includes any word, name, symbol, device, or any combination thereof adopted and used by a manufacturer or merchant to identify its goods and distinguish them from those manufactured or sold by others. This definition originally appeared in the Lanham Act of 1946, as codified in 15 U.S.C. § 1127, and has been widely cited in cases involving common law claims. *See, e.g., New England Butt Co. v. Int'l Trade Comm'n,* 756 F.2d 874, 877 (D.C. Cir. 1985). In the Tradework Law Revision Act of 1988, the definition of trademark contained in 15 U.S.C. § 1127 was expanded to include

> any word, name, symbol, or device or any combination thereof
>
> (1) used by a person, or
> (2) which a person has a bona fide intention to use in commerce and applies to register on the principal register established by this chapter, to identify and distinguish his or her goods, including a unique product, from those manufactured or sold by others and to indicate the source of the goods, even if that source is unknown.

15 U.S.C. § 1129 (Supp. 1992).

This new definition reflects an overall revision in the Lanham Act. Under the 1988 amendments, applications for tradework registration can be based on a bona fide intent to use a mark in interstate commerce in the future, as well as an actual use of a mark before application. *See generally* 1 J. Gilson, *Tradework Protection and Practice* § 1.04[4] (1992).

In practice, trademarks, which identify and distinguish tangible goods, should be differentiated from service marks, which identify and distinguish services. Service mark infringement is, however, governed by the same principles as trademark infringement. *See, e.g., Nat'l Football League Properties, Inc. v. New Jersey Giants, Inc.,* 637 F. Supp. 507, 519, (D.N.J. 1986); *Murphy v. Provident Mut. Life Ins. Co.,* 923 F.2d 923, 927 (2d Cir. 1990). Therefore, for the purposes of these suggested instructions and charges, the word "trademark" will be used generically to refer to both trademarks and service marks. Counsel is advised to consult more specialized treatises for a thorough discussion of service marks. The terminological distinction between trademarks and service marks originated by statute in 1946 with the Lanham Act, 15 U.S.C. § 1127. Before that enactment, goods and services both fell within the rubric of "trademark" law.

In determining what can be protected as trademark subject matter, it is generally recognized that a trademark at common law may be a word, symbol, device, letter, numeral, or any combination of them in any form or arrangement. *See generally* 1 J. McCarthy, *Trademarks & Unfair Competition,* ch. 4 (3d ed. 1992). *See also* Annotation, *Letters, Initials, or Numerals as Common-Law Trademarks,* 56 A.L.R. Fed. 232 (1982). Thus, a word such as "Ivory" may be a trademark; so may an individual letter, a group of letters, numbers, combinations of letters and numbers, abbreviations and nicknames, slogans, the title of a newspaper column, designs, or color configurations. *See, e.g., Singer Mfg. Co. v. Singer Upholstery & Sewing Co.,* 130 F. Supp. 205 (W.D. Pa. 1955) (the letter "S"); *Elec. Communications, Inc. v. Elec. Components for Ind. Co.,* 443 F.2d 487 (8th Cir.), *cert. denied,* 404 U.S. 833 (1971) (letters "ECI"); *Television Enter. Network, Inc. v. Entertainment Network, Inc.,* 630 F. Supp. 244 (D.N.J. 1986) (number "TEN"); *Cytanovich Reading Ctr. v. Reading Game,* 208 Cal. Rptr. 412 (Cal. Ct. App. 1984) (alphanumeric telephone number letters); *Southland Corp. v. Schubert,* 297 F. Supp. 477 (C.D. Cal. 1968) ("7-ELEVEN"); *Coca-Cola Co. v. Pace,* 283 F. Supp. 291 (W.D. Ky. 1968) ("COKE"); *Anheuser-Busch, Inc. v. Power City Brewery, Inc.,* 28 F. Supp. 740 (W.D.N.Y. 1939) ("BUD"); *Application of Kopy Kat, Inc.,* 498 F.2d 1379 (C.C.P.A. 1974) ("We Print-It In A Min-It"); *Metro Publishing, Ltd. v. San Jose Mercury News,* case no. 91-16537, March 8, 1993 WL 57749 (9th Cir. March 8, 1993); *Ideal Toy Corp. v. Plawner Toy Mfg. Corp.,* 685 F.2d 78 (3d Cir. 1982) (color of cube puzzles); *Shakespeare Co. v. Silstar Corp. of Am.,* 802 F. Supp. 1386 (D.S.C. 1992) (color configuration of fishing rod). Even the color pink has been held not barred from protection as a trademark. *See In re Owens-Corning Fiberglass Corp.,* 774 F.2d 1116 (D.C. Cir. 1985). Furthermore, the shapes of packages and containers and the shapes of products may themselves constitute trademarks. *See generally* 1 J. McCarthy, *Trademarks & Unfair Competition* § 723 (3d ed. 1992). *See also* Gary Schumann, *Trademark Protection of Container and Package Configurations—A Primer,* 59 Chi.-Kent L. Rev. 779 (1983).

A product or service may bear more than one protectable trademark. *See, e.g., In re Polar Music Int'l AB.,* 714 F.2d 1567 (Fed. Cir. 1983); *Fleischmann Distilling Corp. v. Maier Brewing Co.,* 314 F.2d 149 (9th Cir.), *cert. denied,* 374 U.S. 830 (1963). There is a limit, however, on the trademark significance of each word, number, picture, slogan, and so on, that appears on a product; that is, not everything that appears on a label can be said to be, by itself, of trademark significance. *See generally* 1 J. McCarthy, *Trademarks & Unfair Competition* § 71 (3d ed. 1992).

Not all items or symbols qualify for legal protection as trademarks. Only those items or symbols that are used by a person in a manner that identifies that person's own goods or services and distinguishes them from those of others will be protected. *See* 1 J. Gilson, *Trademark Protection & Practice* § 2.01 (1992). The reason for this general rule is that unless the words or devices identify and distinguish the goods, the first user of the mark cannot be injured by misappropriation.

If a symbol is inherently distinctive, it is entitled to legal protection as a trademark. In those cases in which a symbol is not inherently distinctive, it may nevertheless be possible to show that the symbol has acquired a "secondary meaning," according to which the symbol may by usage develop a special, secondary, or trade meaning distinguishing such goods or services in a way that merits legal protection. *See* Annotation, *Doctrine of Secondary Meaning of the Law of Trademarks and Unfair Competition,* 150 A.L.R. 1067 (1944). When the right to protection of a word or symbol is founded on the doctrine of secondary meaning, the geographical extent of such protection will generally be limited to that area where the symbol is used or understood in its secondary sense. *See, e.g., Natural Footwear, Ltd. v. Hart Schaffner & Marx,* 760 F.2d 1383, 1384 (3d Cir.), *cert. denied,* 474 U.S. 920 (1985); Annotation, *Unfair Competition: Geographical Extent of Protection of Word or Symbol under Doctrine of Secondary Meaning,* 41 A.L.R.3d 434 (1972).

4.01[2] Trade Name Infringement

A trade name is a word, name, symbol, device, or any combination thereof in any form or arrangement used to identify one's business, vocation, or occupation and to distinguish it from the business, vocation, or occupation of others. A trade name may be a personal name, corporate name, or fictitious name and it may be dominated by words or terms that are merely descriptive of the goods produced or sold, or by a geographical name identifying the location of the business. *See generally* 1 J. Gilson, *Trademark Protection and Practice* § 2.14 (1992); 1 J. McCarthy, *Trademarks & Unfair Competition* § 91 (3d ed. 1992).

4.01[3] Unfair Competition

An unfair competition claim may be premised on, but is not limited to, the following:

(1) The simulation of advertising methods: *e.g, Echo Travel, Inc. v. Travel Assoc., Inc.,* 674 F. Supp. 656 (E.D. Wis. 1987), *aff'd,* 870 F.2d 1264 (7th Cir. 1989); *B.D. Communications, Inc. v. Dial Media, Inc.,* 429 F. Supp. 1011 (S.D.N.Y 1977); Annotation, *Rights and Remedies with Respect to Another's Use of a Deceptively Similar Advertising Slogan,* 2 A.L.R.3d 748 (1965).

(2) Deceptive comparative advertising practice: *e.g., Johnson & Johnson * Merck v. Smithline Beecham,* 960 F.2d 294 (2d Cir. 1992); *W.L. Gore & Assocs., Inc. v. Totes, Inc.,* 788 F. Supp. 800 (D. Del. 1992), *amended,* 1992 U.S. Dist. Lexis 8055 (D. Del. 1992); *U-Haul Int'l, Inc. v. Jartran, Inc.,* 601 F. Supp. 1140 (D. Ariz. 1984), *aff'd in part, modified in part, rev'd in part,* 793 F.2d 1034 (9th Cir. 1986); *Alpo Petfoods, Inc. v. Ralston Purina Co.,* 720 F. Supp. 194 (D.D.C. 1989), *aff'd in part, vacated in part,* 913 F.2d 958 (D.C. Cir. 1990); *c.f. Harper House, Inc. v. Thomas Nelson, Inc.,* 889 F.2d 197 (9th Cir. 1989); Annotation, *Actionable Nature of Advertising Impugning Quality or Worth of Merchandise or Products,* 42 A.L.R.4th 318 (1985).

(3) The appearance of business facilities: *e.g., Rally's, Inc. v. Int'l Shortstop, Inc.,* 776 F. Supp. 451 (E.D. Ark.), *aff'd,* 985 F.2d 565 (8th Cir. 1990); *Fotomat Corp. v. Photo Drive-Thru, Inc.,* 425 F. Supp. 693 (D.N.J. 1977); *White Tower Sys., Inc. v. White Castle Sys.,* 90 F.2d 67 (6th Cir.), *cert. denied,* 302 U.S. 720 (1937); *see also Two Pesos, Inc. v. Taco Cabana, Inc.,* 505 U.S. 615 (1992) and "trade dress," *infra; but cf. Demetriades v. Kaufman,* 680 F. Supp. 658 (S.D.N.Y. 1988); Annotation, *Trade Dress Simulation of Cosmetic Products As Unfair Competition,* 86 A.L.R.3d 505 (1978); *Unfair Competition by Imitation in Sign or Design of Business Place,* 86 A.L.R.3d 884 (1978).

(4) A product's shape or configuration: *e.g., Chemlawn Serv. Corp. v. GNC Pumps, Inc.,* 690 F. Supp. 1560 (S.D. Tex. 1988); *SunDor Brand, Inc. v. Borden, Inc.,* 657 F. Supp. 86

(M.D. Fla. 1986); *Duo-Tint Bulb & Battery Co. v. Moline Supply Co.,* 360 N.E.2d 798 (Ill. App. Ct. 1977); *cf. Truck Equip. Serv. Co. v. Fruehauf Corp.,* 536 F.2d 1210 (8th Cir.), *cert. denied,* 429 U.S. 861 (1976).

(5) The use of similar corporate, business, and professional names: *e.g., Healing the Children, Inc. v. Heal the Children, Inc.,* 786 F. Supp. 1209 (W.D. Pa. 1992); *Dollar Rent A Car Sys., Inc. v. Sand Dollar Car Rentals,* 765 F. Supp. 876 (D.S.C. 1990); *Century 21 Real Estate Corp. v. Sandlin,* 846 F.2d 1175 (9th Cir. 1988); *Caesars World, Inc. v. Caesar's Palace,* 490 F. Supp. 818 (D.N.J. 1980); 47 P.O.F. 2d, *Wrongful Use of Another's Trademark or Tradename* (1987); Annotation, *Use of "Family Name" by Corporation As Unfair Competition,* 72 A.L.R.3d 8 (1976); Annotation, *Right of Benevolent or Fraternal Society or Organization to Protection against Use of Same or Similar Name, Insignia, or Ritual by Another Organization,* 76 A.L.R.2d 1396 (1961).

(6) "Trade dress," a term that refers to everything the consumer sees when the consumer looks at a packaged product, such as the color or color combinations on the package, the shape or configuration of the package, the wording and the form and placement of wording on the package, and the presence of any decorative indicia on the package: *e.g., Two Pesos, Inc. v. Taco Cabana, Inc.,* 505 U.S. 615 (1992); *Storck U.S.A., L.P. v. Farley Candy Co. Inc.,* 785 F. Supp. 730 (N.D. Ill. 1992); *Speedry Prod., Inc. v. Dri Marks Prod., Inc.,* 271 F.2d 646 (2d Cir. 1959); *Tas-T-Nut Co. v. Variety Nut & Date Co.,* 245 F.2d 3 (6th Cir. 1957); *Mr. Gasket Co. v. Travis,* 299 N.E.2d 906 (Ohio Ct. App. 1973). *See generally* 1 J. McCarthy, *Trademarks & Unfair Competition* ch. 8 (3d ed. 1992); 3 P.O.F.2d, *Trade Dress (Packaging) Simulation* 577 (1974).

(7) The dilution of goodwill of a trademark: *e.g., L.L. Bean, Inc. v. Drake Publisher's Inc.,* 811 F.2d 26, 31–32 (1st Cir.), *cert. denied,* 483 U.S. 1013 (1987); *Frances Denney Inc. v. New Process Co.,* 670 F. Supp. 661 (W.D. Va. 1985); *Chem. Corp. of Am. v. Anheuser-Busch, Inc.,* 306 F.2d 433 (5th Cir. 1962), *cert. denied,* 372 U.S. 965 (1963); *cf. E&J Gallo Winery v. Consorizo del Gallo Nero,* 782 F. Supp. 457 (N.D. Cal.

1991). The existence of a common law remedy for dilution, however, is controversial. *See Int'l Order of Job's Daughters v. Lindburgh & Co.,* 633 F.2d 912 (9th Cir. 1980), *cert. denied,* 452 U.S. 941 (1981).

This section does not address all torts that may be considered as falling under the category of unfair competition. For example, this section does not encompass "palming off" or "passing off"—that is, when there is proof that one subjectively and knowingly intended to confuse buyers. The most familiar example of "passing off" is when a seller knowingly substitutes product X in response to an order for product Y (*see* 3 J. McCarthy, *Trademarks & Unfair Competition* § 2501 (3d ed. 1992)), as classically illustrated in the Coca-Cola cases when a customer at a restaurant, having asked for a "Coke" or "Coca-Cola," is served another cola beverage. *See, e.g., Coca-Cola Co. v. Dorris,* 311 F. Supp. 287 (E.D. Ark. 1970). In effect, "passing off" is simply a more direct and flagrant way of confusing purchasers about the source of the product or service. *See, e.g., Boothroyd Dewhurst, Inc. v. Poli,* 783 F. Supp. 670 (D. Mass. 1991); *Worthington Foods, Inc. v. Kellogg Co.,* 732 F. Supp. 1417 (S.D. Ohio 1990); *Pezon et Michel v. E. R. Hewin Assoc.,* 270 F. Supp. 423 (S.D.N.Y. 1967).

4.02 General Instructions: Trademark Infringement

4.02[1] Theory of Trademark Infringement

In this case, the plaintiff, [name], seeks to recover money damages from the defendant, [name], for what the plaintiff claims to be a trademark infringement in the use of [describe symbol] in connection with the sale of [identify goods and/or services]. The legal principles discussed in these instructions regarding the law of trademark infringement have resulted from attempts to balance the following conflicting policy objectives:

(1) there is a need to protect the public from being misled about the nature and source of the goods and services they buy;

(2) there is a need to protect the property rights of a business to identify itself and its goods and services to the public;

(3) there is a need to try to achieve these goals without injury to the free-market economic system, which encourages fair competition among those providing goods and services.

Fair competition is encouraged, but unfair competition is destructive of the competitive process and is illegal.

Because of the conflicting policy objectives involved in cases of this type, each such case must be decided largely on its specific facts, and you, the jury, are the judge of the facts.

Comment

This charge is based upon the one given by Judge Matsch in *Big O Tire Dealers, Inc. v. Goodyear Tire & Rubber Co.,* 408 F. Supp. 1219 (D. Colo. 1976), *modified on other grounds,* 561 F.2d 1365 (10th Cir. 1977), *cert. dismissed,* 434 U.S. 1052 (1978). This charge informs the jury of the competing interests underlying trademark infringement litigation. *See Holiday Inns, Inc. v. Trump,* 617 F. Supp. 1443, 1464 (D.N.J. 1985); *Scott Paper Co. v. Scott's Liquid Gold, Inc.,* 589 F.2d 1225, 1228 (3d Cir. 1978).

4.02[2] Definition of Trademark

The term "trademark" includes any word, name, symbol, device, or any combination thereof adopted and used by a manufacturer or merchant to identify and distinguish its goods [or services], including a unique product, from those manufactured [or sold] by others and to indicate the source of the goods [or services], even if that source is unknown.

The main function of a trademark is to identify and distinguish goods or services as a product of a particular manufacturer or merchant and to protect its goodwill against the sale of another's product or service as its own.

A trademark is also a merchandising symbol that helps a prospective purchaser to select what such purchaser wants. A trademark signifies that all goods bearing that trademark come from a single source and that all goods bearing the trademark are of an equal level of quality. There is, therefore, a public interest in avoiding confusion in the use of trademarks.

When a manufacturer or merchant has established a trademark right by use on, or in connection with, a product or service before anyone else, the right to use it becomes an exclusive right, and the trademark is property of the manufacturer or merchant. No other person can then use the same or similar [symbol] in any manner that makes confusion likely in the consumer's mind regarding the source or origin of those goods [or services].

Comment

This charge is based on the one given by Judge Matsch in *Big O Tire Dealers, Inc. v. Goodyear Tire & Rubber Co.*, 408 F. Supp. 1219 (D. Colo. 1976), *modified on other grounds*, 561 F.2d 1365 (10th Cir. 1977), *cert. dismissed*, 434 U.S. 1052 (1978). Its use is recommended to alert the jury that a wide variety of items may function as trademarks, and that trademarks are not limited to words. The jury should, however, be instructed that a trademark is not a monopoly; rather, its legal relevance is showing the source, identity, sponsorship, or origin of a product. *See Calvin Klein Cosmetics Corp. v. Lennox Lab.,* 815 F.2d 500, 503 (8th Cir. 1987); *see also Citrus Group Inc. v. Cadbury Beverages, Inc.,* 781 F. Supp. 386, 391 (D. Md. 1991) (to be a trademark, words must be indicative of source of origin; not infringement to use words in their ordinary meanings).

The use of this charge also alerts the jury to the functions of a trademark and the legal effect of establishing a trademark. *See Scandia Down Corp. v. Euroquilt, Inc.,* 772 F.2d 1423, 1429–30 (7th Cir. 1985), *cert. denied,* 475 U.S. 11471 (1986); *Processed Plastic Co. v. Warner Communications, Inc.,* 675 F.2d 852 (7th Cir. 1982); *Fleischmann Distilling Corp. v. Maier Brewing Co.,* 314 F.2d 149 (9th Cir.), *cert. denied,* 374 U.S. 830 (1963); *Kentucky Fried Chicken Corp. v. Diversified Packaging Corp.,* 549 F.2d 368 (5th Cir. 1977); *Turner v. HMH Publishing Co.,* 380 F.2d 224 (5th Cir.), *cert. denied,* 389 U.S. 1006 (1967); Julius R. Lunsford, *Trademarks: Prestige, Practice and Protection,* 4 Ga. L. Rev. 322, 324 (1970); Ralph S. Brown, *Advertising and the Public Interest,* 57 Yale L.J. 1165, 1185 (1948). *See generally* 3 R. Callman, *Unfair Competition, Trademarks & Monopolies* § 17.01 (4th ed. 1983).

4.02[3] Elements of Liability

To find liability for trademark infringement, you, the jury, must find from a preponderance of the evidence that

(1) the plaintiff has established [describe symbol] as a trademark for plaintiff's [identify product or service]; and

(2) the plaintiff had established [name or symbol] as a trademark before the defendant began to market plaintiff's [identify product or service] in the area where plaintiff sells its [identify product or service]; and

(3) the defendant used [describe symbol] in a manner likely to cause confusion about the source of the [identify product or service] among a significant number of persons using ordinary care and prudence in the purchase of [identify product or service].

If you find by a preponderance of the evidence that the plaintiff has proved these elements, then and only then may you find the defendant liable of trademark infringement. You will then consider the question of damages under separate instructions.

Comment

This charge reflects the traditional standard for establishing liability for trademark infringement. *See, e.g., Big O Tire Dealers, Inc. v. Goodyear Tire & Rubber Co.,* 408 F. Supp. 1219 (D. Colo. 1976), *modified on other grounds,* 561 F.2d 1365 (10th Cir. 1977), *cert. dismissed,* 434 U.S. 1052 (1978). *See also Bass Buster, Inc. v. Gapen Mfg. Co.,* 420 F. Supp. 144, 156 (W.D. Mo. 1976).

The jury may find liability without also concluding that the defendant intended to deceive the public (*see, e.g., Emerson Elec. Co. v. Emerson Quiet Kool Corp.,* 577 F. Supp. 668, 678 (E.D. Mo. 1983)), and damages may be awarded without a finding that the defendant acted with a wrongful intent. *See generally* 2 J. McCarthy, *Trademarks & Unfair Competition* §§ 23:30, 30:27(1) (3d ed. 1992). However, an accounting of the defendant's profits requires proof of a wrongful intent. *Nalpac, Ltd. v. Corning Glass Works,* 784 F.2d 752, 2 J. McCarthy, *Trademarks & Unfair Competition* § 30:27(a) (3d ed. 1992).

4.02[4] Jury's Reliance on Improper Fact

The fact that the defendant used [a] [describe symbol] that is similar (or even identical in some respects) to plaintiff's [describe symbol], and that the purchasing public is likely to be confused as a result, does not, in and of itself, constitute trademark infringement. To establish its claim against the defendant, the plaintiff must prove by a preponderance of the evidence each of the three elements previously set forth for your consideration. Only then may you find for the plaintiff.

Comment

This charge follows from the authority cited in the comment to § 4.02[3]. Its use is recommended to reinforce the fact that liability for trademark infringement will be established only upon a finding that all three elements have been proved.

4.03 Trademark Infringement: Proof of Identifying Function

4.03[1] Generally

In this case, the plaintiff claims that plaintiff has established [describe symbol] as a trademark for the [goods or services—choose one] that are [sold or produced—choose one] by [him/her].

In determining whether the plaintiff has established [describe symbol] as a trademark, the first question for you, the jury, to decide is whether the public recognizes the plaintiff's [describe symbol] in connection with the sale of plaintiff's [identify product or service] as identifying plaintiff's [identify product or service] and distinguishing it from those of others. To determine whether the plaintiff has proved this, you must consider whether the evidence shows that the plaintiff's [describe symbol] is inherently distinctive or that, even if not inherently distinctive, the [describe symbol] has become distinctive through the acquisition of what the law calls "secondary meaning." If the trademark is inherently distinctive, then no determination regarding "secondary meaning" need be made.

Comment

This charge describes the proof necessary to establish the requisite identifying function. An identifying work is distinctive if either it is inherently so or it has become distinctive through the acquisition of secondary meaning. *Two Pesos, Inc. v. Taco Cabana, Inc.*, 112 S. Ct. 2753, 2758 (1992). *See also Wiley v. Am. Greetings Corp.*, 762 F.2d 139, 141 (1st Cir. 1985); 1 J. McCarthy, *Trademarks & Unfair Competition* § 151 (3d ed. 1992).

It is possible that a court may consider the issue of whether a symbol is inherently distinctive as a question of law. These charges should not be interpreted as resolving this issue. On the other hand, whether a symbol has acquired secondary meaning is a question of fact for the jury. *See, e.g., Suo-Wizard Mfg., Inc. v. Eisemann Prod. Co.*, 791 F.2d 423, 427 (5th Cir. 1986); *Transgo, Inc. v. Ajac Transmissions Parts Corp.*, 768 F.2d

1001 (9th Cir. 1985); *Zatarains, Inc. v. Oak Grove Smokehouse, Inc.*, 698 F.2d 786, 794 (5th Cir. 1983); *Volkswagenwerk Aktiengesellschaft v. Rickard*, 492 F.2d 474, 477 (5th Cir. 1974). *But see Marker Intern v. De Bruler*, 844 F.2d 763 (10th Cir. 1988) (issue of whether trademark has acquired secondary meaning is issue of fact, but when underlying facts not in dispute, question of secondary meaning appropriate for resolution by summary judgment).

4.03[2] Word(s) as Trademark: Strong versus Weak Marks

The plaintiff asserts that the word(s) [insert word(s)] is a trademark for plaintiff's [identify goods or services]. In trademark usage, words can be classified along a continuum from those that are inherently distinctive to those that are not distinctive at all, or generic.

A "coined" word is an artificial word that has no language meaning except as a trademark. A coined word bears no relationship to the product or service with which it is associated. "EXXON," for example, is a coined word used by an oil company.

A "fanciful" word is like a coined word, in that it is invented for the sole purpose of functioning as a trademark. A fanciful word bears no relationship to the product or service with which it is associated. A fanciful word differs from a coined word only in that it may bear a relationship to another word or it may be an obsolete word. "FAB," for example, is a shortened version of the word "fabulous" and is a fanciful word used for detergent.

An "arbitrary" word is one that is commonly used, but when used with the goods in issue neither suggests nor describes any ingredient, quality, or characteristic of those goods, but is used only in an arbitrary capacity. An arbitrary word bears no relationship to the product or service with which it is associated. "WILD TURKEY" for whiskey is an example of arbitrary wording.

A "suggestive" word is one that suggests, rather than describes, a characteristic or quality of a product or service. "STRONGHOLD" for threaded nails is, for example, suggestive of their superior holding power.

A merely "descriptive" word is one that identifies or describes a characteristic or quality of a product, such as its intended use, its ingredients, or its desirable features. "TENDER VITTLES" for cat food is descriptive.

A merely "geographically descriptive" word is one used to indicate the location or origin of goods and services. "CAL-

IFORNIA APPAREL" as applied to clothing produced in California is geographically descriptive. "NORTH POLE" as applied to bananas would, however, be an arbitrary use of geographical wording because it bears no relationship to the product.

A word is merely a "personal name" (surname or first name) if its ordinary significance is that of a personal name. "GALLO" applied to wine is a personal name. "KING'S" as applied to cologne would, however, be an arbitrary use of a personal name.

A "generic" word is one that is the common name for the product. "BUTTER" is the common generic name for butter. There can be no trademark rights in a generic term. Generic words remain in the public domain as a part of our language.

The right to protection of a trademark comes from its utility in identifying a specific product.

We speak of strong and weak marks in terms of the amount of use necessary to create protected rights. A strong mark is one that symbolizes or signifies a single source or origin. Weak marks are those that do not symbolize or signify a single source or origin. Coined, fanciful, arbitrary, and suggestive words are strong marks. Words that are merely descriptive are weak marks.

Weak marks do not obtain protection solely from their use as a trademark. Weak marks must first acquire distinctiveness from the effect of the owner's efforts in the marketplace. This is what is called the development of secondary meaning. For example, a merely descriptive term used as a trademark must have been so used that its primary significance in the minds of the consuming public is not the product itself but the identification of it with a single source. This does not mean that the consuming public must know the identity of that single source in the sense that the consumer knows the corporate name of the [producer or seller—choose one]. All that is necessary is that the ordi-

nary consumer associates the symbol with a single source, regardless of whether the buyer knows who or what that source is. Once secondary meaning has been established for a mark, that mark is entitled to protection as a trademark.

Comment

This charge is suggested for use when the plaintiff asserts that a word or words are the trademark, in contrast to those situations that involve nonword symbols. The language is generally based upon the charge in *Big O Tire Dealers, Inc. v. Goodyear Tire & Rubber Co.,* 408 F. Supp. 1219 (D. Colo. 1976), *modified on other grounds,* 561 F.2d 1365 (10th Cir. 1977), *cert. dismissed,* 434 U.S. 1052 (1978). *See generally* 1 J. McCarthy, *Trademarks & Unfair Competition* chs. 11–14 (3d ed. 1992); 1 J. Gilson, *Trademark Protection & Practice* ch. 2 (1992); Annotation, *When Does Product Mark Become Generic Term or "Common Descriptive Name" So As to Warrant Cancellation of Registration of Mark, Pursuant to § 14 of Lanham Act (15 U.S.C.S. § 1064* by George K. Chamberlain, J.D. 55 A.L.R. Fed. 241 (1981) (when product mark becomes generic term or common descriptive name so as to warrant cancellation of registration of mark).

In some instances, it may be preferable to limit the categories of words included in the previous charge, as not all categories may be necessary or relevant. *See Two Pesos, Inc. v. Taco Cabana, Inc.,* 505 U.S. 615 (1992); *Wiley v. Am. Greetings Corp.,* 762 F.2d 139, 141 (1st Cir. 1985); *Centour Communications, Ltd. v. A/S/M Communications, Inc.,* 830 F.2d 1217 (2d Cir. 1987); *Bernard v. Commerce Drug Co.,* 964 F.2d 1338, 1340 (2d Cir. 1992) (citing *Abercrombie & Fitch Co. v. Hunting World, Inc.,* 537 F.2d 4 (2d Cir. 1976)); *Branoff-Perlstein Assocs. v. Sklar,* 967 F.2d 852, 855 (3d Cir. 1992); *Perini Corp. v. Perini Constr., Inc.,* 915 F.2d 121, 124 (4th Cir. 1990); *Union Nat'l Bank of Texas, Laredo, Texas v. Union Nat'l Bank of Texas, Austin, Texas,* 909 F.2d 839, 844 (5th Cir. 1990). When applicable, it is appropriate to weigh the interest a person has in doing business in its own name. *See S.C. Johnson & Son, Inc. v. Johnson,* 175 F.2d 176, 180 (2d Cir.), *cert. denied,* 338 U.S. 860 (1949).

4.03[3] Word(s) as Trademark: Secondary Meaning—Permissible Considerations

The mere fact that the plaintiff is using the [describe symbol], or that the plaintiff began using it before the defendant, does not establish or create secondary meaning.

Similarly, the mere fact that you might consider plaintiff's [describe symbol] to be unique is not enough to establish secondary meaning. Additionally, the mere fact that a product is popular is not itself sufficient to show secondary meaning.

There is no particular length of time within which secondary meaning is established. The question for you to determine is whether secondary meaning has been established, not in how long or short a time this was done.

Comment

This charge is suggested for use when the issue at trial is whether plaintiff's symbol is arbitrary, fanciful, or suggestive on the one hand or descriptive, geographically descriptive, a personal name, or generic on the other hand. It is based upon the jury charge in *Big O Tire Dealers, Inc. v. Goodyear Tire & Rubber Co.*, 408 F. Supp. 1219 (D. Colo. 1976), *modified on other grounds*, 561 F.2d 1365 (10th Cir. 1977), *cert. dismissed*, 434 U.S. 1052 (1978), and the charges used in *Gordon v. Warner Brothers Pictures, Inc.*, 74 Cal. Rptr. 499 (Cal. Ct. App. 1969). *See WLWC Ctrs., Inc. v. Winners Corp.*, 563 F. Supp. 717, 723 (M.D. Tenn. 1983) (popularity in sales alone cannot establish secondary meaning). *See also* 1 J. McCarthy, *Trademarks & Unfair Competition* ch. 15 (3d ed. 1992); 1 J. Gilson, *Trademark Protection & Practice* ch. 2 (1992); Annotation, *Application of Secondary Meaning Test in Action for Trademark Infringement*, 86 A.L.R. Fed. 489 (1988).

Depending upon the specific facts of the case, counsel may expand upon what is descriptive, generic, and so forth, and why the symbol at issue does or does not fall within such a category, using the evidence introduced at trial. The law relating to whether a trademark is generic or descriptive is developing, and there are differences among jurisdictions.

Counsel should consider the point raised in the comment to § 4.03[1] that the issue of whether the symbol is inherently distinctive may be one of law for the court to decide.

4.03[4] Word(s) as Trademark: Dispute between Arbitrary, Fanciful, or Suggestive Word(s), and Descriptive, Generic, Geographically Descriptive, or Personal Name Word(s)

Plaintiff claims that [describe symbol] is inherently distinctive because it is a [coined, fanciful, arbitrary, and/or suggestive—choose one or more adjectives as applicable] word(s).

Defendant, however, contends that plaintiff has not established [describe symbol] as a trademark because it constitutes a word(s) that is [insert "merely descriptive of a quality or characteristic of plaintiff's goods and/or services," "geographically descriptive of the origin of plaintiff's goods and/or services," "merely a personal name," and/or "a generic name for plaintiff's goods and/or services"—choose one or more phrases as appropriate].

This is a question for you, the jury, to decide. Is the [describe symbol] a [coined, fanciful, arbitrary, and/or suggestive—choose one or more adjectives as applicable] word(s), or ["merely descriptive," "merely geographically descriptive," "merely a personal name," and/or "generic"—choose one or more phrases as applicable] in accordance with what I have just charged you?

If your answer to that question is that the [describe symbol] is inherently distinctive, you will then consider whether the quantity and quality of the plaintiff's use of [describe symbol] has established plaintiff's priority so as to earn legal protection of the [describe symbol] as a trademark.

On the other hand, if you decide that the plaintiff's [describe symbol] is [insert "merely descriptive," "merely geographically descriptive," "merely a personal name," and/or "generic"—choose one or more phrases as applicable] as applied to plaintiff's goods and/or services, then you will consider whether the evidence shows that plaintiff's [describe symbol] has developed secondary meaning.

Comment

This text clarifies and defines the differences between "descriptive" and "generic" words, and "arbitrary" and "suggestive" words.

4.03[5] Word(s) as Trademark: Secondary Meaning Defined

By the term "secondary meaning," the law means that a symbol has been so used that its primary significance in the minds of the consuming public is not the [product or service—choose one] itself but the identification of such [product or service] with a single source. This does not mean that the consuming public must know the exact identity of that single source in the sense that it knows the corporate name of the [producer or seller—choose one]. All that is necessary to establish secondary meaning is that the ordinary consumer associates the [product or service] with a single source, regardless of whether the consumer knows who or what that source is.

You must find, therefore, from a preponderance of the evidence, that a significant number of the consuming public associates the [describe symbol] involved in this case with a single source. It is for you to decide how many constitute a significant number, keeping in mind that the plaintiff need not prove that all or even a majority of the consuming public understands this secondary meaning.

In determining whether the plaintiff's [describe symbol] has attained secondary meaning, it is appropriate for you to consider the evidence (if any) relating to

(1) the length and manner of its use;
(2) the nature and extent of advertising and promotion;
(3) sales volume;
(4) other efforts made by the plaintiff to promote the connection in the consuming public's mind between the [symbol] and the plaintiff;
(5) properly designed and conducted consumer surveys;
(6) the testimony of consumers relating to the identity of source or the origin of the [describe symbol] in the minds of the consuming public; and
(7) copying by others.

Comment

This text includes a composite of the factors that may be considered in determining whether secondary meaning has been established as set forth by various courts. Counsel is advised to refer to the law of the appropriate jurisdiction, as various courts have delineated different sets of factors. *See, e.g., Laureyssens v. Idea Group, Inc.*, 964 F.2d 131, 136 (2d Cir. 1992); *Faberge, Inc. v. Saxony Prods., Inc.*, 605 F.2d 426, 428 (9th Cir. 1979); *Essie Cosmetics, Ltd. v. Dae Do Int'l Ltd.*, 808 F. Supp. 952, 958 (E.D.N.Y. 1992); *Sprinklets Water Ctr., Inc. v. McKesson Corp.*, 806 F. Supp. 656, 661 (E.D. Mich. 1992); *Spraying Sys. Co. v. Delavan, Inc.*, 762 F. Supp. 772, 778 (N.D. Ill. 1991); *Ginger Group, Ltd. v. Beatrice Cos., Inc.*, 678 F. Supp. 555, 560 (E.D. Pa. 1988); *Shen Mfg. Co., Inc. v. Suncrest Mills, Inc.*, 673 F. Supp. 1199, 1204 (S.D.N.Y. 1987); *Southwestern Bell Tel. Co. v. Nationwide Indep. Directory Serv., Inc.*, 371 F. Supp. 900, 909 (W.D. Ark. 1974); *Filter Dynamics Int'l, Inc. v. Astron Battery, Inc.*, 311 N.E.2d 386 (Ill. App. Ct. 1974); *Gordon v. Warner Bros. Pictures, Inc.*, 74 Cal. Rptr. 499 (Cal. Ct. App. 1969). *See generally* 1 J. Gilson, *Trademark Protection & Practice* § 2.09 (1986); 3 R. Callman, *Unfair Competition, Trademarks & Monopolies* § 18.01 (4th ed. 1992).

Several cases in the Southern District of New York conclude that when "incipient secondary meaning" or "secondary meaning in the making" is shown, a court may dispense with most, if not all, of the normal secondary meaning proof requirements. *See, e.g., Mets Kane Imports, Ltd. v. Federated Dep't Stores, Inc.*, 625 F. Supp. 313, 316 (S.D.N.Y. 1985), *aff'd sub nom.*, 800 F.2d 1128 (2d Cir. 1986); *West & Co., Inc. v. Arica Inst., Inc.* 35 n.10 (S.D.N.Y. 1976), *aff'd*, 557 F.2d 338 (2d Cir. 1977); *Nat'l Lampoon, Inc. v. Am. Broadcasting Cos.*, 376 F. Supp. 733, 747 (S.D.N.Y.), *aff'd*, 497 F.2d 1343 (2d Cir. 1974). *See also* 3 R. Callman, *Unfair Competition, Trademarks & Monopolies* § 77.3 at 356 (3d ed. 1971).

Some courts have held that evidence of deliberate copying establishes a prima facie case of secondary meaning, with the defendant bearing the ultimate burden of proof once deliberate copying is shown. *M. Kramer Mfg. Co., Inc. v. Andrews*, 783 F.2d 421, 449 (4th Cir. 1986). *See also Two Pesos, Inc. v. Taco Cabana, Inc.*, 112 S. Ct. 2757 (1992) (inherently distinctive trade dress held protectable from infringement without proof of secondary meaning); *Ideal Toy Mfg.Corp. v. Plawner Toy Mfg. Corp.*, 685 F.2d 78, 82 (3d Cir. 1982) (admission of copying persuasive evidence of secondary meaning); *Am. Greetings Corp. v. Dan-Dee Imports, Inc.*, 619 F. Supp. 1204, 1221 (D.N.J. 1985) (court's finding that plaintiff in fact copied design persuasive evidence of secondary meaning); *Maryland Stadium Auth. v. Becker*, 806 F. Supp. 1236, 1241 (D. Md. 1992) ("Intentional copying of a mark. . . raises a presumption of secondary meaning."). This view has been criticized. *See Mr. Gasket Co. v. Travis*, 299 N.E.2d 906 (Ohio Ct. App. 1973); *Developments in the Law—Competitive Torts*, 77 Harv. L. Rev. 888, 916 (1963).

4.03[6] Nonword Symbols as Trademarks

In this case, the plaintiff claims that plaintiff has established [describe nonword symbol] as a trademark for the [goods or services—choose one] that are [sold or produced—choose one] by [him/her]. Not only words constitute valid and protectable trademarks. The term trademark includes any word, name, symbol, device, or combination thereof adopted and used by a manufacturer or merchant to identify and distinguish its goods or services, including a unique product, from those manufactured or sold by others.

In determining whether the plaintiff has established [describe nonword symbol] as a trademark, the first question for you, the jury, to decide is whether the public recognizes plaintiff's [describe nonword symbol] in connection with the sale of plaintiff's [identify product or service] as identifying plaintiff's [identify product or service] and distinguishing plaintiff's [describe goods and services] from those of others. To determine whether plaintiff has proved this, you must consider whether the evidence shows that the plaintiff's [describe nonword symbol] is inherently distinctive or, even if it is not inherently distinctive, the [describe nonword symbol] has become distinctive through the acquisition of what the law calls "secondary meaning."

Comment

Word symbols as well as nonword symbols, such as letters, numbers, product and container shapes, designs, and pictures may be regarded as being inherently distinctive in an appropriate case. *See generally* 1 J. McCarthy, *Trademarks & Unfair Competition* §§ 11.02–11.04 (3d ed. 1992); Richard P. Shafer, Annotation, *Letters, Initials, or Numerals as Commonlaw Trademarks,* 56 A.L.R. Fed. 232 (1992). Some symbols ordinarily require proof of secondary meaning, however. These include ordinary geometric shapes, descriptive symbols, geographically descriptive symbols, personal name symbols, and noninherently distinctive designs and product and container shapes. *See, e.g., Brooks Shoe Mfg. Co. v. Suave Shoe Corp.,* 716 F.2d 854, 857 (11th Cir. 1983) ("V" design on side of shoe not distinctive); *Application of David Crystal, Inc.*, 296 F.2d 771, 773 (C.C.P.A. 1961) (stripes on top of men's socks not inherently distinctive). *See generally* 1 J. McCarthy, *Trademarks & Unfair Competition* § 7.12 (3d ed. 1992).

Section 43(a) of the Lanham Trademark Act, 15 U.S.C. § 1125(a), has also been interpreted to provide a cause of action for trade dress infringement. *See e.g., Am. Greetings Corp. v. Dan-Dee Imports, Inc.*, 807 F.2d 1136, 1140 (3d Cir. 1986). For the purposes of an infringement action, "trade dress" is defined as the total image of a product and may include features such as size, shape, color or color combinations, textures, graphics, or particular sales techniques. *Bauer Lamp Co., Inc. v. Slatter*, 941 F.2d 1165, 1170 (11th Cir. 1991); *Stormy Cline Ltd. v. Pro Group, Inc.*, 809 F.2d 971, 974 (2d Cir. 1987); *Vision Sports, Inc. v. Melville Corp.*, 888 F.2d 609, 613 (8th Cir. 1988). Secondary meaning is a required element of a cause of action for trade dress infringement. *Am. Greetings Corp.*, 807 F.2d at 1141; *Bauer Lamp Co.*, 941 F.2d at 1170.

The issue of distinctiveness may be one of law for the court to decide. *See* § 4.03[1], cmt., *supra.*

When trademark protection is sought for a design used as a background for a word or other marks, it may be contended that the design is simply a decorative or ornamental feature, and thus has no trademark function. *See, e.g., Ventura Travelware, Inc. v. Baltimore Luggage Co.*, 322 N.Y.S.2d 93 (N.Y. App. Div. 1971), *aff'd*, 328 N.Y.S.2d 811 (N.Y. App. Div. 1972). In such a case, it will be necessary to include an additional charge:

> To be a trademark, the design's principal function must be to identify and distinguish the plaintiff's goods. This function will be present if you find that the design creates a separate impression upon the consuming public. In other words, you must find that the consuming public recognizes the plaintiff's [nonword symbol] as a mark to identify and distinguish the plaintiff's goods and services when they see the design alone, apart from any other marks used in connection with the [nonword symbol].

4.03[7] Nonword Symbols as Trademarks: Secondary Meaning—Permissible Considerations

The mere fact that the plaintiff is using [describe nonword symbol], or that the plaintiff began using it before the defendant, does not establish or create secondary meaning.

Similarly, the mere fact that you might consider the plaintiff's [describe nonword symbol] to be unique is not enough to establish secondary meaning. Additionally, the mere fact that a product is popular is not itself sufficient to show secondary meaning.

There is no particular length of time within which secondary meaning is established. The question for you to determine is whether secondary meaning has been established, not in how long or short a time this was done.

Comment

"Secondary meaning" is the circumstance when a nonword symbol identifies one's goods or services and distinguishes them from those of others. *See* 1 J. McCarthy, *Trademarks & Unfair Competition* §§ 7:7–7:15 (3d ed. 1992). The issue of distinctiveness may be one of law for the court to decide.

This charge concerning secondary meaning is identical to that contained in § 4.03[3] for word symbols.

4.03[8] Nonword Symbols as Trademarks: Dispute between Inherently Distinctive and Noninherently Distinctive Nonword Symbols

Nonword symbols that are fanciful or arbitrary, in contrast to descriptive or generic, are inherently distinctive and can be protected as common law trademarks. For example, nonword symbols that comprise designs that are not commonly used at the time of adoption may be inherently distinctive. Pictures of products that create or present arbitrary or fanciful impressions may also be inherently distinctive. On the other hand, common basic designs such as circles, ovals, triangles, diamonds, or stars are not examples of inherently distinctive symbols.

The plaintiff claims that [describe nonword symbol] is inherently distinctive. The defendant, however, contends that the [describe nonword symbol] is not inherently distinctive. This is a question for you, the jury, to decide in accordance with what I have just read to you.

If you decide that the [describe nonword symbol] is inherently distinctive, you will then consider whether [insert the following in an appropriate case:] the [describe nonword symbol] is functional and whether the quantity and quality of the plaintiff's use of the [describe nonword symbol] has established plaintiff's priority so as to have earned legal protection for the [describe nonword symbol] under instructions to be given.

If you decide that plaintiff's [describe nonword symbol] is not inherently distinctive, then you will consider whether the evidence shows that the plaintiff's [describe nonword symbol] has developed secondary meaning.

By the term "secondary meaning," the law means that one's nonword symbol has been so used that its primary significance in the minds of a significant number of the consuming public is not the [product or service—choose one] itself but the identification of it with a single source. This does not mean that the consuming public knows the identity of that single source in the sense that the consumer knows the corporate name of the [producer or seller—choose one]. All that is necessary to establish secondary meaning is that the ordinary consumer associates the nonword symbol with a single source, regardless of whether the buyer knows who or what that source is.

You must find, therefore, from a preponderance of the evidence, that a significant number of the consuming public has associated the [describe nonword symbol] involved in this case with a single source. It is for you to decide how many constitute a significant number, keeping in mind that it is not necessary for the plaintiff to prove that all or even a majority of the consuming public understand this secondary meaning.

In determining whether the plaintiff's [describe nonword symbol] has attained secondary meaning, it is appropriate for you to consider the evidence (if any) relating to:

(1) the length and manner of its use;
(2) the nature and extent of the plaintiff's advertising and promotion;
(3) sales volume;
(4) other efforts made by the plaintiff to promote the connection in the consuming public's mind between the [describe nonword symbol] and the plaintiff;
(5) properly designed and conducted consumer surveys;
(6) the testimony of consumers relating to the identity of source or origin in the minds of the consuming public; and
(7) copying by others.

Comment

See §§ 4.03[1], 4.03[3], 4.03[4], cmts., *supra. See also Wiley v. Am. Greetings Corp.*, 762 F.2d 139 (1st Cir. 1985).

4.03[9] Nonword Symbols as Trademarks: Functional or Nonfunctional

In this case, the defendant claims that the [describe nonword symbol] used by the plaintiff is functional, and that the defendant may therefore also use the [describe nonword symbol].

Under the law of trademark infringement, any feature of goods or services that is functional cannot be legally protected. That is, the use of such a feature cannot constitute trademark infringement. For plaintiff to establish liability in this case, it will therefore be necessary for you to find that the [describe nonword symbol] is nonfunctional.

Design features that are useful or practical or that serve a utilitarian purpose are merely functional and cannot be legally protected. Moreover, if the [describe nonword symbol] functions primarily to beautify a product, then the [describe nonword symbol] must also be considered merely functional. In short, any feature that gives the consumer a substantial reason for purchasing the goods or services because the feature adds to either the utility or the style and attractiveness of the goods or services is functional. For example, a twist-off bottle cap is functional because it adds to the utility of the product. Conversely, a feature that serves only to distinguish the goods or services from other goods and services is nonfunctional. For example, a logo is an arbitrary symbol of source and is nonfunctional.

If you find from the evidence that the plaintiff's [describe nonword symbol] substantially contributes to the usefulness, utility, or practicality of the product, then you must find that the [describe nonword symbol] is functional and that the defendant was free to copy or simulate it.

If you find from the evidence that the plaintiff's [describe nonword symbol] substantially contributes to the general appeal of its product, because of the design of the [describe nonword symbol] itself and not because it indicates a source for the goods the consumer desires to purchase, then

you must also find that the [describe nonword symbol] is functional and that the defendant was free to copy or simulate it.

If you find, however, that the plaintiff's [describe nonword symbol] is used to distinguish the product from others, the [describe nonword symbol] is nonfunctional.

Comment

The issue of functionality may arise when trademark rights are asserted in nonword symbols such as designs or container shapes. *See, e.g., Fabrica, Inc. v. El Dorado Corp.*, 697 F.2d 890 (9th Cir. 1983). This charge reflects the generally accepted standard in determining whether such nonword symbols are functional.

The landmark case pertaining to functionality is *Pagliero v. Wallace China Co.*, 198 F.2d 339 (9th Cir. 1952). "Functionality," as defined in *Pagliero*, is a measure of the effect of a design or physical detail in the marketplace. If a design functions in the marketplace (1) by means of aesthetic appeal, (2) by increasing the utility or practicality of a product, or (3) by saving the consumer or producer time or money, then the design may be legally functional. *Fabrica, Inc. v. El Dorado Corp.*, 697 F.2d 890, 894 (9th Cir. 1983). *See also J. C. Penney Co. v. H. D. Lee Mercantile Co.*, 120 F.2d 949 (8th Cir. 1941); *Zippo Mfg. Co. v. Rogers Imports, Inc.*, 216 F. Supp. 670 (S.D.N.Y. 1963). *But see Wallace Intern. Silversmiths, Inc. v. Godinger Silver Art Co., Inc.*, 916 F.2d 76, 80 (2d Cir.) (rejecting *Pagliero* on the grounds that "[b]y allowing the copying of an exact design without any evidence of market foreclosure, the *Pagliero* test discourages both originators and later competitors from developing pleading designs"), *cert. denied*, 499 U.S. 976 (1991).

It should be noted, however, that some courts may not accept this broad definition of functionality. *See W. T. Rogers Co., Inc. v. Keene*, 778 F.2d 334, 343 (7th Cir. 1985) (attractiveness of design feature does not preclude its being trademarked); *Sicilia di R. Biebow & Co. v. Cox*, 732 F.2d 417, 427–29 (5th Cir.

1984). *But see Unital, Ltd. v. Sleepco Mfg., Ltd.*, 627 F. Supp. 285, 290 (W.D. Wash. 1985) (if eye appeal essential, purely aesthetic design functional). Specifically, there is a conflict about whether aesthetic features of a product may be termed functional. For a fuller discussion, see Bradford J. Duft, *"Aesthetic" Functionality*, 73 Trademark Rep. 151 (1983). *See also* § 4.09[2], cmt., *infra*.

In *Inwood Laboratories, Inc. v. Ives Laboratories, Inc.*, 456 U.S. 844, 850 n.10 (1982), the Supreme Court held that a product feature is functional if it is essential to the product's use or if it affects the cost or quality of the article. Case law also defines nonfunctionality in terms of the dispensability of a feature (*e.g., W. T. Rogers Co., Inc. v. Keene*, 778 F.2d 334, 342 (7th Cir. 1985)), and/or whether a given feature is essential to effective competition. *E.g., Essie Cosmetics Ltd. v. Dae Do Int'l, Ltd.*, 808 F. Supp. 952, 958 (E.D.N.Y. 1992); *New England Butt Co. v. Int'l Trade Comm'n*, 756 F.2d 874, 877–78 (D.C. Cir. 1985). *See also U.S. Golf Assoc. v. St. Andrews Sys.*, 749 F.2d 1028, 1033 (3d Cir. 1984) (asserting that functionality depends on "whether a particular feature of a product or service is substantially related to its value *as a product or service*, i.e., if the feature is part of the 'function' served, or whether the primary value of a particular feature is the identification of the provider"). It is important to frame this charge in accordance with the current view of the appropriate jurisdiction.

The Supreme Court has interpreted federal patent law as preempting state law insofar as the latter restricts the ability of a competitor to copy the functional features of a competitor's unpatented product. *Sears, Roebuck & Co. v. Stiffel Co.*, 376 U.S. 225 (1964); *Compco Corp. v. Day Brite Lighting, Inc.*, 376 U.S. 234 (1964); *Sunbeam Corp. v. Equity Indus. Corp.*, 635 F. Supp. 625, 637–38 (E.D. Va. 1986). *But see Towle Mfg. Co. v. Godinger Silver Art Co. Ltd.*, 612 F. Supp. 986, 995 (S.D.N.Y. 1985) (statute still permits states to afford common law remedies to limited degree); 1 J. McCarthy, *Trademarks & Unfair Competition* § 8:7 (3d ed. 1992) ("Since the shape of a container or package may be an essential element of similarity in simulation of trade dress, and has always been so considered, it can be argued that there is no federal preemption of unfair competition protection, even though the shape is not protected by a design patent").

Finally, it is important to note that courts may construe functionality as a question of law or as a mixed question of fact and law. *See Unital, Ltd. v. Sleepco Mfg., Ltd.*, 627 F. Supp. 285, 290 (W.D. Wash. 1985).

4.04 Trademark Infringement: Acquisition and Priority of Trademark Rights

4.04[1] Generally

If you find that the public recognizes the plaintiff's [describe symbol] as identifying plaintiff's [identify product or service] and distinguishing it from those of others, you must then find that plaintiff had used the [describe symbol] as a trademark before the defendant began to market its [identify product or service] in the area where the plaintiff sells its [identify product or service].

Comment

See § 4.02[3], cmt., *supra.* This charge is important when the plaintiff and defendant both assert that they are the "owner" of the trademark in litigation.

4.04[2] Priority of Use: Inherently Distinctive Trademarks

If you find that the plaintiff's [describe symbol] is inherently distinctive, you must then consider whether the evidence shows that the plaintiff used [describe symbol] as a trademark for plaintiff's [identify product or service] before the defendant began to use the [describe symbol]. That is, the plaintiff must have attached the symbol to plaintiff's [identify product or service] or its label or container before the defendant made such use of the [describe symbol].

You must also determine whether the evidence shows that the plaintiff's use of the [describe symbol] as a trademark for its [identify product or service] was continuous. That is, the plaintiff's use of the [describe symbol] must not have constituted merely a token use of the [describe symbol]. Token use is sporadic, casual, or transitory use that is not part of an ongoing program to exploit the trademark commercially. The number of sales does not conclusively establish continuous use, but there must be a bona fide attempt to establish a trade or a market in the product.

The date that the party conceived the idea of the symbol does not constitute use.

Comment

This charge reflects the traditional view that trademark rights are obtained by the party who first makes an actual, bona fide use of the trademark in a going business. *See, e.g., Bell v. Streetwise Records, Ltd.*, 640 F. Supp. 575 (D. Mass. 1986); *Blue Bell, Inc. v. Farah Mfg. Co.*, 508 F.2d 1260 (5th Cir. 1975); *Blisscraft of Hollywood v. United Plastics Co.*, 294 F.2d 694 (2d Cir. 1961); *Rolley v. Younghusband*, 204 F.2d 209 (9th Cir. 1953). *See generally* 1 J. McCarthy, *Trademarks & Unfair Competition* ch. 16 (3d ed. 1992); 1 J. Gilson, *Trademark Protection & Practice* § 3.03 (1992).

4.04[3] Priority of Use: Secondary Meaning Trademarks

If you find that the plaintiff's [describe symbol] is not inherently distinctive, but that the plaintiff has established secondary meaning in it, you must then consider whether the plaintiff can prove, by a preponderance of the evidence, that plaintiff's [describe symbol] possessed secondary meaning before the defendant first began use of [describe symbol].

Comment

This charge reflects the well-established rule that for secondary meaning marks—unlike inherently distinctive marks—the issue of priority is resolved in favor of the party who first uses the mark with secondary meaning. The senior user must prove the existence of secondary meaning in its mark at the time and place that the junior user first began use of that mark. *See Scott Paper Co. v. Scott's Liquid Gold, Inc.*, 589 F.2d 1225, 1231 (3d Cir. 1978); *Carter-Wallace, Inc. v. Procter & Gamble Co.*, 434 F.2d 794 (9th Cir. 1970); 1 J. McCarthy, *Trademarks & Unfair Competition* § 16:12 (1992).

4.04[4] Failure to Establish Priority

If you determine that the plaintiff has not established that plaintiff used [describe symbol] before the defendant's use of [describe symbol], then you must find for the defendant, as there can be no trademark infringement.

Comment

This charge follows from the law discussed in the three previous sections. *See, e.g., Scott Paper Co. v. Scott's Liquid Gold, Inc.*, 589 F.2d 1225, 1231 (3d Cir. 1978); *Ball v. United Artists Corp.*, 214 N.Y.S.2d 219 (N.Y. App. Div. 1961).

4.05 Trademark Infringement: Likelihood of Confusion

4.05[1] Generally

If you decide that the plaintiff established [describe symbol] as a trademark for plaintiff's [identify product or service] before the defendant did, then you must consider whether the defendant used [describe symbol] in a manner likely to cause confusion regarding the source of [identify product or service] among consumers using ordinary care and prudence in the purchase of [identify product or service].

In other words, you must find that ordinary purchasers, buying under the usual conditions and exercising ordinary care, would be likely to purchase the defendant's [identify product or service] in the belief that it was [produced or provided—choose one] by the plaintiff.

It is unnecessary that the evidence show that any specific person has been confused or misled. It is enough if you find that the consequences of the sale of the [describe symbol] complained of in all reasonable probability would be to confuse the public regarding the source, sponsorship, approval, or affiliation of the [identify product or service].

The fact that the [identify product or service] could be distinguished by careful or discriminating purchasers is not enough to lead you to conclude that there is no likelihood of confusion.

Comment

This charge reflects the traditional standard of likelihood of confusion. *See, e.g., Plus Prods. v. Plus Discount Foods Inc.*, 722 F.2d 999, 1003 (2d Cir. 1983); *Seven-Up Co. v. Cheer Up Sales Co.*, 148 F.2d 909 (8th Cir.), *cert. denied*, 326 U.S. 727 (1945); *Omega Importing Corp. v. Petri-Kine Camera Co.*, 451 F.2d 1190 (2d Cir. 1971); *Union Carbide Corp. v. Ever-Ready, Inc.*, 531 F.2d 366 (7th Cir.), *cert. denied*, 429 U.S. 830 (1976); *Thomas J. Lipton, Inc. v. Borden, Inc.*, 340 N.Y.S.2d 328 (N.Y. App. Div. 1972); 2

J. McCarthy, *Trademarks & Unfair Competition* ch. 23 (2d ed. 1984); 1 J. Gilson, *Trademark Protection & Practice* ch. 5 (1986).

The charge is generally based upon the ones used in *El Rancho, Inc. v. First National Bank of Nevada,* 406 F.2d 1205 (9th Cir. 1968), *cert. denied sub. nom. Gerber v. First National Bank of Nevada,* 396 U.S. 875 (1969), and *Big O Tire Dealers, Inc. v. Goodyear Tire & Rubber Co.,* 408 F. Supp. 1219 (D. Colo. 1976), *modified on other grounds,* 561 F.2d 1365 (10th Cir. 1977), *cert. dismissed,* 434 U.S. 1052 (1978).

4.05[2] Factors for the Jury's Consideration

In determining whether there is or will be a likelihood of confusion caused by use of [describe symbol] by both plaintiff and defendant in connection with [identify product or service], you may draw on your common experience as citizens of the community. Likelihood of confusion is also determined by evaluating the following factors:

(1) the degree of similarity between the original [describe symbol] and the allegedly infringing [describe symbol];
(2) the manner and method in which the plaintiff and defendant used the [describe symbol];
(3) the strength of the [describe symbol];
(4) the price of the goods and other factors indicative of the degree of care and attention likely to be used by consumers when making a purchase;
(5) the length of time the defendant has used the [describe symbol] without evidence of actual confusion;
(6) the intent of the defendant in adopting the [describe symbol]; that is, whether there was an intent to confuse;
(7) evidence (if any) of instances of actual confusion;
(8) other factors about the [describe symbol] that would tend to reduce any tendency to confuse the purchaser about the source or origin of the [describe product];
(9) the extent to which the target of the parties' sales efforts is the same; and
(10) other facts suggesting that the consuming public might expect the first user to manufacture a product in the defendant's market.

No one factor or consideration is conclusive, but each aspect should be weighed in light of the total evidence presented at the trial.

In light of these considerations and your common experience, you must determine if ordinary consumers, neither overly careless nor overly careful, would be confused about the origin, sponsorship, approval, or affiliation of the [identify product or service] upon encountering the [describe

symbol] as the respective parties have used it in connection with [identify product or service].

Comment

The charge is based upon the one used in *Big O Tire Dealers, Inc. v. Goodyear Tire & Rubber Co.,* 408 F. Supp. 1219 (D. Colo. 1976), *modified on other grounds,* 561 F.2d 1365 (10th Cir. 1977), *cert. dismissed,* 434 U.S. 1052 (1978), and the charge in *Control Components, Inc. v. Valtek, Inc.,* 609 F.2d 763, 770 (5th Cir.), *cert. denied,* 449 U.S. 1022 (1980).

The charge includes a composite of the factors, as set forth by various courts, that may be weighed in determining whether there is a likelihood of confusion. *See generally* 2 J. McCarthy, *Trademarks & Unfair Competition* ch. 23 (3d ed. 1992); 1 J. Gilson, *Trademark Protection & Practice* ch. 5 (1992). Because various courts have delineated different sets of factors, counsel is advised to refer to the law of the appropriate jurisdiction. *See, e.g., Holiday Inns, Inc. v. Trump,* 617 F. Supp. 1443, 1465 (D.N. J. 1985) (five factors are strength of mark, degree of similarity, defendant's intent, similarity of products or services involved, and evidence of actual confusion); *Emerson Elec. Co. v. Emerson Quiet Kool Corp.,* 577 F. Supp 668, 676 (E.D. Mo. 1983) (eight factors are similarity of marks, similarity of products, identity of channels of trade, identity of advertising, type of purchasers, evidence of actual confusion, defendant's intent, and strength of mark); *Moore Business Forms, Inc. v. Ryu,* 960 F.2d 486, 489–90 (5th Cir. 1992) (seven factors are type of trademark at issue [that is, strength of trademark], degree of similarity between the two marks, similarity of products, identity of retail outlets and purchasers, identity of advertising media utilized, defendant's intent, and actual confusion); *Mut. of Omaha Ins. Co. v. Novak,* 836 F.2d 397, 399 (8th Cir. 1987) (six factors are strength of trademark, similarity between trademarks, competitive proximity of products, defendant's intent, indications of actual confusion, and degree of care likely to be exercised by potential customers).

4.06 Trademark Infringement: Damages

4.06[1] Generally

Two kinds of damages can be considered in this case: compensatory damages and punitive damages.

Compensatory damages consist of the plaintiff's direct economic losses and out-of-pocket expenses resulting from the effect of the defendant's conduct on the plaintiff. In other words, if you determine that the defendant is liable to the plaintiff in accordance with the instructions already given to you, the defendant is liable for all damages suffered by the plaintiff that were caused by the defendant's conduct. The question you should attempt to answer is: What is the amount of money required to right the wrong done to the plaintiff by the defendant?

Punitive damages consist of that amount of money awarded by you that is not to be considered as compensation to the plaintiff for the wrong done, but which instead serves as a punishment to the defendant and as an example, warning, or deterrent to others not to engage in such conduct.

Comment

In jurisdictions where punitive damages are allowable in tort cases, they are equally allowable in cases of trademark infringement and unfair competition. *See, e.g., Transgo, Inc. v. Ajac Transmission Parts Corp.*, 768 F.2d 1001 (9th Cir. 1985), *cert. denied*, 474 U.S. 1059 (1986); *Big O Tire Dealers, Inc. v. Goodyear Tire & Rubber Co.*, 408 F. Supp. 1219 (D. Colo. 1976), *modified on other grounds*, 561 F.2d 1365 (10th Cir. 1977), *cert. dismissed*, 434 U.S. 1052 (1978); *Five Platters, Inc. v. Purdie*, 419 F. Supp. 372 (D. Md. 1976); 2 J. McCarthy, *Trademarks & Unfair Competition* §§ 3027, 3029 (3d ed. 1992); Annotation, *Punitive or Exemplary Damages as Recoverable for Trademark Infringement or Unfair Competition*, 47 A.L.R.2d 1117 (1956). Most states restrict the award of punitive damages in tort cases to circumstances in which some level of wrongful intent has been shown. For example, California state law limits the availability of punitive damages to cases "where defendant has been guilty of oppression, fraud or malice." Cal. Civ. Code § 3294 (West or Deering 1995). The Ninth Circuit affirmed punitive damages for trademark infringement when defendant acted with "reckless disregard" for plaintiff's rights. *Transgo, Inc. v. Ajac Transmission Parts, Corp.*, 768 F.2d 1001 (9th Cir. 1985). New York law will allow punitive damages for unfair competition if the defendant "acted knowingly and with reckless disregard." *Murphy Door Bed Co. v. Interior Sleep Sys., Inc.*, 874 F.2d 95 (2d Cir. 1989). Other jurisdictions place similar intent requirements on the availability of punitive damages. *See, e.g., Charles Jacquin Et Cie, Inc. v. Distileria Serralles, Inc.*, 921 F.2d 467 (3d Cir. 1990) (to support punitive damages, defendant's conduct must be "outrageous," resulting from ill motive or reckless indifference); *see also, Bandig, Inc. v. Al Bolser's Tire Stores, Inc.*, 750 F.2d 903 (D.C. Cir. 1984). In at least one state, punitive damages have been limited to an amount that will compensate the plaintiff to the extent of plaintiff's litigation expenses less taxable costs. *Triangle Sheet Metal Works, Inc. v. Silver*, 222 A.2d 220 (Conn. 1966).

Counsel should be aware that an award to the plaintiff may be measured by the defendant's profits, the ascertainment of which will be accomplished through an accounting. *Cuisinarts, Inc. v. Robot-Coupe Int'l Corp.*, 580 F. Supp. 634 (S.D.N.Y. 1984); *Hamilton-Brown Shoe Co. v. Wolf Bros. & Co.*, 240 U.S. 251 (1916); 2 J. McCarthy, *Trademarks & Unfair Competition* §§ 3025–26 (3d ed. 1992). In an appropriate case, the plaintiff may be awarded damages in addition to the defendant's profits.

4.06[2] Compensatory Damages

In determining compensatory damages, the difficulty or uncertainty in ascertaining or measuring the precise amount of any damages does not preclude recovery, and the jury should use its best judgment in determining the amount of such damages, if any, based upon the evidence. You may not, however, determine damages by speculation or conjecture.

In determining compensatory damages, you may consider whether the plaintiff suffered any measurable loss to its goodwill.

The goodwill of a company is an intangible business value that reflects the basic human tendency to do business with merchants who offer products of the type and quality the customer desires and expects. Service to the customer, and a willingness to stand behind a warranty and other representations about the quality of the products sold by a merchant, are factors that help establish the goodwill of a business.

The goodwill associated with a particular product or a business may be symbolized in whole or in part by the consuming public's acceptance and recognition of a trademark. The goodwill attached to a product is a part of the overall business value that is the goodwill of the company. It is possible, therefore, that the general goodwill of a company may be damaged by the loss of goodwill to a particular product. Whether this has occurred is a question of fact for you to determine.

If you find that the plaintiff's goodwill has been damaged either by injury to its general business reputation or by damage to a particular product, you may assess such compensatory damages as you may find to be shown by evidence. The measure of the plaintiff's damage is the difference between the value of such goodwill before and after the acts of the defendant. In determining compensatory damages, you may also consider other losses for which the plaintiff may seek recovery.

The fact that the defendant did not actually intend, anticipate, or contemplate that these losses would occur is not a relevant factor to be considered by you.

If you find that the plaintiff is entitled to a verdict in accordance with these instructions, but you do not find that the evidence before you is sufficient to show that the plaintiff has sustained any substantial damages, then you may return a verdict for the plaintiff on one or more of the theories of liability and fix the amount of the compensatory damages in a nominal sum such as one dollar.

Comment

Plaintiff's damages are "measured by the tort standard under which the infringer-tortfeasor is liable for all injuries caused to plaintiff by the wrongful act, whether or not actually anticipated or contemplated by the defendant when it performed the acts of infringement." 2 J. McCarthy, *Trademarks & Unfair Competition* § 30.27[1] (3d ed. 1992).

The above instruction seeks compensatory damages for injury to goodwill. A plaintiff may also recover damages based on lost profits. *Broan Mfg. Co. v. Associated Distrib. Inc.*, 923 F.2d 1232 (6th Cir.) (plaintiff manufacturer entitled to lost profits it claims would have accrued from future sales but for defendant's infringement scheme, provided plaintiff can demonstrate amount of future losses), *reconsideration denied, appeal discussed*, 932 F.2d 1146 (6th Cir. 1991); *see also, e.g., Blue Ribbon Feed Co. v. Farmers Union Cent. Exch. Inc.*, 731 F.2d 415, 421 (7th Cir. 1984); *Obear-Nester Glass Co. v. United Drug Co.*, 149 F.2d 671 (8th Cir.), *cert. denied*, 326 U.S. 761 (1945). Recoverable damages may include amounts lost due to nullification of plaintiff's advertising expenditures. *W. Des Moines State Bank v. Hawkeye Bancorporation*, 722 F.2d 411 (8th Cir. 1983). *See also Cuisinarts, Inc. v. Robot-Coupe Int'l Corp.*, 580 F. Supp. 634 (S.D.N.Y. 1984) (rebuttal advertising). These losses are simply illustrative and should not be interpreted as excluding other kinds of losses. According to at least one court, the plaintiff is not required to prove the amount of damages with mathematical certainty. *W. Des Moines State Bank v. Hawkeye Bancorporation,* 722 F.2d 411 (8th Cir. 1983). However, to be recoverable, damages for lost profits must be supported by more than mere speculation. *Bundy Corp. v. Teledyne Indus., Inc.* 584 F. Supp. 656, 669 (Dist. Ct. 1984).

4.06[3] Punitive Damages

The purpose of awarding punitive or exemplary damages is to punish a wrongdoer for some extraordinary conduct and to serve as an example, warning, or deterrent to others not to engage in such conduct.

If you find that [insert the applicable state legal standard for the circumstances under which an award of punitive damages is appropriate], then, in addition to compensatory damages, you may also award the plaintiff a reasonable sum as punitive damages.

Whether to make any award of punitive or exemplary damages, in addition to actual damages, is a matter exclusively within the discretion of the jury. You should bear in mind the conditions under which, and the purposes for which, the law permits an award of punitive or exemplary damages to be made. You must also bear in mind, however, the requirement of the law that the amount of such extraordinary damages, when awarded, must be fixed with calm discretion and sound reason, and must never either be awarded, or fixed in amount, because of any sympathy, bias, or prejudice you may feel toward any party in the case.

The award of a nominal sum for compensatory damages does not prevent your awarding punitive damages if you find that the award of punitive damages is justified.

Comment

As noted in § 4.06[1], in jurisdictions where punitive damages are allowable, they are also permitted in trademark infringement actions. Because the standard for the award of punitive damages varies from state to state, counsel should insert the appropriate local standard where indicated in the charge. For some examples of factors and criteria applicable to punitive damages instructions, see the various subsections of § 1.07.

4.07 General Instruction: Trade Name Infringement

Comment

Because trade names are protectable under the same basic principles that govern trademarks (see § 4.01[2]), the same charges that are found in the trademark infringement sections can be used in an action involving alleged trade name infringement, substituting "trade name" for "trademark" and "business" for "goods or services."

4.08 General Instruction: Unfair Competition

4.08[1] Theory of Unfair Competition

In this case, the plaintiff, [name], seeks to recover money damages from the defendant, [name], for what the plaintiff claims to be unfair competition in the use of [describe symbol], in connection with the sale of [identify goods and/or service]. The legal principles discussed in these instructions regarding the law of unfair competition have evolved from attempts to balance the following conflicting policy objectives:

(1) there is a need to protect the public from being misled about the nature and source of the goods and services they buy;

(2) there is a need to protect the property rights of a business to identify itself and its goods and services to the public;

(3) there is a need to try to achieve these goals without injury to the free-market economic system, which encourages fair competition among those providing goods and services.

Fair competition is encouraged, but unfair competition is destructive of the competitive process and is illegal.

Because of the conflicting policy objectives involved in cases of this type, each such case must be decided largely on its specific facts, and you, the jury, are the judge of the facts.

Comment

This charge is identical to § 4.02[1] for trademark infringement. *See* § 4.02[1], cmt., *supra.*

4.08[2] Elements of Liability

To find liability for unfair competition, you, the jury, must find from a preponderance of the evidence

(1) that the public recognizes the plaintiff's [describe symbol] in connection with the sale of plaintiff's [identify product or service] as identifying plaintiff's [identify product or service] and distinguishing it from those of others; and
(2) that such recognition has occurred before the defendant entered the market in which the plaintiff sells its [identify product or service]; and
(3) that the defendant uses [describe symbol] in a manner likely to cause confusion about the source of the [identify product or service] among persons using ordinary care and prudence in the purchase of [identify product or service].

If you find by a preponderance of the evidence that the plaintiff has proved these elements, then and only then may you find the defendant liable for unfair competition. You will then consider the question of damages under separate instructions.

Comment

This charge reflects the traditional standard for establishing liability for unfair competition. *See* 1 J. McCarthy, *Trademarks & Unfair Competition* §§ 8.01–.07 (3d ed. 1992). A jury may find liability without also concluding that the defendant intended to deceive the public. 2 J. McCarthy, *Trademarks & Unfair Competition* § 23.30[2] (3d ed. 1992). Moreover, damages may be awarded without a finding that the defendant acted with a wrongful intent. 2 J. McCarthy, *Trademarks & Unfair Competition* § 30.25[2] (3d ed. 1992).

There is a developing aspect of unfair competition jurisprudence that will encompass the situation that occurs when a second manufacturer enters the market before the time a first distributor has established its trade dress in the consumer's mind. It is possible that a successful cause of action based on unfair competition can be sustained under these circumstances regardless of whether public recognition of the first user's product exists, if the defendant is aware of plaintiff's preexisting product and fails to make defendant's product sufficiently dissimilar. *See, e.g., Thompson v. Tega-Rand Int'l*, 740 F.2d 762 (9th Cir. 1984). *Cf. Dominion Bankshares Corp. v. Devar Holding Co., Inc.*, 690 F. Supp. 338, 347 (E.D. Pa. 1988) (imposing on defendant, who entered market subsequent to plaintiff, an "affirmative duty to choose a [trademark] or a trade name so as to avoid all confusion as to the source of origin of its services").

4.08[3] Jury's Reliance on Improper Fact

The fact that the defendant uses [describe symbol] that is similar (or even identical in some respects) to plaintiff's [describe symbol] and that the purchasing public is likely to be confused as a result, does not in and of itself constitute unfair competition. To establish its claim against the defendant, the plaintiff must prove by a preponderance of the evidence each of the three elements I just mentioned to you. Only then may you find for the plaintiff.

Comment

This charge follows from the authority cited in the comment to § 4.08[2]. It is recommended to reinforce and remind the jury that liability will be established only upon a finding that all three elements have been proved. Reference is made to the comment to § 4.08[2] regarding the possibility that public recognition of a symbol may not be a necessary element for a cause of action based on unfair competition.

4.09 Unfair Competition: Proof of Identifying Function

4.09[1] Secondary Meaning

The first question for you, the jury, to decide is whether the public recognizes the plaintiff's [describe symbol] in connection with the sale of plaintiff's [identify product or service] as identifying its [product or service] and distinguishing it from those of others. To determine whether the plaintiff has proved this, you must consider whether the evidence shows that the plaintiff's [describe symbol] has developed secondary meaning.

By the term "secondary meaning," the law means that a symbol has been so used that its primary significance in the minds of the consuming public is not the [product or service] itself but the identification of such [product or service] with a single source. This does not mean that the consuming public must know the exact identity of that single source in the sense that it knows the corporate name of the [producer or seller]. All that is necessary to establish secondary meaning is that the ordinary consumer associates the [product or service] with a single source, regardless of whether the consumer knows who or what that source is.

You must find, therefore, from a preponderance of the evidence, that a significant number of the consuming public has associated the [describe symbol] involved in this case with a single source. It is for you to decide how many constitute a significant number, keeping in mind that it is not necessary for the plaintiff to prove that all or even a majority of the consuming public understand this secondary meaning.

In determining whether the plaintiff's [describe symbol] has attained secondary meaning, it is appropriate for you to consider the evidence (if any) relating to

(1) the length and manner of its use;
(2) the nature and extent of advertising and promotion;
(3) sales volume;

(4) other efforts made by the plaintiff in the direction of promoting the connection in the consuming public's mind between the [describe symbol] and the plaintiff;

(5) properly designed and conducted consumer surveys; and

(6) testimony of consumers relating to the identity of the source or origin of the [describe symbol] in the minds of the consuming public.

The mere fact that plaintiff is using [describe symbol], or that the plaintiff began using it before the defendant, does not establish or create secondary meaning.

Similarly, the mere fact that you might consider the plaintiff's [describe symbol] to be unique is not enough to establish secondary meaning.

There is no particular length of time within which secondary meaning is established. The question for you to determine is whether secondary meaning has been established, not in how long or short a time this was accomplished.

Comment

This charge reflects the traditional view of what must initially be established in unfair competition cases. *See, e.g., Walt Disney Prod. v. Air Pirates,* 581 F.2d 751 (9th Cir. 1978), *cert. denied sub nom., O'Neill v. Walt Disney Prod.,* 439 U.S. 1132 (1979); *Tas-T-Nut Co. v. Variety Nut & Date Co.,* 245 F.2d 3 (6th Cir. 1957); *Wembley, Inc. v. Diplomat Tie Co.,* 216 F. Supp. 565 (D. Md. 1963); *Filter Dynamics Int'l Inc. v. Astron Battery, Inc.,* 311 N.E.2d 386 (Ill. App. Ct. 1974). In some cases, however, proof of the identifying function could be established by showing that the item the plaintiff is attempting to protect is inherently distinctive. *Cf. Application of McIlhenny Co.,* 278 F.2d 953C, 47 C.C.P.A. 985 (C.C.P.A. 1960). *But see Truck Equip. Serv. Co. v. Fruehauf Corp.,* 536 F.2d 1210 (8th Cir.), *cert. denied,* 429 U.S. 861 (1976). Again, as in § 4.03[1], the caveat is raised that the issue of distinctiveness may be one of law for the court to decide.

This charge also reflects the traditional standard for secondary meaning. *See, e.g.*, 1 J. McCarthy, *Trademarks & Unfair Competition* §§ 15:1–15:2 (2d ed. 1984); Julius R. Lunsford, *The Mechanics of Proof of Secondary Meaning*, 60 Trademark Rep. 263 (1970). It is primarily drawn from the charge used in *Big O Tire Dealers, Inc. v. Goodyear Tire & Rubber Co.*, 408 F. Supp. 1219 (D. Colo. 1976), *modified on other grounds*, 561 F.2d 1365 (10th Cir. 1977), *cert. dismissed*, 434 U.S. 1052 (1978), and the charges used in *Gordon v. Warner Brothers Pictures, Inc.*, 74 Cal. Rptr. 499 (Cal. Ct. App. 1969).

It is also important to note that proof of secondary meaning may not be essential to an action for trade dress infringement. *See, e.g., 20th Century Wear, Inc. v. Sanmark-Stardust, Inc.*, 747 F.2d 81, 92 n.16 (2d Cir. 1984), *cert. denied*, 470 U.S. 1052 (1985). Similarly, in *Gemveto Jewelry Co. v. Jeff Cooper, Inc.*, 568 F. Supp. 319, 335 (S.D.N.Y. 1983), the court found that the deliberate use of a competitor's nonfunctional marks or trade dress is actionable without a showing of secondary meaning.

The charge also reflects the traditional types of evidence that are accepted by the courts. *See, e.g., Artus Corp. v. Nordic Co.*, 512 F. Supp. 1184 (W.D. Pa. 1981); 1 J. Gilson, *Trademark Protection & Practice* § 2.09 (1986); 4 R. Callmann, *Unfair Competition, Trademarks & Monopolies* ¶ 77.3 at 349 (3d ed. 1969). Although some courts have held that proof of secondary meaning is sufficiently made by the inferences to be drawn from mere copying (*see, e.g., Audio Fidelity, Inc. v. High Fidelity Recordings, Inc.*, 283 F.2d 551, 558 (9th Cir. 1960)), this view has been criticized. *See Mr. Gasket Co. v. Travis*, 299 N.E.2d 906 (Ohio Ct. App. 1973); *Developments in the Law—Competitive Torts*, 77 Harv. L. Rev. 888, 916 (1963).

4.09[2] Functional or Nonfunctional

In this case, the defendant claims that the [describe symbol] used by the plaintiff is functional, and therefore the defendant may also simulate the [describe symbol]. Under the law of unfair competition, items that are functional cannot be legally protected. That is, use of such items cannot constitute unfair competition. For the plaintiff to establish liability in this case, you therefore must find that the [describe symbol] is nonfunctional.

The requirement of nonfunctionality involves an evaluation regarding whether the [describe symbol] at issue has any purpose other than the identification of the product. You must determine whether the [describe symbol] is substantially related to its value as a product or service; that is, if the [describe symbol] is part of the "function" served, or whether the primary value of the [describe symbol] is the identification of the product.

A feature of goods, or of their wrappers or containers, may be functional because it contributes to efficiency or economy in manufacturing them or in handling them through the marketing process. It may also be functional because it contributes to their utility, to their durability, or to the effectiveness or ease with which they serve their function or are handled by users. A feature that adds to the utility or the style and attractiveness of a product may also be functional. A feature that, if omitted, would prevent a seller or manufacturer from competing effectively is functional. A feature is nonfunctional if, when it is omitted, nothing of substantial value in the goods is lost. A feature that merely associates goods with a particular source may be a substantial factor in increasing the marketability of the goods. But if that is the entire significance of the feature, it is nonfunctional because its value then lies only in the demand for goods associated with a particular source.

For example, the ribbed or corrugated design on the top of a construction worker's hard hat may be functional because of the design's ability to strengthen the crown. On the other

hand, a FOTOMAT Film kiosk structure with a steep, yellow, three-tiered roof may not be functional because the distinctive shape of the roof was not dictated by the function it was to serve; that is, to shelter personnel from the elements. That the roof may perform a function does not prevent unfair competition protection. It is only when the design or packaging is primarily functional that it will be deemed functional for purposes of unfair competition.

If you find from the evidence that the plaintiff's [describe symbol] falls within the boundaries of the foregoing definition of functionality, then there can be no unfair competition, and the defendant was free to copy and imitate [describe symbol].

Comment

This charge becomes pertinent in those cases when an issue raised is that the item for which protection is claimed is functional. *See, e.g., Bristol-Meyers Squibb Co. v. McNeil-P.P.C., Inc.,* 973 F.2d 1033 (2d Cir. 1992); *Merchant & Evans, Inc. v. Roosevelt Bldg. Prods. Co., Inc.,* 963 F.2d 628 (3d Cir. 1992); In re *Morton-Norwich Prods., Inc.,* 671 F.2d 1332 (C.C.P.A. 1982). This charge is in part derived from section 742 of the *Restatement of Torts,* which provides a commonly cited definition and explanation of functionality. The *Restatement (Second) of Torts* (1977) does not deal with the question of functionality because its drafters felt that this issue had become a separate area of the law. Courts, however, continue to cite to the first *Restatement of Torts.*

The charge reflects the generally accepted view about what is functional. *See* 4 A R. Callmann, *The Law of Unfair Competition, Trademarks & Monopolies* § 25.29 n.11 (4th ed. 1992); 1 J. McCarthy, *Trademarks & Unfair Competition* § 7.26 (3d ed. 1992); 1 J. Gilson, *Trademark Protection & Practice* § 7.02[7] (1992); Annotation, *Applicaton of Functionality Doctrine Under § 43 (a) of Lanham Act* (15 U.S.C.S. § 1125 (a)), by Colleen R. Courtade, J.D. 78 A.L.R. Fed. 712 (application of functionality doctrine); *Filter Dynamics Int'l, Inc. v. Astron Battery, Inc.,* 311

N.E.2d 386 (Ill. App. Ct. 1974); *Fisher Stores, Inc. v. All Nighter Stove Works, Inc.,* 626 F.2d 193, 195 (1st Cir. 1980); In re *Morton-Norwich Prods., Inc.,* 671 F.2d 1332 (C.C.P.A. 1982). There is, however, some dispute about whether aesthetic features are functional. *See* 1 J. McCarthy, *Trademarks & Unfair Competition* § 7.26[4] (3d ed. 1992); *Gemveto Jewelry Co. v. Jeff Cooper, Inc.,* 613 F. Supp. 1052, 1061 (S.D.N.Y. 1985), *vacated on other grounds,* 800 F.2d 256 (Fed. Cir. 1986). At least one court has held that a certain design was nonfunctional as a matter of law. *Artus Corp. v. Nordic Co.,* 512 F. Supp. 1184, 1189 (W.D. Pa. 1981).

When substantially all of an overall design otherwise eligible for trademark protection is nonfunctional, as is the fluting of the glass in a Coca-Cola bottle, it should not matter that the shape of an insignificant element of the design is arguably functional. *See Textron, Inc. v. Int'l Trade Comm'n,* 753 F.2d 1019 (D.C. Cir. 1985); 1 J. McCarthy, *Trademarks & Unfair Competition* § 7.31 (3d ed. 1992). *See also* § 4.03[9], cmt., *supra.*

4.10 Unfair Competition: Acquisition and Priority of Rights

4.10[1] Generally

If you find that the plaintiff has established secondary meaning in [describe symbol], you must then consider whether the evidence shows that the plaintiff's [describe symbol] possessed secondary meaning before the defendant first began use of [describe symbol].

If you determine that the plaintiff has not established that plaintiff's [describe symbol] possessed secondary meaning before the defendant's use of [describe symbol], then you must find for the defendant, as there can then be no unfair competition.

Comment

When the plaintiff and defendant both assert that they are the "owner" of the item in litigation, the court must determine the priority of each right. This reflects the well-established rule that the requisite secondary meaning be developed before the defendant uses the item. *See, e.g., Artus Corp. v. Nordic Co.,* 512 F. Supp. 1184, 1189 (W.D. Pa. 1981); *Marion Lab., Inc. v. Michigan Pharmacal Corp.,* 338 F. Supp. 762 (E.D. Mich. 1972), *aff'd,* 473 F.2d 910 (6th Cir. 1973); 1 J. Gilson, *Trademark Protection & Practice* § 3.03 (1986).

4.11 Unfair Competition: Likelihood of Confusion

4.11[1] Generally

If you find that the [describe symbol] used by the plaintiff possessed secondary meaning before the time that the defendant first began use of [describe symbol], then you must consider whether the defendant used [describe symbol] in a manner likely to cause confusion about the source of [identify product or service] among persons using ordinary care and prudence in the purchase of [identify product or service].

In other words, you must find that ordinary purchasers, buying under the usual conditions and exercising ordinary care, would be likely to purchase the defendant's [identify product or service] in the belief that it was [produced or provided—choose one] by the plaintiff.

It is not necessary that the evidence show that any specific person has been confused or misled. It is enough if you find that the probable consequences of the use of the [describe symbol] complained of in all reasonable probability would be to confuse the public about the source, sponsorship, approval, or affiliation of the [identify product or service].

The fact that the [identify product or service] could be distinguished by careful or discriminating purchasers is not enough to lead you to conclude that there is no likelihood of confusion.

Comment

This charge reflects the traditional standard of likelihood of confusion. *See, e.g., Jean Patou, Inc. v. Jacqueline Cochran, Inc.*, 201 F. Supp. 861 (S.D.N.Y.), *aff'd*, 312 F.2d 125 (2d Cir. 1963); *Don Alvarado Co. v. Porganan*, 21 Cal. Rptr. 495 (Cal. Ct. App. 1962); 1 J. McCarthy, *Trademarks & Unfair Competition* §§ 8:3; 23:1–23:29 (1992). A showing of likelihood of confusion is sometimes not necessary. Some courts have held that when a defendant intentionally copies, the second comer will be presumed to have intended to create a confusingly similar appearance and will be presumed to have succeeded. *Morex S.P.A. v. Design Inst. Am., Inc.*, 779 F.2d 799, 801 (2d Cir. 1985); *Perfect Fit Indus., Inc. v. Acme Quilting Co. Inc.*, 618 F.2d 950, 952–53 (2d Cir. 1980), *cert. denied*, 459 U.S. 832 (1982).

Some courts, though in a minority, have held that proof of actual confusion is required to obtain a damages remedy. *See 20th Century Wear Inc. v. Sanmark-Stardust, Inc.*, 747 F.2d 81, 93 (2d Cir. 1984), *cert. denied*, 470 U.S. 1052 (1985); *Warner Bros. v. Gay Toys, Inc.*, 658 F.2d 76, 79 (2d Cir. 1981).

4.11[2] Factors for the Jury's Consideration

In determining whether there is or will be a likelihood of confusion caused by the use of [describe symbol] by both plaintiff and defendant in connection with [identify product or service], you may draw on your common experience as citizens of the community. Likelihood of confusion is also determined by evaluating the following factors:

(1) the degree of similarity between the original [describe symbol] and the allegedly infringing [describe symbol];
(2) the manner and method in which the plaintiff and defendant used the [describe symbol];
(3) the strength of the [describe symbol];
(4) the price of the goods and other factors indicative of the degree of care and attention likely to be used by consumers when making a purchase;
(5) the length of time the defendant has used the [describe symbol] without evidence of actual confusion;
(6) the intent of the defendant in adopting the [describe symbol]; that is, whether there was an intent to confuse;
(7) evidence (if any) of instances of actual confusion;
(8) other factors about the [describe symbol] that would tend to reduce any tendency to confuse the purchaser about the source or origin of the [describe symbol];
(9) the extent to which the target of the parties' sales efforts is the same; and
(10) other facts suggesting that the consuming public might expect the first user to manufacture a product in the defendant's market.

No one factor or consideration is conclusive, but each aspect should be weighed in light of the total evidence presented at the trial.

Similarity of appearance of [describe symbols] is to be determined on the basis of the total effect of the [describe symbols] on the consumer. One cannot avoid liability simply by showing that individual features of the [describe symbols] are dissimilar. Rather, it is the total combination

of elements and the similarity of the total, overall impression to the consumer that is to be considered by you.

In light of these considerations and your common experience, you must determine whether ordinary consumers, neither overly careful nor overly careless, would be confused about the origin, sponsorship, approval, or affiliation of the [identify product or service] upon encountering the [describe symbol] as the respective parties have used it in connection with [identify product or service].

Comment

This text lists the usual factors considered in determining whether there is a likelihood of confusion. *See* § 4.05[2], *supra. See also Nat'l Football League Properties, Inc. v. New Jersey Giants, Inc.,* 637 F. Supp. 507, 516 (D.N.J. 1986); *Scott Paper Co. v. Scott's Liquid Gold, Inc.,* 589 F.2d 1225 (3d Cir. 1978); *Caesar's World, Inc. v. Caesar's Palace,* 490 F. Supp. 818, 827 (D.N.J. 1980); *Scarves by Vera, Inc. v. Todo Imports, Ltd. (Inc.),* 554 F.2d 1167, 1173 (2d Cir. 1976); *Am. Greetings Corp. v. Dan-Dee Imports, Inc.,* 619 F. Supp. 1204, 1222 (D.N.J. 1985).

In general, the same factors are considered in cases premised on trademark (or trade name) infringement as in those based on unfair competition. *See, e.g., Am. Footwear Corp. v. Gen. Footwear Co.,* 609 F.2d 655, 664 (2d Cir. 1979), *cert. denied,* 445 U.S. 951 (1980). Some courts have indicated, however, that in cases involving only unfair competition, the defendant's use of his/her own trademark in connection with an allegedly infringing item may be sufficient to prevent likelihood of confusion. *See, e.g., T & T Mfg. Co. v. A. T. Cross Co.,* 449 F. Supp. 813 (D.R.I.), *aff'd,* 587 F.2d 533 (1st Cir. 1978), *cert. denied,* 441 U.S. 908 (1979); *Ralston Purina Co. v. Thomas J. Lipton, Inc.,* 341 F. Supp. 129 (S.D.N.Y. 1972). In appropriate cases, the charges should be modified accordingly.

4.11(3) Unfair Competition: Damages

[See § 4.06, *supra.*]

Chapter Five

Racketeer Influenced and Corrupt Organizations (RICO) Act

5.01 Introduction

Edward F. Mannino and Marguerite S. Walsh[1]

This chapter presents jury instructions for use in cases arising under the Racketeer Influenced and Corrupt Organizations Act, 18 U.S.C. §§ 1961–68 (RICO). Although RICO's Statement of Findings and Purpose clearly states that the act was directed primarily toward the problem of the infiltration of legitimate business by organized crime, it is now well settled that RICO reaches far beyond traditional notions of "organized crime." *See, e.g., Sedima, S.P.R.L. v. Imrex Co.*, 473 U.S. 479 (1985); *H.J., Inc. v. Northwestern Bell Tel. Co.*, 492 U.S. 229 (1989). These instructions are designed to address the "heart" of the RICO elements as they may apply in business tort litigation; in an actual trial, as with any case, the instructions should be tailored to address the factual context of the particular case.

Although section 1962 of RICO, in four separate subsections, declares it unlawful for any person to engage in any one of four categories of activities, it is the third subsection—section 1962(c)—under which virtually all business-related RICO cases have been brought. Subsection (c) prohibits the "(1) conduct (2) of an enterprise (3) through a pattern (4) of racketeering activity," terms that are discussed more fully below and in the instructions that follow. *Sedima S.P.R.L. v. Imrex Co.*, 473 U.S. 479, 496 (1985). Subsection (d), the conspiracy subpart, is also employed, although to a lesser extent, in business RICO cases, which makes it unlawful to conspire to violate any of the other subsections of section 1962.

The three elements of section 1962(c) that have most lent themselves to varying interpretations by courts are the "pattern," "conduct," and "enterprise" requirements. The pattern controversy has largely been settled by the Supreme Court's decision in *H.J., Inc. v. Northwestern Bell Telephone Co.*,

[1]The authors gratefully acknowledge the contributions of Gregory P. Joseph, who reviewed a prior draft of these instructions.

492 U.S. 229 (1989), upon which the instruction in § 5.11[1] is based. Similarly, questions about the proper interpretation of the conduct requirement have been resolved by the Supreme Court's decision in *Reves v. Ernst & Young,* 113 S. Ct. 1163 (1993). The instructions in §§ 5.08[1] and [2] are based upon that decision.

The enterprise requirement has raised two important issues under section 1962(c). The first issue is whether the person and enterprise must be separate and distinct. The circuit courts are nearly unanimous in holding that they must be, and that only the person can be held liable for damages under section 1962(c). *See* § 5.07[1], cmt., *infra.* The second issue focuses on the proper use and structural requirements of association-in-fact enterprises, principally whether the person may be part of such an enterprise and still liable for damages. This issue has created at least semantic conflicts among the courts that have considered it. *See* § 5.07[2], cmt., *infra.*

Once a RICO violation has been established, section 1964(c) mandates an award of treble damages, attorneys' fees, and costs to a person whose business or property has been injured by reason of the RICO violation. With the Supreme Court's rejection in *Sedima* of the concept of a special "racketeering injury" as a condition of relief, and its subsequent decision in *Holmes v. Securities Investor Protection Corp.,* 503 U.S. 258 (1992), requiring some direct relation between the injury asserted and the injurious conduct alleged, the "by reason of" language has taken on enhanced importance as a traditional proximate-cause screening device. This requirement is discussed in § 5.14[2].

It is important to remember that many substantive elements of section 1962(c) violations may be appropriate for resolution by motions for summary judgment or for directed verdict in some cases, and should not reach the jury. These include both some of the elements covered in the instructions that follow (such as association-in-fact enterprises [§ 5.07[2]], interstate commerce [§ 5.07[3]], and pattern of racketeering activity, the latter in cases in which the alleged pattern involves closed-end conduct of less than twelve months in duration threatening no future harm, or single-victim, single-scheme activity [§ 5.11[1]]), and additional elements that are not covered in these instructions because they are appropriate for resolution by the court as a matter of law. These latter elements include standing, (*see* Gregory P. Joseph, *Civil RICO: A Definitive Guide* 26–30 (1992); Edward F. Mannino, *Lender Liability and Banking Litigation* § 4.03[5][c] (1989–92)), and vicarious liability of the "enterprise" (*see generally* Edward F. Mannino, *Lender Liability and Banking Litigation* § 4.03[2][b][iii] (1989–92)). Note that vicarious liability may be appropriate in cases filled under section 1962(a) or (b). *See generally* Gregory P. Joseph, *Civil RICO: A Definitive Guide* 105–08 (1992); and the existence *vel non* of any compensable injury. *See* Gregory P. Joseph, *Civil RICO: A Definitive Guide* 25–26 (1992); Edward F. Mannino, *Lender Liability and Banking Litigation* § 4.03[5][d] (1989–92). This issue is covered in instruction 5.14[1].

Given the significant number of cases being decided every month on these and other key RICO elements, it is essential to review and update the applicable case law regularly to assure the continued accuracy of these instructions. In addition, proposed legislation has been introduced to amend the existing RICO statute in many significant respects. Thus, H.R. 1717, which was reported out favorably from the House Judiciary Committee in the 102d Congress, but was not acted on thereafter, would have created a judicial "gatekeeper" screen, permitting trial courts to determine if a particular RICO action alleged sufficiently egregious activity to warrant a RICO treble damages remedy. That proposed legislation would also have imposed a "clear and convincing evidence" burden of proof in civil RICO actions. The legislation was not acted on by the full House of Representatives, nor considered in the Senate. Future legislative efforts to amend RICO are anticipated, however, and should be monitored carefully for potentially significant changes to key elements of the current legislation.

Finally, so-called state "baby RICO" statutes should be consulted for possible additional claims and relief that may be available in a particular jurisdiction, including extraordinary equitable remedies and prejudgment relief.

These and other legal issues covered in these instructions are discussed in length in Gregory P. Joseph, *Civil RICO: A Definitive Guide* (ABA 1992) [hereinafter Joseph, *Civil RICO*], Edward F. Mannino, *Lender Liability and Banking Litigation* (Law Journal Seminars Press 1989–92) [hereinafter Mannino, *Lender Liability*], and *Business Torts Litigation* (ABA 1992).

For an excellent brief summary of some legal issues on which the courts have split under RICO, see Gregory P. Joseph, *Circuits in Disarray on Six Key Issues,* Nat'l L.J., Oct. 26, 1992, at 17. Since that article was written, the Supreme Court has resolved one of those issues by ruling in *National Organization for Women, Inc. v. Scheidler,* 510 U.S. (1994) that RICO does not require proof of an economic motivation for the predicate acts of racketeering.

5.02 General Instruction

The plaintiff claims that the defendant has violated the Racketeer Influenced and Corrupt Organizations Act, commonly referred to by the abbreviation RICO.

5.03 No Organized Crime Requirement

Although the RICO statute uses the terms "racketeering" and "corrupt organizations," the RICO statute does not require you to determine whether the defendant is a "racketeer" in the everyday sense of the word, or whether it is associated with "organized crime" in the everyday sense of the word.

Comment

This instruction is obviously favorable to the plaintiff and should be requested as part of a RICO plaintiff's charge. See the "Requested Defense Instructions" in *United States v. Scotto,* 641 F.2d 47 (2d Cir. 1980), *cert. denied,* 452 U.S. 961 (1981).

5.04 "Preponderance" Standard Applies

Although the RICO statute refers to the term "racketeering activity," I instruct you that this is a civil case, not a criminal case, and that the plaintiff's RICO allegations do not need to be proved beyond a reasonable doubt, but only by a preponderance of the evidence.

Comment

This instruction is supported by *Sedima, S.P.R.L. v. Imrex Co., Inc.*, 473 U.S. 479, 491 (1985) (dictum). *See also Grogan v. Garner*, 498 U.S. 279 (1991). Many circuit courts have expressly held that the preponderance standard governs civil RICO actions. *See, e.g., Matter of EDC, Inc.*, 930 F.2d 1275, 1280 (7th Cir. 1991); *Wilcox v. First Interstate Bank*, 815 F.2d 522, 530–32 (9th Cir. 1987).

The proposed legislation discussed in the introduction would establish a "clear and convincing evidence" burden of proof.

5.05 General Elements of Section 1962(c)

Section 1962(c) of RICO prohibits the conduct of an enterprise through a pattern of racketeering activity. To prove liability under section 1962(c), the plaintiff must establish each of the following elements by a preponderance of the evidence:

- ***first,* that the defendant was a person employed by or associated with an enterprise;**
- ***second,* that the enterprise was engaged in, or its activities affected, interstate commerce;**
- ***third,* that the defendant conducted or participated, directly or indirectly, in the conduct of that enterprise's affairs; and**
- ***fourth,* that the defendant's conduct of, or participation in, the enterprise's affairs was through a pattern of racketeering activity.**

To recover damages from the defendant, the plaintiff must further prove that the defendant's acts proximately caused injury to plaintiff's business or property.

Some of these elements are matters for the Court to decide, while others are for you the jury to decide. I will instruct you about those matters that are for you to decide.

Comment

This instruction tracks the statutory language of 18 U.S.C. §§ 1962(c) and 1964(c). Because the vast majority of RICO cases involving businesses are brought under section 1962(c) (as well as section 1962(d), the conspiracy subpart), this general instruction should be requested in most cases.

5.06 Person

Before I further explain the elements of a RICO violation, I need to define for you some of the terms used in the RICO statute. The first is the term "person." A person includes any individual or entity capable of holding a legal or beneficial interest in property. [I instruct you that as a matter of law, the plaintiff and the defendant are both legal entities capable of holding a legal or beneficial interest in property and are therefore persons under the RICO statute.]

Comment

This instruction tracks the statutory language of 18 U.S.C. § 1961(3). Because it would be a rare case when the existence of a "person" would be disputed, the bracketed material will usually be appropriate to include in the instruction.

Two areas pose questions regarding the existence of a RICO "person." First, unincorporated associations may not qualify as persons under section 1961(3) unless the applicable law permits them to hold an interest in property. *See* Joseph, *Civil RICO, supra* at 25 (citing *Fleischhauer v. Feltner,* 879 F.2d 1290, 1298–99 (6th Cir.), *cert. denied,* 493 U.S. 1074 (1989) and *Jund v. Town of Hempstead,* 941 F.2d 1271, 1283–84 (2d Cir. 1991)). Second, some courts have also held that the United States is not a person authorized to sue under section 1964(c). *See United States v. Bonnano Organized Crime Family,* 879 F.2d 20 (2d Cir. 1989).

5.07 Enterprise

5.07[1] Enterprise—General Instruction

The next term I must define for you is "enterprise." An enterprise includes any individual, partnership, corporation, association, or other legal entity, and any union or group of individuals associated in fact although not a legal entity.

I instruct you that for purposes of the RICO statute in this case the "person" and the "enterprise" cannot be the same, but must be separate and distinct.

Comment

The first paragraph of this instruction tracks the statutory language of 18 U.S.C. § 1961(4).

The proposition that the person and enterprise must be different to establish liability under section 1962(c) has met with nearly universal agreement in all the circuits. *See, e.g.*:

- First Circuit: *Schofield v. First Commodity Corp.*, 793 F.2d 28 (1st Cir. 1986);
- Second Circuit: *Bennett v. U.S. Trust Co.*, 770 F.2d 308 (2d Cir. 1985), *cert. denied*, 474 U.S. 1058 (1986);
- Third Circuit: *B.F. Hirsch v. Enright Ref. Co.*, 751 F.2d 628, 634 (3d Cir. 1984);
- Fourth Circuit: *United States v. Computer Sciences Corp.*, 689 F.2d 1181, 1190 (4th Cir. 1982), *cert. denied*, 459 U.S. 1105 (1983), *overruled on other grounds in Busby v. Crown Supply, Inc.*, 896 F.2d 833, 840–42 (4th Cir. 1990);
- Fifth Circuit: *Bishop v. Corbitt Marine Ways, Inc.*, 802 F.2d 122 (5th Cir. 1986);
- Seventh Circuit: *Masi v. Ford City Bank & Trust Co.*, 779 F.2d 973 (7th Cir. 1985);
- Eighth Circuit: *Bennett v. Berg*, 685 F.2d 1053, 1061 (8th Cir. 1982), *cert. denied*, 464 U.S. 1008 (1983);

- Ninth Circuit: *Schreiber Distrib. Co. v. Serv-Well Furniture Co.,* 806 F.2d 1393, 1396 (9th Cir. 1986);
- Tenth Circuit: *Bd. of County Comm'rs v. Liberty Group,* 965 F.2d 879, 885 (10th Cir. 1992); and
- D.C. Circuit: *Yellow Bus Lines, Inc. v. Local Union 639,* 883 F.2d 132, 139–40 (D.C. Cir. 1989).

Contra, United States v. Hartley, 678 F.2d 961 (11th Cir.), *cert. denied,* 459 U.S. 1170 (1983). *See generally* Mannino, *Lender Liability, supra* at § 4.03[2][b]; Joseph, *Civil RICO, supra* at 42–46.

The requirement that the person and enterprise be different entities applies under section 1962(c), but not under sections 1962(a) and (b). *See, e.g., Busby v. Crown Supply, Inc.,* 896 F.2d 833, 840–42 (4th Cir. 1990) (en banc); *Haroco, Inc. v. Am. Nat'l Bank & Trust Co.,* 747 F.2d 384, 401–02 (7th Cir. 1984), *aff'd on other grounds,* 473 U.S. 606 (1985).

5.07[2] Enterprise—Association-in-Fact

In this case the plaintiff asserts that the enterprise is an informal, de facto association rather than a structured organization, and that the enterprise is composed of [describe components of alleged association-in-fact]. I instruct you that such an association-in-fact can be considered an enterprise, provided that it (1) is ongoing, (2) functions as a continuing unit, (3) has some type of organization, whether formal or informal, (4) has a common or shared purpose, and (5) constitutes an entity separate and apart from the pattern of racketeering activity in which it is alleged to have engaged.

Comment

Courts have offered various formulations regarding when an association-in-fact can satisfy the enterprise requirement. *See, e.g., United States v. Turkette,* 452 U.S. 576, 583 (1981); *Calcasieu Marine Nat'l Bank v. Grant,* 943 F.2d 1453, 1461–63 (5th Cir. 1991); *Atlas Pile Driving Co. v. DiCon Fin. Co.,* 886 F.2d 986, 995–96 (8th Cir. 1989); *Town of Kearny v. Hudson Meadows Urban Renewal Corp.,* 829 F.2d 1263, 1266 (3d Cir. 1987); *Atkinson v. Anadarko Bank & Trust Co.,* 808 F.2d 438 (5th Cir.), *cert. denied,* 483 U.S. 1032 (1987); *Shaffer v. Williams,* 794 F.2d 1030 (5th Cir. 1986); *Miller Hydro Group v. Popovitch,* 793 F. Supp. 24, 27–28 (D. Me. 1992). *See generally* Joseph, *Civil RICO, supra* at 53–56, 59–62.

Many courts have also imposed the requirement that an association-in-fact have an "ascertainable structure." *See, e.g., Atlas Pile Driving Co. v. DiCon Fin. Co.,* 886 F.2d 986, 995–96 (8th Cir. 1989). *See generally* Mannino, *Lender Liability, supra* at § 4.03[2][b][iv]. For a criticism of this requirement, see Joseph, *Civil RICO, supra* at 54–56.

5.07[3] Enterprise—Interstate Commerce

I have previously instructed you that the enterprise must be one that was engaged in, or whose activities affected, interstate commerce. This requirement is satisfied if you determine that the activities of the enterprise itself, or the defendant's conduct with respect to the enterprise, had even a slight or minimal impact on commerce between separate states or between one or more states and foreign countries.

Comment

This instruction is supported by *Jund v. Town of Hempstead,* 941 F.2d 1271, 1284–85 (2d Cir. 1991); *Rose v. Bartle,* 871 F.2d 331, 356–57, 358 n.42 (3d Cir. 1989); and *United States v. Robinson,* 763 F.2d 778, 781 (6th Cir. 1985). *But see Musick v. Burke,* 913 F.2d 1390 (9th Cir. 1990). *See generally* Joseph, *Civil RICO, supra* at 96–97.

This issue should rarely go to the jury, and typically will be appropriate for determination by the trial court as a matter of law.

5.08 Conduct

5.08[1] Conduct—Insiders

Among the other elements the plaintiff must prove to establish RICO liability on the part of the defendant are that the defendant was employed by or associated with the enterprise and conducted or participated in the conduct of the affairs of the enterprise through a pattern of racketeering activity. In this regard, you must find that the defendant participated in the operation or management of the enterprise itself, and was involved in the alleged unlawful activities.

To participate in the operation or management of an enterprise, a defendant must have had some part in directing the enterprise's affairs. A defendant need not be a member of upper management to satisfy this requirement, but may be a lower-rung participant in the enterprise who is acting under the direction of upper management.

Comment

This instruction should be employed when the defendant holds some formal position with the enterprise, such as officer, director, partner, principal, or employee. The language in the second paragraph of this instruction is based upon the language of the majority opinion in *Reves v. Ernst & Young,* 507 U.S. (1993).

The *Reves* decision resolved a conflict among the circuits on the proper interpretation of section 1962(c). Some courts had followed variations of the operation or management standard adopted in *Reves,* while others had employed a more liberal standard under which performing activities necessary or helpful to the operation of the enterprise was sufficient. *See generally,* Mannino, *Lender Liability, supra* at § 4.03[4]; Joseph, *Civil RICO, supra* at 46–49.

5.08[2] Conduct—Outsiders

Among the other elements the plaintiff must prove to establish RICO liability on the part of the defendant are that the defendant was employed by or associated with the enterprise and conducted or participated in the conduct of the affairs of the enterprise through a pattern of racketeering activity. In this regard, you must find that the defendant participated in the operation or management of the enterprise itself, and was involved in the alleged unlawful activities.

To participate in the operation or management of an enterprise, a defendant must have had some part in directing the enterprise's affairs. This does not require that the defendant hold a formal position in the enterprise. Even an outsider may participate in the operation or management of an enterprise if the outsider is associated with the enterprise and participates in the conduct of its affairs. An example of such association and participation would be if the outsider exerted control over the enterprise through bribery.

Comment

This instruction should be employed when the defendant does not hold any formal position with the enterprise but rather, is an outsider, such as an outside auditor, outside counsel, a lender, or some other third party. The language in the second paragraph of this instruction is based upon the language of the majority opinion in *Reves v. Ernst & Young,* 507 U.S. (1993).

Courts applying the *Reves* outsider standard have dismissed suits against outsider auditors, outside counsel, and lenders, among others. *See, e.g., Univ. of Maryland v. Peat, Marwick, Main & Co.,* 996 F.2d (3d Cir. 1993) (outside auditors); *Nolte v. Pearson,* 994 F.2d 1311 (8th Cir. 1993) (outside counsel); *Info. Exch. Sys., Inc. v. First Bank Nat'l Ass'n,* 994 F.2d 478 (8th Cir. 1993) (lender).

Given the restrictive reach of section 1962(c) when outsider parties are involved, such parties are more likely to be named as defendants on conspiracy or aiding and abetting theories. These theories are covered in the instructions in § 5.12 and § 5.13 (conspiracy), and in the comment to § 5.12[1] (aiding and abetting).

5.09 Racketeering Activity

The next term I will define for you is the term "racketeering activity." Racketeering activity includes any act or threat that is chargeable under certain state criminal laws, or an act that is indictable as a violation of certain federal statutes. Here the plaintiff contends that defendant engaged in [describe the RICO violations that are alleged].

Comment

Section 1961(1) sets forth a long list of predicate acts that are helpfully categorized in Sheehy, *RICO Forfeitures: The Development of* In Personam *Forfeitures as a Sanction in Federal Criminal Cases, in Civil RICO* 101, 176–80 (Pa. Bar Inst. 1990). *See also* Joseph, *Civil RICO, supra* at 62–81.

The most commonly charged RICO predicate act is mail fraud, and the elements of proof necessary to establish a mail fraud violation are set forth in § 5.10.

5.10 Mail Fraud

5.10[1] General Elements of Mail Fraud

The plaintiff has charged the defendant with mail fraud as a predicate act under RICO. Under Title 18, United States Code, section 1341, a person who has devised or intended to devise a scheme or artifice to defraud, or to obtain money or property by means of false or fraudulent pretenses, representations, or promises, and who uses the mails to execute or attempt to execute the scheme or artifice to defraud, has committed mail fraud.

To state a violation of the mail fraud statute, plaintiff must establish each of the following elements:

(1) the existence of a scheme or artifice to defraud;

(2) participation by the defendant in that scheme or artifice to defraud;

(3) specific intent to defraud on the part of the defendant;

(4) deception of the plaintiff as a result of the scheme or artifice to defraud; and

(5) the use of the United States mails in furtherance of the scheme or artifice to defraud.

Comment

See, e.g., United States v. Burks, 867 F.2d 795 (3d Cir. 1989); In re *Phillips Petroleum Sec. Litig.,* 881 F.2d 1236 (3d Cir. 1989); *Lavery v. Kearns,* 792 F. Supp. 847 (D. Me. 1992). *See also* Joseph, *Civil RICO, supra* at 66; 3 Devitt, Blackmar & Wolff, *Federal Jury Practice and Instructions: Civil* § 100.06 (4th ed. 1987); *Manual of Model Jury Instructions for the Ninth Circuit* (1984) [hereinafter *Ninth Circuit Model Instructions*] at 135–36.

It should be noted that the requirements of the wire fraud statute, 18 U.S.C. § 1343, are essentially similar, so that this instruction may be adapted by substituting "telephone lines" (or "wires") for "mails" in item (5), when wire fraud is charged. *See United States v. Computer Sciences Corp.,* 689 F.2d 1181 (4th Cir. 1982), *cert. denied,* 459 U.S. 1105 (1983).

5.10[2] Scheme/Artifice and Specific Intent

I will now explain to you the terms "scheme or artifice" and "specific intent." To employ a scheme or artifice to defraud means to use misrepresentations, omissions, or other dishonest means that are reasonably calculated to deceive persons of ordinary prudence and intelligence. It is necessary that the defendant have a specific intent to defraud, which may be established by proof that the defendant made material misrepresentations of fact with knowledge of their falsity or with reckless disregard for their truth, or that the defendant knowingly or recklessly omitted to state material facts.

Comment

For cases addressing the "scheme/artifice" requirement, see *Pereira v. United States,* 347 U.S. 1 (1954); *Associates in Adolescent Psychiatry, S.C. v. Home Life Insurance Co.,* 941 F.2d 561 (7th Cir. 1991); *Walters v. First National Bank,* 855 F.2d 267 (6th Cir. 1988), *cert. denied,* 489 U.S. 1067 (1989); *Lavery v. Kearns,* 792 F. Supp. 847 (D. Me. 1992); *Zee-Bar, Inc.-N.H. v. Kaplan,* 792 F. Supp. 895 (D.N.H. 1992). *See also* Joseph, *Civil RICO, supra* at 66–67; 3 Devitt, Blackmar & Wolff, *Federal Jury Practice and Instructions: Civil* § 100.07 (4th ed. 1987); *Ninth Circuit Model Instructions, supra* at § 8.03.

For cases addressing the "specific intent" requirement, see *Landry v. Air Line Pilots Ass'n,* 901 F.2d 404 (5th Cir.), *cert. denied,* 498 U.S. 895 (1990); *Atlas Pile Driving Co. v. DiCon Financial Co.,* 886 F.2d 986 (8th Cir. 1989); *Lavery v. Kearns,* 792 F. Supp. 847 (D. Me. 1992). *See also* Joseph, *Civil RICO, supra* at 66–67.

5.10[3] Mailing May Be Incidental

The alleged scheme or artifice to defraud need not contemplate the use of the mails as an essential element. It is sufficient if the mailing is incidental to an essential part of the scheme, as long as the mailing contributes to the completion of the scheme or artifice to defraud the plaintiff.

Comment

Although this instruction, which is generally favorable to a RICO plaintiff, emphasizes that the mailing in question need not be an essential element of the scheme, it nonetheless recognizes that the mailing must be related to the execution or completion of the scheme. Thus, fraudulent mailings that do not have the effect of deceiving the plaintiff are generally insufficient, even if they have the effect of deceiving third parties. *See, e.g., McEvoy Travel Bureau, Inc. v. Heritage Travel, Inc.*, 904 F.2d 786 (1st Cir.), *cert. denied*, 498 U.S. 992 (1991); *United States v. Shelton*, 848 F.2d 1485 (10th Cir. 1988). *But see Shaw v. Rolex Watch USA, Inc.*, 726 F. Supp. 969 (S.D.N.Y. 1989). *See generally* Joseph, *Civil RICO, supra* at 67; 3 Devitt, Blackmar & Wolff, *Federal Jury Practice and Instructions: Civil* § 100.08 (4th ed. 1987).

Similarly, if the mailings are undertaken after the completion or fruition of the fraudulent scheme, they are generally insufficient to support a claim of mail fraud. *See, e.g., Dennis v. Gen. Imaging, Inc.*, 918 F.2d 496 (5th Cir. 1990).

5.10[4] Good Faith Belief in Truth

Even if you find that the defendant misstated or omitted to state certain facts, I instruct you that if the defendant believed in good faith that the statements made were true at the time of mailing, then there is no mail fraud.

Comment

This instruction, which is favorable to a RICO defendant, simply expands upon the "specific intent" requirement discussed in § 5.10[2]. *See generally* Joseph, *Civil RICO, supra* at 66; 3 Devitt, Blackmar & Wolff, *Federal Jury Practice and Instructions: Civil* § 100.08 (4th ed. 1987).

5.11 Pattern of Racketeering Activity

5.11[1] Pattern of Racketeering Activity—Definition

Now I will define the term "pattern of racketeering activity." A pattern of racketeering activity requires at least two acts of racketeering activity within ten years of each other, [one of which must have occurred after October 15, 1970]. Those acts must be *related* to each other and must also amount to, or pose a threat of, *continuing criminal activity*. [Here describe the alleged pattern of racketeering activity.]

In determining whether these alleged acts, if proved, constituted a pattern of racketeering activity, you should consider the following factors.

First, acts are "related" within the meaning of RICO if they embrace criminal acts that have the same or similar purposes, results, participants, victims, or methods of commission. Acts may also be related for purposes of RICO liability if they otherwise are interrelated by distinguishing characteristics and are not isolated events.

Second, acts may be found to amount to, or pose a threat of, "continuing criminal activity" in two general ways. If the activity has ended, this requirement is satisfied if you find that the defendant committed a series of related unlawful acts extending over a substantial period of time and involving long-term criminal conduct. Unlawful acts extending over a few weeks or months and threatening no future criminal activity do not satisfy this requirement. [Ordinarily, a period of at least twelve months is required to establish sufficient continuity.]

A second way for the plaintiff to satisfy this requirement is by showing either that the unlawful activity is part of the enterprise's regular way of doing business, or that the related unlawful acts themselves involve a distinct threat of long-term racketeering activity. For example, a threat of long-term racketeering activity would be established in a case in which a hoodlum attempted to sell "insurance" to neighborhood storekeepers to cover them against breakage

of their windows, telling his victims that hoodlum would be reappearing each month to collect the "premium" that would continue their "coverage."

[In determining whether plaintiff has proved the existence of a pattern of racketeering activity in this case, you may also consider the following factors:

(1) the number, type, and variety of the alleged unlawful acts;
(2) the duration or time span of the alleged unlawful acts;
(3) the number of perpetrators;
(4) the number of victims;
(5) the number and separateness of "transactions," "schemes," or "episodes" involving unlawful conduct; and
(6) the presence of distinct injuries.]

Comment

The second sentence of this instruction tracks the language of 18 U.S.C. § 1961(5). The bracketed material in that sentence can be omitted in most cases. The remainder of the first paragraph, and all of the second through fifth paragraphs, with the exception of the bracketed material at the end of the fourth paragraph, are based on the language of the majority opinion in *H.J., Inc. v. Northwestern Bell Telephone Co.,* 492 U.S. 229, 236–39 (1989).

The bracketed material in the fourth paragraph, suggesting a litmus test of a twelve-month minimum period, finds considerable support in the circuit and district court opinions postdating the *H.J., Inc.* case. *See, e.g., Feinstein v. RTC,* 942 F.2d 34, 44–47 (1st Cir. 1991); *Kehr Packages, Inc. v. Fidelcor, Inc.,* 926 F.2d 1406 (3d Cir.), *cert. denied,* 501 U.S. 1222 (1991); *Johnston v. Wilbourn,* 760 F. Supp. 578, 588–89 n.16 (S.D. Miss. 1991) (collecting cases). This point is discussed further, and additional cases cited, in Mannino, *Lender Liability,* § 4.03[3][d], and in Edward F. Mannino, *"Less Corn and More Hell": The Application of RICO to Financial Institutions,* 35 Vill. L. Rev. 883, 899–901 (1990).

The bracketed material in the sixth and final paragraph of this proposed instruction incorporates elements from those circuit court opinions that followed the so-called "multifactor" test before the *H.J., Inc.* case. Although some circuits have concluded that the test is inconsistent with *H.J.* (*see, e.g., Fleet Credit Corp. v. Sion,* 893 F.2d 441, 445–46 (1st Cir. 1990)), others still follow it. *See, e.g., Banks v. Wolk,* 918 F.2d 418, 423 (3d Cir. 1990); *U.S. Textiles, Inc. v. Anheuser-Busch Cos., Inc.,* 911 F.2d 1261, 1267–69 (7th Cir. 1990). This point is discussed further, and additional cases cited, in Joseph, *Civil RICO,* at 93–95.

The existence of a pattern of racketeering activity may be a question of law in some cases. As noted above, when a closed-end scheme lasts less than twelve months and threatens no future harm, or affects only a single victim, courts have increasingly held that no pattern exists as a matter of law.

5.11[2] Pattern of Racketeering Activity—Additional Instruction for Mail Fraud

In this case, plaintiff contends that defendant violated RICO by committing acts of mail fraud that constituted a pattern of racketeering activity. I instruct you that in determining whether a pattern of racketeering activity has been proved, you may consider only defendant's deceptive or fraudulent activity; you may not consider innocent mailings even though they may have continued for a substantial period of time.

Comment

This instruction is based upon *Kehr Packages, Inc. v. Fidelcor, Inc.*, 926 F.2d 1406, 1418 (3d Cir.), *cert. denied*, 501 U.S. 1222 (1991). *Accord, Feinstein v. RTC*, 942 F.2d 34, 46 (1st Cir. 1991); *Delta Pride Catfish, Inc. v. Marine Midland Business Loans, Inc.*, 767 F. Supp. 951, 968 (E.D. Ark. 1991).

This instruction should be coordinated with those on mail fraud to avoid confusion between the pattern element, for which innocent mailings cannot be considered, and the elements of a mail fraud violation, for which the mailings may be incidental as long as they contribute to completion of the fraudulent scheme. *See* § 5.10[3], *supra*.

5.12 General Elements of Section 1962(d)

5.12[1] In Circuits Requiring Overt Acts to Be Predicate Acts

The plaintiff also claims that the defendant violated section 1962(d). Section 1962(d) states that it is unlawful for any person to conspire to violate any of the other subsections of section 1962. The plaintiff alleges that the defendant conspired with others to violate section 1962 [insert applicable subsection], the section that I have just described to you.

For the plaintiff to prove a violation of section 1962(d), the RICO conspiracy claim, the plaintiff must establish each of the following:

(1) that the defendant conspired with others to violate section 1962 [insert applicable subsection];
(2) that the defendant knowingly agreed with others to become part of the alleged conspiracy; and
(3) that the defendant agreed to commit, or to aid and abet another to commit, at least two unlawful acts that are predicate acts of racketeering under RICO, and knew that those acts were part of a pattern of racketeering activity.

If you find that the plaintiff has proven each of these elements, then you must find that the defendant has violated section 1962(d).

Comment

The RICO conspiracy subsection requires *an agreement to commit* unlawful activity, not simply the commission of such activity. *See, e.g., United States v. Pepe,* 747 F.2d 632, 660 n.44 (11th Cir. 1984); *United States v. Taruglio,* 731 F.2d 1123, 1133 (4th Cir.), *cert. denied,* 469 U.S. 862 (1984); *United States v. Brooklier,* 685 F.2d 1208, 1220 (9th Cir. 1982), *cert. denied,* 459 U.S. 1206 (1983); *United States v. Winter,* 663 F.2d 1120, 1136 (1st Cir. 1981), *cert. denied,* 460 U.S. 1011 (1983). However, an agreement to commit unlawful activity, without more, is not enough; there must also be agreement to join the conspiracy and knowledge that such activity is part of a pattern of racketeering activity under RICO. *See, e.g., Glessner v. Kenny,* 952 F.2d 702, 714 (3d Cir. 1991); *Seville Indus. Mach. Corp. v. Southmost Mach. Corp.,* 742 F.2d 786, 792 n.8 (3d Cir. 1984), *cert. denied,* 469 U.S. 1211 (1985).

There is a split among the circuits that have considered the issue about whether the overt acts committed in furtherance of the conspiracy must themselves be predicate acts. The foregoing instruction applies in those jurisdictions, including the First, Second, Eighth, and Ninth Circuits, which require that such overt acts be predicate acts. *See Miranda v. Ponce Fed. Bank,* 948 F.2d 41, 48 (1st Cir. 1991); *Hecht v. Commerce Clearing House, Inc.,* 897 F.2d 21 (2d Cir. 1990); *Bowman v. W. Auto Supply Co.,* 985 F.2d 383, 386–88 (8th Cir. 1993); *Reddy v. Litton Indus., Inc.,* 912 F.2d 291 (9th Cir. 1990), *cert. denied,* 112 S. Ct. 332 (1991). The Third and Seventh Circuits have reached the opposite conclusion. *See* § 5.12[2], *infra. See also* Joseph, *Civil RICO, supra* at 49–50; Mannino, *Lender Liability, supra* at § 4.01[3][d].

Conspiracy liability under section 1962(d) is different from liability for aiding and abetting a violation of any of the other subsections of section 1962. Several courts have held that a defendant may be liable for aiding and abetting such a violation. *See, e.g., Petro-Tech, Inc. v. W. Co. of N. Am.,* 824 F.2d 1349, 1357–58 (3d Cir. 1987) (civil liability for aiding and abetting under RICO appropriate as long as other statutory requirements met; however, alleged aider/abettor cannot be same as RICO enterprise); *Armco Indus. Credit Corp. v. SLT Warehouse Co.,* 782 F.2d 475, 485–86 (5th Cir. 1986); *Rodriguez v. Banco Cent.,* 727 F. Supp. 759 (D.P.R. 1989) (recognizing aiding and abetting liability under RICO as long as aider/abettor and RICO enterprise different), *modified on other grounds,* 917 F.2d 664 (1st Cir. 1990). These decisions, however, predate the Supreme Court's decision, by a 5 to 4 majority, in *Central Bank v. First Interstate Bank,* 114 S. Ct. 1439 (1994), in which the majority held that a private plaintiff may not maintain an aiding and abetting suit under section 10(b) of the Securities Exchange Act of 1934. The impact of the *Central Bank* decision on RICO aiding and abetting claims is presently unclear. *See* Mannino, *Lender Liability, supra* at § 7.01[1][b] (discussing this issue).

To establish an aiding and abetting violation, some courts have held that a civil RICO plaintiff must prove that the defendant was associated with the primary violation, participated in it as something that defendant wished to bring about, and sought, by defendant's actions, to make it succeed. *See, e.g., Armco Indus. Credit Corp. v. SLT Warehouse Co.,* 782 F.2d 475 (5th Cir. 1986).

Both aiding and abetting and conspiracy claims are more likely to be brought against enterprise outsiders, such as accountants, lawyers, and lenders, as a result of the Supreme Court's decision on the scope of section 1962(c) in *Reves v. Ernst & Young,* 113 S. Ct. 1163 (1993). *See* § 5.08[2], cmt. *supra.* In the majority opinion in *Reves,* the Supreme Court noted that section 1962(c) participation liability required more than aiding and abetting liability, which the Court characterized as "a term of breadth indeed, for 'aid and abet' 'comprehends all assistance rendered by words, acts, encouragement, support, or presence.' " *Reves v. Ernst & Young,* 113 S. Ct. 1163, 1170 (1993) (quoting *Blacks Law Dictionary*).

5.12[2] In Circuits Where Overt Acts Need Not Be Predicate Acts

The plaintiff also claims that the defendant violated section 1962(d). Section 1962(d) states that it is unlawful for any person to conspire to violate any of the other subsections of section 1962. The plaintiff alleges that the defendant conspired with others to violate section 1962 [insert applicable subsection], the section that I have just described to you.

For the plaintiff to prove a violation of section 1962(d), the RICO conspiracy claim, the plaintiff must establish each of the following:

(1) that the defendant conspired with others to violate section 1962 [insert applicable subsection];
(2) that the defendant knowingly agreed with others to become part of the alleged conspiracy; and
(3) that the defendant agreed to commit, or to aid and abet another to commit, overt acts in furtherance of the alleged conspiracy, even if those acts were not unlawful acts under RICO, and knew that those acts were part of a pattern of racketeering activity.

Comment

This instruction reflects the more liberal approach, adopted by the Third and Seventh Circuits, that the overt acts committed in furtherance of a RICO conspiracy need not themselves be predicate acts. *See Shearin v. E.F. Hutton Group, Inc.*, 885 F.2d 1162 (3d Cir. 1989); *Schiffels v. Kemper Fin. Serv., Inc.*, 978 F.2d 344 (7th Cir. 1992). *See also* Joseph, *Civil RICO, supra* at 49–50; Mannino, *Lender Liability, supra* at § 4.01[3][d].

5.13 Conspiracy, Predicate Acts, Multiple Defendants

5.13[1] Liberal Approach

As you know, there are [number of] defendants in this lawsuit, each of whom is being charged with conspiring to violate RICO. I instruct you that to impose liability upon a defendant for conspiring to violate RICO, you need not find that the defendant agreed to commit at least two predicate acts itself. It is sufficient if a particular defendant agreed that some member of the enterprise would commit the predicate acts.

Comment

This instruction should be requested by a RICO plaintiff in cases involving multiple defendants or alleged wrongdoers. *See United States v. Neapolitan,* 791 F.2d 489, 492 (7th Cir.), *cert. denied,* 479 U.S. 939 (1986); *United States v. Tille,* 729 F.2d 615, 623–24 (9th Cir.), *cert. denied,* 469 U.S. 819 (1984); *Airlines Reporting Corp. v. Barry,* 666 F. Supp. 1311 (D. Minn. 1987). *See also* Joseph, *Civil RICO, supra* at 102.

5.13[2] Conservative Approach

As you know, there are [number of] defendants in this lawsuit, each of whom is being charged with conspiring to violate RICO. I instruct you that to impose liability upon a defendant for conspiring to violate RICO, you must find that the defendant agreed to commit at least two predicate acts itself.

Comment

This conservative approach has been adopted by the First and Second Circuits. *See Miranda v. Ponce Fed. Bank,* 948 F.2d 41 (1st Cir. 1991); *United States v. Angiulo,* 847 F.2d 956 (1st Cir.), *cert denied,* 488 U.S. 852 (1988); *United States v. Rastelli,* 870 F.2d 822 (2d Cir.), *cert. denied,* 493 U.S. 892 (1989); *United States v. Ruggiero,* 726 F.2d 913, 921 (2d Cir.), *cert. denied,* 469 U.S. 831 (1984); *United States v. Winter,* 663 F.2d 1120, 1136 (1st Cir. 1981), *cert. denied,* 460 U.S. 1011 (1983). *See also United States v. Martino,* 648 F.2d 367 (5th Cir. 1981), *cert. denied,* 456 U.S. 943 (1982); Joseph, *Civil RICO, supra* at 102. See § 5.13[1] for a discussion of the liberal approach.

5.14 Injury and Proximate Cause

5.14[1] Injury

If you find that the defendant violated [insert applicable subsection], then the plaintiff must next prove that it was injured in its business or property by reason of the defendant's violation of [insert applicable subsection].

For the plaintiff to prevail on its RICO claim, you must find that the plaintiff suffered an injury to its business or property and that this injury was proximately caused by reason of the defendant's violation of RICO. I will explain this proximate cause requirement to you in more detail in the next instruction, but I will first describe for you the types of damages that are and are not recoverable under RICO. Damages that are recoverable include, for example, the payment of money, lost profits, and overcharges. They do not include, for example, claims for personal injury or mental anguish. However, before any damages are recoverable at all, the plaintiff must prove that such damages were proximately caused by the defendant's RICO violation, as I will now explain to you.

Comment

This instruction focuses upon the types of damages recoverable in RICO cases, while the instruction in § 5.14[2] discusses the proximate cause requirement. Many cases discuss the types of damages recoverable under RICO. *See, e.g., Advanced Business Sys., Inc. v. Philips Infor. Sys. Co.,* 750 F. Supp. 774 (E.D. La. 1990) (lost profits recoverable if proximate cause requirement satisfied); *Sound Video Unlimited, Inc. v. Video Shack, Inc.,* 700 F. Supp. 127 (S.D.N.Y. 1988) (same holding); *Rodonich v. House Wreckers Union,* 627 F. Supp. 176, 180 (S.D.N.Y. 1985) (lost wages recoverable); *Brandenberg v. Seidel,* 859 F.2d 1179, 1187 (4th Cir. 1988) (lost interest income recoverable); *Haroco, Inc. v. Am. Nat'l Bank & Trust Co.,* 747 F.2d 384, 398 (7th Cir. 1984) (excessive interest charges recoverable), *aff'd on other grounds,* 473 U.S. 606 (1985); *Genty v. Resolution Trust Corp.,* 937 F.2d 899 (3d Cir. 1991) (physical and emotional injuries not compensable under RICO); *Moore v. Eli Lilly & Co.*, 626 F. Supp. 365 (D. Mass. 1986) (same holding; loss of consortium not compensable under RICO); *Drake v. B.F. Goodrich Co.*, 782 F.2d 638 (6th Cir. 1986) (wrongful death not compensable under RICO); *Bast v. A.H. Robins Co.*, 616 F. Supp. 333, 335 (E.D. Wis. 1985) (illness and injury based on products liability claim not compensable); *Zimmerman v. HBO Affiliate Group*, 834 F.2d 1163, 1169–70 (3d Cir. 1987) (damage to reputation and mental anguish not compensable under RICO). *Compare Hunt v. Weatherbee*, 626 F. Supp. 1097 (D. Mass. 1986) (claims for discrimination and sexual harassment compensable under RICO, at least when plaintiff forced from job and prevented from pursuing similar work in future). *See also* Joseph, *Civil RICO, supra* at 111–14; Mannino, *Lender Liability, supra* at § 4.03[5].

5.14[2] Proximate Cause

Now I will explain the concept of proximate cause as it applies to RICO. For you to find that defendant's violation of RICO proximately caused injury to plaintiff's business or property, plaintiff must establish a direct relationship between the injury asserted and the injurious conduct alleged. In other words, plaintiff must prove that defendant's conduct was a substantial factor in the sequence of responsible causation, and that plaintiff's injury was reasonably foreseeable or anticipated as a natural consequence of such conduct. It is not enough that the defendant has committed a RICO violation and that the plaintiff has suffered some injury; rather, there must be a direct and proximate link between the two.

A determination of proximate cause depends on the facts of each case. For example, if a defendant engages in a scheme to defraud a plaintiff who is in the construction business by submitting and collecting inflated invoices, and the plaintiff goes out of business—not because of defendant's conduct but rather because of an economic recession affecting the construction industry—then there would be no proximate cause under RICO for the destruction of the business. On the other hand, if it were shown that plaintiff's loss of the business was the reasonably foreseeable and natural consequence of defendant's scheme of submitting and collecting inflated invoices, then the RICO proximate cause requirement would be met.

Comment

The foregoing instruction is derived from the Supreme Court's decision in *Holmes v. Securities Investor Protection Corp.,* 503 U.S. 258 (1992), in which the Supreme Court held that a RICO plaintiff had to establish a direct causal connection between the injury alleged and the conduct in question. In *Holmes,* the Ninth Circuit reversed the lower court's entry of summary judgment in favor of a broker-dealer on standing grounds. The Ninth Circuit held that in liquidation proceedings, the Securities Investor Protection Corporation (SIPC) had standing to pursue claims under section 1964(c) on the basis that it had been required to advance funds to certain customers of its member broker-dealers in reimbursement of defendants' allegedly fraudulent stock manipulation scheme. The Supreme Court reversed the Ninth Circuit's decision and rejected a "but for" analysis in favor of a more stringent "direct relation" requirement between the alleged injury and the conduct in question. The Court concluded that the harm suffered as a result of the fraudulent scheme was actually to the member broker-dealers who were then unable to pay customers' claims, thus requiring the SIPC to step in and reimburse those customers. Such harm, the Court determined, was too remote from the alleged violation to fulfill the proximate cause requirement. The "responsible causation" language is found in *Hecht v. Commerce Clearing House, Inc.*, 879 F.2d 21 (2d Cir. 1990). *See also* Joseph, *Civil RICO, supra* at 30–32; Mannino, *Lender Liability, supra* at § 4.03[5][b].

Chapter Six

Fraud, Misrepresentation, Nondisclosure, and Concealment

6.01 Introduction

M. Stanford Blanton and Daniel C. Johnson

The model jury instructions contained in this chapter address the liability and damage aspects of the common law torts of fraudulent misrepresentation, negligent misrepresentation, innocent misrepresentation, fraudulent concealment, and fraudulent nondisclosure.

The model instructions closely follow the *Restatement (Second) of Torts* (1977) for three reasons. First, not every tort contained in this chapter is recognized by every jurisdiction. Second, not all jurisdictions distinguish between and among the torts contained in this chapter. For example, see the comment to the instruction in § 6.02[3], which identifies a jurisdiction that allows a cause of action for fraudulent misrepresentation to be predicated upon the communication of a negligent representation. Third, due to their common law development, the precise jury charges for each element may vary slightly from jurisdiction to jurisdiction. This is especially true for the tort of fraudulent misrepresentation. For these reasons, the model instructions follow the *Restatement,* with important distinguishing information contained in each instruction's comment section.

No attempt has been made to survey the statutory liability for similar causes of action, due to the intent that these instructions have the broadest possible application. The practitioner is advised, however, that the legislature of the relevant jurisdiction may have enacted legislation that allows a litigant to pursue a statutory cause of action based upon a state of facts that create a common law cause of action of the type addressed by these instructions. These statutory causes of action may allow an enhanced compensatory damage award similar to the federal antitrust and RICO statutes.

6.02 Fraudulent Misrepresentation

6.02[1] Requirement of Fraudulent Misrepresentation: General Rule

For the plaintiff to recover from the defendant, the plaintiff must prove by a preponderance of the evidence that the defendant has made a fraudulent misrepresentation. A misrepresentation can include spoken or written words, or any other conduct that amounts to an assertion not in accordance with the truth. Asserting the existence of a fact, by words or conduct, is a misrepresentation if the fact does not exist. A fraudulent misrepresentation may be either oral or written, and either express or implied.

Comment

This instruction sets forth the principle that a misrepresentation may be made orally or in writing and may be express or implied. *See generally Restatement (Second) of Torts* § 525 cmt. b (1977); 37 Am. Jur. 2d *Fraud and Deceit* § 42 (1968).

6.02[2] Elements of Liability

In this case, to recover money damages, the plaintiff must establish that the defendant made a fraudulent misrepresentation. To find liability for fraudulent misrepresentation, you, the jury, must find from a preponderance of the evidence all of the following:

(1) that the defendant made a fraudulent misrepresentation of fact, opinion, intention, or law;

(2) that the misrepresentation was made with the purpose or expectation of inducing the plaintiff to act or refrain from action in reliance upon the misrepresentation; and

(3) that the plaintiff justifiably relied on the misrepresentation to its injury.

Comment

This instruction is modeled on section 525 of the *Restatement (Second) of Torts* (1977). *See Pinney & Topliff v. Chrysler Corp.*, 176 F. Supp. 801 (S.D. Cal. 1959); *Knight v. E.F. Hutton and Co., Inc.*, 750 F. Supp. 1109 (M.D. Fla. 1990); *Arbour v. Hazelton*, 534 A.2d 1303 (Me. 1987); *Southwestern Indem. Co. v. Cimarron Ins. Co.*, 334 S.W.2d 831 (Tex. Civ. App. 1960). *Cf. Farrar v. Churchill*, 135 U.S. 609 (1890); 37 Am. Jur. 2d *Fraud and Deceit* § 12 (1968).

6.02[3] Conditions under Which Misrepresentation Is Fraudulent

A misrepresentation is fraudulent in any of the following situations:

(1) the defendant knows or believes the matter was not as the defendant represents it to be;

(2) the defendant does not have the confidence in the accuracy of the representation that the defendant states or implies; or

(3) the defendant knows it did not have the basis for the representation that the defendant states or implies.

Comment

This instruction is modeled on section 526 of the *Restatement (Second) of Torts* (1977). *See Wishnick v. Frye,* 245 P.2d 532 (Cal. Ct. App. 1952); *Young v. Johnson,* 538 So. 2d 1387 (Fla. Dist. Ct. App. 1989); *Dundee Land Co. v. Simmons,* 49 S.E.2d 488 (Ga. 1948); *Lambert v. Smith,* 201 A.2d 491 (Md. Ct. Spec. App. 1964).

Some jurisdictions allow recovery if the defendant should have known of the falsity of the representation under the circumstances, even though the defendant had no such actual knowledge. These jurisdictions allow a plaintiff to pursue an action for fraudulent misrepresentation for what is, in effect, negligent misrepresentation. *See Cameron v. Outdoor Resorts of Am., Inc.,* 611 F.2d 105 (5th Cir. 1980); *Burgess v. Premier Corp.,* 727 F.2d 826 (9th Cir. 1984).

6.03 Types of Misrepresentation

6.03[1] Ambiguous Misrepresentation

A representation is fraudulent if the defendant knows it to be capable of two interpretations, one of which [he or she] knows to be false and the other true, and if the misrepresentation is made

(1) with the intention that it be understood in the false sense; or

(2) without any belief or expectation about how it will be understood; or

(3) with reckless indifference regarding how it will be understood.

Comment

This instruction is modeled on section 527 of the *Restatement (Second) of Torts* (1977). *See Thiele v. Davidson,* 440 F. Supp. 585 (M.D. Fla. 1977); *John R. Cowley & Bros., Inc. v. Brown,* 569 So. 2d 375 (Ala. 1990); *Berger v. Sec. Pac. Info. Sys.,* 795 P.2d 1380 (Colo. Ct. App. 1990). *Cf. New York Yellow Pages, Inc. v. Growth Personnel Agency,* 414 N.Y.S.2d 260 (N.Y. Civ. Ct. 1979); 37 Am. Jur. 2d *Fraud and Deceit* §§ 42–43 (1968).

Subsection (3) should not be used in an action for negligent misrepresentation. As set forth in this instruction, a defendant is liable if the defendant intentionally makes what he or she knows to be an ambiguous representation, with reckless indifference regarding how it will be understood.

6.03[2] Negligent Representation

A representation is not fraudulent if the defendant believed it stated the truth but, because of negligent expression, stated what is false. Such a statement is a negligent, but not a fraudulent, representation.

Comment

This instruction is modeled on section 528 of the *Restatement (Second) of Torts* (1977) and is consistent with the comment to instruction 6.03[1]. *Cf. Slater Trust Co. v. Gardiner,* 183 F. 268 (Comm. Ct. N.Y. 1910); 37 Am. Jur. 2d *Fraud and Deceit* § 208 (1968). The practitioner should be aware, however, that some jurisdictions hold negligent representations actionable as fraudulent representations. *First Union Discount Brokerage Servs., Inc. v. Milos,* 744 F. Supp. 1145 (S.D. Fla. 1990).

6.03[3] Incomplete Representation Becoming Misleading

A representation that is technically accurate but that the defendant knows or believes to be materially misleading because of a failure to state additional or qualifying matter is a fraudulent misrepresentation.

If the defendant knows, has reason to know, or believes that a reasonable person or the plaintiff would regard the incomplete representation as important in determining the defendant's choice of action in the transaction involved, then this incomplete representation becomes a fraudulent misrepresentation.

Comment

This instruction is modeled on sections 529 and 538 of the *Restatement (Second) of Torts* (1977). *Cf. V.S.H. Realty, Inc. v. Texaco, Inc.*, 757 F.2d 411, 414 (1st Cir. 1985); *Jacobs v. Freeman*, 163 Cal. Rptr. 680 (Cal. Ct. App. 1980); *Amtruck Factors v. Int'l Forest Prods.*, 795 P.2d 742 (Wash. Ct. App. 1990); 36 Am. Jur. 2d *Fraud and Deceit* § 183 (1968).

6.03[4] Misrepresentation of Defendant's Intention

A representation of the defendant's own intention to do or not to do a particular thing is fraudulent if the representation is made when the defendant does not have that intention.

Comment

This instruction is modeled on section 530 of the *Restatement (Second) of Torts* (1977). *Cf. Gifford v. Wichita Falls & S. R4. Co.,* 211 F.2d 494 (5th Cir. 1954); *E&S Facilities, Inc. v. Precision Chippers Corp.,* 565 So. 2d 54 (Ala. 1990); *McEvoy Travel Bureau, Inc. v. Norton Co.,* 563 N.E.2d 188 (Mass. 1990); 37 Am. Jur. 2d *Fraud and Deceit* § 68 (1968).

6.03[5] Misrepresentation of a Third Person's Intention

A misrepresentation of the intention of a third person is fraudulent in any of the following circumstances:

(1) the defendant knows or believes the matter was not as the defendant represents it to be;
(2) the defendant does not have the confidence in the accuracy of the representation that the defendant stated or implied; or
(3) the defendant knows it did not have the basis for the representation that the defendant stated or implied.

Comment

This instruction is modeled on section 530 of the *Restatement (Second) of Torts* (1977). *Cf. Cofield v. Griffin,* 78 S.E.2d 131 (N.C. 1953); 37 Am. Jur. 2d *Fraud and Deceit* § 67 (1968).

6.04 Requirement of Intention or Expectation of Influencing Conduct

6.04[1] General Rule

For the plaintiff to recover against the defendant, the plaintiff must prove by a preponderance of the evidence that the fraudulent misrepresentation was made with the purpose or expectation of inducing the plaintiff to act or refrain from action in reliance upon the misrepresentation. The plaintiff must show that the defendant intended or expected the fraudulent misrepresentation to cause or influence the plaintiff's action or decision not to act.

Comment

This instruction is modeled on section 531 of the *Restatement (Second) of Torts* (1977). *See Clark v. Haggard,* 109 A.2d 358 (Conn. 1954); *Sherban v. Richardson,* 445 So. 2d 1147 (Fla. Dist. Ct. App. 1984). *Cf. City Deposit Bank v. Green,* 115 N.W. 893 (Iowa 1908); *Hoffman v. Ryan,* 422 N.Y.S.2d 288 (N.Y. Civ. Ct. 1979); 37 Am. Jur. 2d *Fraud and Deceit* § 189 (1968); *Black's Law Dictionary* 397 (5th ed. 1983).

6.04[2] Representation to More Than One Person

The requirement that [the defendant] intended or expected to influence [the plaintiff's] conduct is satisfied if [the defendant] made a fraudulent misrepresentation intending, or with reason to expect, that more than one person or a class of persons would be induced to rely on it, or that there will be action or inaction as a result of the representation.

Comment

This instruction is modeled on section 534 of the *Restatement (Second) of Torts* (1977) and represents a modification of the general rule set forth in § 6.04[1] to the special circumstances surrounding the publication of the representation to more than one person. *See Holloway v. Forsyth,* 115 N.E. 483 (Mass. 1917). *Cf. Berkowitz v. Baron,* 428 F. Supp. 1190 (S.D.N.Y. 1977); 37 Am. Jur. 2d *Fraud and Deceit* § 193 (1968).

6.04[3] Representation Made to Third Person

The requirement that [the defendant] intend or expect to influence the plaintiff's conduct is satisfied if

(1) a fraudulent misrepresentation is made to a third person; and

(2) the defendant intended or had reason to expect that

(a) its terms would be repeated or its substance communicated to a plaintiff; and

(b) the representation would influence the plaintiff's conduct in the transaction or type of transaction involved in this suit.

Comment

This instruction is modeled on section 533 of the *Restatement (Second) of Torts* (1977) and represents a modification of the general rule set forth in § 6.04[1] to the special circumstances surrounding the publication of the representation to third persons. *See Varwig v. Anderson-Bethel Porsche/Audi, Inc.*, 141 Cal. Rptr. 539 (Cal. Ct. App. 1977); *Joseph v. Norman LaPorte Reality, Inc.*, 508 So. 2d 496 (Fla. Dist. Ct. App. 1987). *Cf. Colonial Bank v. Ridley & Schweigert*, 551 So. 2d 390 (Ala. 1990); *Metric Inv., Inc. v. Paterson*, 244 A.2d 311 (N.J. Super. Ct. App. Div. 1968); *Credit Alliance Corp. v. Arthur Anderson & Co.*, 483 N.E.2d 110 (N.Y. 1985); 37 Am. Jur. 2d *Fraud and Deceit* § 190 (1968).

6.04[4] Misrepresentation Incorporated in Document or Other Thing

The inclusion of a fraudulent misrepresentation in an article of commerce, a muniment of title, a negotiable instrument, or a similar commercial document satisfies the requirement that the misrepresentation be made with the purpose or expectation of inducing the plaintiff to act or refrain from acting in reliance upon the misrepresentation.

Comment

This instruction is modeled on section 532 of the *Restatement (Second) of Torts* (1977). *See Herskowitz v. Nutri-System,* 857 F.2d 179 (3d Cir. 1988), *cert. denied,* 489 U.S. 1054 (1989); *U.S. v. Puerto,* 730 F.2d 627 (11th Cir. 1984). *Cf.* 37 Am. Jur. 2d *Fraud and Deceit* § 194 (1968).

6.04[5] Continuing Misrepresentation

A defendant expected to influence the plaintiff's conduct if the defendant knew that the plaintiff was relying on the defendant's fraudulent misrepresentation involving a previous transaction and the defendant enters into a second transaction without disclosing the falsity of the original misstatement. The law treats the defendant's allowance of this continuing misrepresentation the same as if the defendant repeated the misrepresentation to influence the plaintiff's conduct in the later transaction.

Comment

This instruction is modeled on section 535 of the *Restatement (Second) of Torts* (1977) and represents a modification of the general rule set forth in § 6.04[1] to the special circumstances when the defendant knows the plaintiff is relying on an earlier fraudulent misrepresentation made by defendant to plaintiff and the defendant enters into a second transaction without disclosing the falsity of the earlier fraudulent misrepresentation. *Cf. Sedco Int'l S.A. v. Cory,* 683 F.2d 1201, 1208 (8th Cir.) *cert. denied,* 459 U.S. 1017 (1982); *Guastella v. Wardell,* 198 So. 2d 227 (Miss. 1967); *Shogyo Int'l Corp. v. First Nat'l Bank of Clarksdale,* 475 So. 2d 425, 427 (Miss. 1985); 37 Am. Jur. 2d *Fraud and Deceit* § 242 (1968).

6.04[6] Liability for Misrepresentation Based upon Information Required by Statute

The requirement of a defendant's expectation of influencing conduct is satisfied if a statute requires information to be furnished, filed, recorded, or published for the protection of a particular class of persons and the defendant has made a fraudulent misrepresentation concerning a type of transaction and involving persons whom the statute was intended to protect.

Comment

This instruction is modeled on section 536 of the *Restatement (Second) of Torts* (1977). *Cf. Handy v. Beck,* 581 P.2d 68 (Or. 1978); *Woodward v. Dietrich,* 548 A.2d 301 (Pa. Super. Ct. 1988); 37 Am. Jur. 2d *Fraud and Deceit* § 194 (1968).

6.05 Materiality of Misrepresentation

For the plaintiff to recover against the defendant you must find that the matter misrepresented was material. A matter is material if either

(1) a reasonable person would attach importance to it in determining his or her choice of action in the transaction in question; or

(2) the defendant knew or had reason to know that its plaintiff regards, or is likely to regard, the matter as important in determining his or her choice of action, regardless of whether a reasonable person would regard the misrepresentation as important.

Comment

This instruction is modeled on section 538 of the *Restatement (Second) of Torts (1977). See Basic v. Levinson,* 485 U.S. 224 (1988); *Hauben v. Harmon,* 605 F.2d 920 (5th Cir. 1979); *Cf. Long v. Ins. Co. of North Am.,* 670 F.2d 930 (10th Cir. 1982); *Weitzman v. Stein,* 436 F. Supp. 895 (S.D.N.Y. 1977); 37 Am. Jur. 2d *Fraud and Deceit* § 178 (1968).

Before addressing the issue of justifiable reliance, the plaintiff must prove plaintiff relied on a material matter. The inclusion of the reasonable person standard may cause some confusion. The comments to the *Restatement* authorize the use, depending on the circumstances of a reasonable person standard and a purely subjective standard. The former is employed for the proposition that a case should be taken away from a jury "if the fact misrepresented is so obviously unimportant that the jury could not reasonably find that a reasonable man would have been influenced by it." *Restatement (Second) of Torts* § 538 cmt. e (1977). However, the authors of the *Restatement* also endorse a purely subjective standard to allow recovery by a plaintiff who, because of peculiarities, is likely to attach significance to a misrepresentation even though a reasonable person would not attach any importance to the same misrepresentation, because to do otherwise would reward a defendant who plays upon the known idiosyncrasies of a plaintiff.

Restatement (Second) of Torts § 538 cmt. f (1977). Presumably to avoid potential confusion, some jurisdictions apply a subjective test to determine materiality, based on whether the plaintiff's actions were influenced by the misrepresentation. *See Saxton v. Harris,* 395 P.2d 71 (Ala. 1964); *Morris v. Ingraffia,* 18 So. 2d 1 (Fla. 1944).

6.06 Requirement of Justifiable Reliance on Part of Plaintiff of Misrepresentation

6.06[1] General Rule

For the plaintiff to recover against defendant, the plaintiff must prove by a preponderance of the evidence that the plaintiff's loss resulted from plaintiff's justifiable reliance on the misrepresentation in acting or refraining from action. The plaintiff relied on the misrepresentation if it caused the plaintiff to act in a way that plaintiff would otherwise not have acted without this misrepresentation. The plaintiff's reliance is justified if the situation makes it reasonable to accept the representation made, in light of the circumstances and the plaintiff's intelligence, experience, and knowledge.

Comment

This instruction is modeled on section 537 of the *Restatement (Second) of Torts* (1977) and sections 12.51 and 12.52 of *California Jury Instructions* (7th ed. Supp. 1992). *See Slaymaker v. Westgate State Bank,* 739 P.2d 444 (Kan. 1987); *Hershmann v. Univ. of Toledo,* 519 N.E.2d 871, 875 (Ohio Ct. Cl. 1987). *Cf. Galego v. Knudsen,* 578 P.2d 769 (Or. 1978); 37 Am. Jur. 2d *Fraud and Deceit* § 236 (1968).

6.06[2] Representations of Opinions

6.06[2][a] General Rule

A plaintiff's reliance on a fraudulent misrepresentation is not justifiable if the representation was one of opinion. A representation is an opinion if it expresses only

(1) the belief of the defendant, without certainty, about the existence of a fact; or

(2) the defendant's judgment about quality, value, authenticity, or other matters of judgment.

Comment

This instruction is modeled on section 538A of the *Restatement (Second) of Torts* (1977). *See Presidio Enter., Inc. v. Warner Bros. Dist. Corp.,* 784 F.2d 674 (5th Cir. 1986); *Vaughn v. Gen. Foods Corp.,* 797 F.2d 1403 (7th Cir. 1986), *cert. denied,* 479 U.S. 1087 (1987); *Taggert V. Ford Motor Credit Co.,* 462 N.W.2d 493 (S.D. 1990); *Cavic v. Grand Bahama Dev. Co., Ltd.,* 701 F.2d 879 (11th Cir. 1983). *Cf. Borba v. Thomas,* 138 Cal. Rptr. 565 (Cal. Ct. App. 1977); 37 Am. Jur. 2d *Fraud and Deceit* §§ 45–46 (1968). A statement of pure opinion is not intended to be a statement of fact and is, therefore, not generally actionable. A classic example is a salesperson's "puffing."

6.06[2][b] Representation of Opinion Implying Justifying Facts

A plaintiff may justifiably rely on a statement of opinion only if it concerns facts not disclosed and not otherwise known to the plaintiff, the plaintiff did not believe that the defendant had an interest adverse to plaintiff, and only if the statement reasonably may be interpreted as an implied statement

(1) that the facts known to the defendant are not inconsistant with the opinion represented; or

(2) that the defendant is aware of facts that support the opinion represented.

Comment

This instruction is modeled on section 539 of the *Restatement (Second) of Torts* (1977) and is an exception to the general rule relating to statements of opinions. The distinction is based upon the implication that facts exist to support the opinion or, at a minimum, that there are no facts incompatible with the statement. *See Restatement (Second) of Torts* § 539 cmt. a (1977). *Cf. Pub. Serv. Enter. Group, Inc. v. Philadelphia Elec. Co.,* 722 F. Supp. 184, 217 (D.N.J. 1989); *S. California Dist. Counsel v. Sheppard of Hills Evangelical Lutheran Church,* 144 Cal. Rptr. 46 (Cal. Ct. App. 1976); 37 Am. Jur. 2d *Fraud and Deceit* § 49 (1968).

6.06[2][c] Opinion of Adverse Party

A plaintiff is not justified in relying on a defendant's fraudulent misrepresentation solely of the defendant's opinion, unless the fact to which the opinion relates is material, and the defendant

(1) claims to have special knowledge of the matter that the plaintiff does not have; or

(2) stands in a fiduciary or similar relation of trust to the plaintiff; or

(3) has successfully attempted to secure the confidence of the plaintiff; or

(4) has a special reason to expect the plaintiff would rely on the defendant's opinion.

Comment

This instruction is modeled on section 542 of the *Restatement (Second) of Torts* (1977) and is an exception to the general rule relating to statements of opinions. *See Astor Chauffeured Limousine v. Runnfeldt Inv. Corp.*, 910 F.2d 1540 (7th Cir. 1990); *Kociemba v. G.D. Searle Co.*, 707 F. Supp. 1517, 1525 (D. Minn. 1989); *Koagel v. Ryan Homes, Inc.*, 562 N.Y.S.2d 312 (N.Y. App. Div. 1990); *Hall v. Edge*, 782 P.2d 122, 127 (Okla. 1989). *Cf. Walters v. First Fed. S&L Ass'n*, 641 P.2d 235 (Ariz. 1982); 37 Am. Jur. 2d *Fraud and Deceit* §§ 51–53 (1968). *But see Doherty v. S. College of Optometry*, 862 F.2d 570, 576 (6th Cir. 1988) (applying Tennessee law), *cert. denied*, 493 U.S. 810 (1989).

6.06[2][d] Opinion of Apparently Disinterested Person

(i) A plaintiff is justified in relying upon a fraudulent misrepresentation of opinion if the opinion is that of a person the plaintiff reasonably believes to be disinterested and the opinion is one on which a reasonable person would place reliance.

Comment

Instruction (i) is modeled on section 543 of the *Restatement (Second) of Torts* (1977) and is applicable to situations (1) in which the defendant has an interest adverse to the plaintiff in the transaction, (2) in which the defendant has an interest adverse to the plaintiff but purports to be disinterested, and (3) in which a party to a transaction misrepresents that an apparently disinterested person has expressed the opinion at issue (or has done an act from which the opinion may be implied). *See Restatement (Second) of Torts* § 543 cmt. a (1977); *Hanberry v. Hearst Corp.,* 81 Cal. Rptr. 519 (Cal. Ct. App. 1969). *See also Friedman v. Manfuso,* 620 F. Supp. 109, 115 (D.D.C. 1985) (court found plaintiff could not reasonably believe defendant was disinterested).

6.06[3] Plaintiff Not Required to Investigate

(i) A plaintiff has no duty to investigate the statement's truth or falsity and is justified in relying on a defendant's fraudulent misrepresentation although the plaintiff might have learned the falsity of the representation had the recipient investigated the misrepresentation.

or

(ii) The plaintiff has no duty to investigate the truth or falsity of the statement unless you find that the plaintiff had facts in plaintiff's possession sufficient to discover the falsity of the statement.

Comment

This instruction is modeled on section 540 of the *Restatement (Second) of Torts* (1977). *See Besett v. Barnett,* 389 So. 2d 995 (Fla. 1980). *Cf. Ashburn v. Miller,* 326 P.2d 229 (Cal. Ct. App. 1958); 37 Am. Jur. 2d *Fraud and Deceit* § 247 (1968). Some jurisdictions impose a duty to investigate, especially if there is reason to suspect that the statement is false. Instruction (ii) is modeled on this body of law. *See Mallis v. Bankers Trust Co.,* 615 F.2d 68 (2d Cir. 1980), *cert. denied,* 449 U.S. 1123 (1981); *K-B Trucking Co. v. Riss Int'l Corp.,* 763 F.2d 1148, 1158 (10th Cir. 1985); *Feak v. Marion Steam Shovel Co.,* 84 F.2d 670 (9th Cir. 1936).

6.06[4] Representation Known to Be or Obviously False

A plaintiff is not justified in relying on a fraudulent misrepresentation if the plaintiff knows the misrepresentation is false or it is obvious to the plaintiff that the misrepresentation is false.

Comment

This instruction is modeled on section 541 of the *Restatement (Second) of Torts* (1977). *See Sun Bank, N.A. v. E.F. Hutton & Co., Inc.*, 926 F.2d 1030 (11th Cir. 1991); *Phoenix Canada Oil Co., Ltd. v. Texaco, Inc.*, 749 F. Supp. 525 (S.D.N.Y. 1990); *Grimes v. Liberty Nat'l Life Ins. Co.*, 551 So. 2d 329 (Ala. 1989). *Cf. Letellier v. Small,* 400 A.2d 371 (Me. 1979); *Gross v. Sussex, Inc.,* 630 A.2d 1156 (Md. Ct. Spec. App. 1993); 37 Am. Jur. 2d *Fraud and Deceit* § 237 (1968). The second prong of this test may be at odds with the rationale advanced by those jurisdictions that rely on purely subjective tests on the issue of materiality. *See* § 6.05, cmt., *supra.*

6.06[5] Representation of Fact by Adverse Party

A plaintiff of a fraudulent misrepresentation may justifiably rely on the defendant's misrepresentation of fact even though the plaintiff believes or knows the defendant has an interest adverse to the plaintiff in the transaction.

Comment

This instruction is modeled on section 541A of the *Restatement (Second) of Torts* (1977). This instruction relates only to misrepresentation of fact by an adverse party. See the instructions in §§ 6.06[2][a]–6.06[2][d] for misrepresentations of opinion. *Williams v. Collins,* 600 P.2d 1235 (Or. Ct. App. 1979).

6.06[6] Statement of Intention

The plaintiff of a fraudulent misrepresentation of intention is justified in relying upon it if

(1) the existence of the intention is material; and

(2) the plaintiff has reason to believe that the defendant will carry out the intention.

Comment

This instruction is modeled on section 544 of the *Restatement (Second) of Torts* (1977). *See E&S Facilities, Inc. v. Precision Chipper Corp.*, 565 So. 2d 54 (Ala. 1990); *Travelodge Int'l, Inc. v. Eastern Ins., Inc.*, 382 So. 2d 789 (Fla. Dist. Ct. App. 1980); *Floyd v. Morgan*, 9 S.E.2d 717 (Ga. Ct. App. 1940); *McEvoy Travel Bureau, Inc. v. Norton Co.*, 563 N.E.2d 188 (Mass. 1990).

Generally, a defendant's misrepresentation of intent must be made without any intention of performing, or with a present intent not to perform, in accordance with the represented intention. *See Palmer v. Sante Fe Health Care Sys., Inc.*, 582 So. 2d 1234 (Fla. Dist. Ct. App. 1991). *Cf. Vance Peerson, Inc. v. Alexander*, 408 N.E.2d 782 (Ill. App. Ct. 1980); 37 Am. Jur. 2d *Fraud and Deceit* § 60 (1968).

6.06[7] Misrepresentations of Law

6.06[7][a] Misrepresentations of Law: Including Misrepresentation of Fact

A plaintiff is justified in relying upon a misrepresentation regarding a matter of law that includes, expressly or impliedly, a misrepresentation of fact, just as the plaintiff would be justified in relying upon any other misrepresentation of fact.

Comment

This instruction is modeled on section 545(1) of the *Restatement (Second) of Torts* (1977). *See Chino Elec., Inc. v. U.S. Fidelity & Guar. Co.,* 578 So. 2d 320 (Fla. Dist. Ct. App. 1991). *Cf. Pieh v. Fitton,* 211 N.W. 964 (Minn. 1927); *Sorenson v. Gardner,* 334 P.2d 471 (Or. 1959); 37 Am. Jur. 2d *Fraud and Deceit* § 77 (1968).

6.06[7][b] Misrepresentations of Law: Opinion about Legal Consequences

A plaintiff is not justified in relying upon a misrepresentation regarding a matter of law that misrepresents only the legal consequences of facts, just as the plaintiff would not be justified in relying upon any other representation of any other opinion.

Comment

This instruction is modeled on section 545(2) of the *Restatement (Second) of Torts* (1977). *See Elliot Megdal & Assoc. v. Hawaii Planning Mill,* 814 F. Supp. 898 (D. Haw. 1993); *Nagashima v. Busch,* 541 So. 2d 783 (Fla. Dist. Ct. App. 1989). *Cf.* 37 Am. Jur. 2d *Fraud and Deceit* § 74 (1968). A plaintiff is justified in relying upon statements regarding foreign law. *Restatement (Second) of Torts* § 545 cmt. e (1977).

6.06[8] Reliance on Truth of Misrepresentation

A defendant is not liable to a plaintiff who did not rely on the truth of the defendant's fraudulent misrepresentation but merely on the expectation that the defendant will be held liable in damages for the falsity of the misrepresentation.

Comment

This instruction is modeled on section 548 of the *Restatement (Second) of Torts* (1977) and articulates the principle that a plaintiff must rely on the truth of the misrepresentation that results in the action or inaction required to create a cause of action. The plaintiff is not entitled to recover if the plaintiff acts (or refrains from acting) based upon the expectation that the plaintiff will be compensated for the falsity of the misrepresentation, unless the plaintiff, in fact, believes in the truth of the misrepresentation. *Cf. State Farm Mut. Auto Ins. Co. v. Wall,* 222 A.2d 282 (N.J. Super. Ct. App. Div. 1965); 37 Am. Jur. 2d *Fraud and Deceit* § 226 (1968).

6.07 Plaintiff's Contributory Negligence

Even if you find that the plaintiff was negligent in relying on a fraudulent misrepresentation, the plaintiff may still recover damages from the defendant if the plaintiff was justified in relying on the misrepresentation.

Comment

This instruction is modeled on section 545A of the *Restatement (Second) of Torts* (1977). *See Hyma v. Lee,* 60 N.W.2d 920 (Mich. 1953); *Adam v. Steinbrecher,* 133 N.W. 477 (Minn. 1911). *Cf. Edwards v. Travelers Ins. Co.,* 563 F.2d 105 (6th Cir. 1977); 37 Am. Jur. 2d *Fraud and Deceit* § 384 (1968). As fraudulent misrepresentation is an intentional tort, the issue of the plaintiff's contributory negligence is irrelevant. The defendant can prevail only when a plaintiff knows the representation is false (or it is obviously false to plaintiff). *See* § 6.06[4], *supra.*

But see 37 Am. Jur. 2d *Fraud and Deceit* § 248 (1968) (plaintiff has some duty to exercise precaution to protect his or her interest).

6.08 Requirement That Fraudulent Misrepresentation Cause Damage

6.08[1] General Rule

For the plaintiff to recover from the defendant, the plaintiff must prove, by a preponderance of the evidence,

(1) that the plaintiff suffered some harm or damage as a result of plaintiff's reliance upon the defendant's fraudulent misrepresentation; and

(2) that the defendant's fraudulent misrepresentation was both the cause-in-fact and legal cause of plaintiff's damages.

Comment

Cf. Sedco Int'l, S.A. v. Cory, 683 F.2d 1201, 1208 (8th Cir.), *cert. denied,* 459 U.S. 1017 (1982); 37 Am. Jur. 2d *Fraud and Deceit* § 293 (1968).

6.08[2] Causation-in-Fact

You must determine whether defendant's alleged fraudulent misrepresentation was the cause-in-fact of plaintiff's damages. If you find that the plaintiff's reliance upon defendant's fraudulent misrepresentation was a substantial factor in determining the course of conduct that resulted in plaintiff's alleged loss, then causation-in-fact exists.

Comment

This instruction is modeled on section 546 of the *Restatement (Second) of Torts* (1977). *See Sult v. Bolenbach,* 327 P.2d 1023 (Ariz. 1958); *Sherban v. Richardson,* 445 So. 2d 1147 (Fla. Dist. Ct. App. 1984). *Cf. Anderson v. Hawdley,* 308 P.2d 368 (Cal. Dist. Ct. App. 1957); 37 Am. Jur. 2d *Fraud and Deceit* § 227 (1968). As with negligence instructions, some jurisdictions seem to be abandoning an instruction on cause-in-fact in favor of relying on an instruction for proximate or legal cause. *See* § 6.08[3], *infra.*

6.08[3] Legal Causation for Pecuniary Loss

You must determine whether defendant's alleged fraudulent misrepresentation was the legal cause of plaintiff's alleged damages. A fraudulent misrepresentation is a legal cause of damages resulting from action or inaction in reliance upon it if, but only if, the loss might reasonably be expected to result from the reliance.

Comment

This instruction is modeled on section 548A of the *Restatement (Second) of Torts* (1977). This instruction limits recoverable damages to those that compensate for a reasonably foreseeable loss. *See Boatman's Nat'l. Co. v. M.W. Elkins & Co., Inc.*, 63 F.2d 214 (8th Cir. 1933). *Cf. Day v. Avery*, 548 F.2d 1018 (D.C. Cir. 1976); 37 Am. Jur. 2d *Fraud and Deceit* §§ 227, 293 (1968).

6.08[4] Plaintiff Relying on Its Own Investigation

The defendant of a fraudulent misrepresentation is not liable if the plaintiff's decision to [engage in the transaction the representation was intended to induce] was the result of an independent investigation by the plaintiff rather than being caused by the plaintiff's belief that the defendant's representation was true, unless the defendant intentionally prevented the plaintiff's investigation from being effective.

Comment

This instruction is modeled on section 547 of the *Restatement (Second) of Torts* (1977). *See Carpenter v. Hamilton,* 62 P.2d 1397 (Cal. Ct. App. 1936); *Czarnecki v. Roller,* 726 F. Supp. 832 (S.D. Fla. 1989). *Cf. Peterson Indus., Inc. v. Lakeview Trust & Savings Bank* 584 F.2d 166 (7th Cir. 1978); 37 Am. Jur. 2d *Fraud and Deceit* § 237 (1968).

6.09 Damages for Fraudulent Misrepresentation

6.09[1] General Rule

If you find for plaintiff and against defendant, the next issue for your determination is the amount, if any, of plaintiff's damages.

Two kinds of damages can be considered in this case. They are compensatory damages and punitive damages.

Compensatory damages will consist of the plaintiff's direct economic losses and out-of-pocket expenses resulting from the defendant's conduct.

Punitive damages will consist of the amount awarded by you, if any, not as compensation to the plaintiff for wrong done, but as punishment to the defendant and as a deterrent to others.

Comment

In an action for fraudulent misrepresentation, the plaintiff may generally be awarded compensatory and punitive damages. Some states, however, prohibit or restrict the award of punitive damages. *Cf.* 37 Am. Jur. 2d *Fraud and Deceit* § 342 (1968).

6.09[2] Compensatory Damages

6.09[2][a] Compensatory Damages: Nonbusiness Transaction

A plaintiff of a fraudulent misrepresentation is entitled to recover from the defendant, as damages, any monetary loss caused by the defendant's fraudulent misrepresentation. This amount includes the difference between the value of what was received by the plaintiff in the transaction and its purchase price or other value given for it by the plaintiff. The plaintiff is also entitled to recover other monetary loss suffered as a result of the plaintiff's reliance upon the fraudulent misrepresentation.

Comment

This instruction is modeled on section 549 of the *Restatement (Second) of Torts* (1977). *See Gregg v. U.S. Indus., Inc.,* 887 F.2d 1462 (11th Cir. 1989); *Zimpel v. Trawick,* 679 F. Supp. 1502 (W. D. Ark. 1988); *Martin v. Brown,* 566 So. 2d 890 (Fla. Dist. Ct. App. 1990). *Cf. Steinberg v. Carey,* 470 F. Supp. 471 (S.D.N.Y. 1978); 37 Am. Jur. 2d *Fraud and Deceit* § 342 (1968).

6.09[2][b] Compensatory Damages: Additional Damages for Business Transaction

In addition to the damages just described, the plaintiff of a fraudulent misrepresentation in a business transaction is also entitled to recover damages sufficient to give plaintiff the benefit of plaintiff's contract or bargain with the defendant, if these damages are proved with reasonable certainty.

Comment

This instruction is modeled on section 549 of the *Restatement (Second) of Torts* (1977) and Graham Douthwaite, *Jury Instruction on Damages in Tort Actions* 622 at § 15-2 (2d ed. 1988), and states the principle that the plaintiff in a business transaction is entitled to recover plaintiff's expectancy damages in addition to plaintiff's reliance damages. Note that these damages are subject to the limiting requirement that they be proved with reasonable certainty. Note further that damage awards must be foreseeable. *See* § 6.08[3], *supra*. *Cf. Osofsky v. Zipf*, 645 F.2d 107 (2d Cir. 1981); *Bates v. Allied Mut. Ins. Co.*, 467 N.W.2d 255, 260 (Iowa 1991); 37 Am. Jur. 2d *Fraud and Deceit* § 345 (1968).

6.09[3] Punitive Damages

If you find for plaintiff and against defendant, you may consider whether, in the circumstances of this case, it is appropriate to award punitive damages, in addition to compensatory damages, as punishment to the defendant and as a deterrent to others.

Comment

As a general rule, punitive damages may be assessed in fraudulent misrepresentation cases. *Cf.* 37 Am. Jur. 2d *Fraud and Deceit* § 347 (1968). *See Nader v. Allegheny Airlines, Inc.,* 445 F. Supp. 168, 178 (D.D.C. 1978); *Zimpel v. Trawick,* 679 F. Supp. 1502 (W.D. Ark. 1988); *Delahanty v. First Pennsylvania Bank,* 464 A.2d 1243 (Pa. Super. Ct. 1983). The rules surrounding punitive damages vary among the jurisdictions. The practitioner should be aware that some jurisdictions require an award of nominal compensatory damages before punitive damages may be assessed. Some jurisdictions require evidence of the net worth of the defendant to be introduced. Finally, some jurisdictions limit punitive damage awards by rule or statute.

6.10 Negligent Misrepresentation

6.10[1] Elements of Liability

In this case, plaintiff seeks to recover money damages from the defendant for what plaintiff claims to be a negligent misrepresentation made by the defendant. To find liability for negligent misrepresentation, you, the jury, must find from a preponderance of the evidence, all of the following:

(1) that the defendant supplied false information when guiding the plaintiff or others in its or their business transactions;

(2) that the defendant failed to exercise reasonable care or competence in obtaining or communicating information in the course of business or any other transaction in which defendant had a monetary interest;

(3) that the defendant intended the information to influence plaintiff or knew that a recipient intended to supply the information to plaintiff and the information influenced plaintiff's conduct;

(4) that the plaintiff's loss resulted from plaintiff's reliance on defendant's misrepresentation and plaintiff's reliance was justifiable; and

(5) that the defendant's misrepresentation caused plaintiff pecuniary loss.

Comment

This instruction is modeled on section 552 of the *Restatement (Second) of Torts* (1977). Some jurisdictions hold negligent representations actionable as fraudulent representations. *See First Union Discount Brokerage Servs., Inc. v. Milos,* 744 F. Supp. 1145 (S.D. Fla. 1990); *Kent v. Bartlett,* 122 Cal. Rptr. 615 (Cal. Ct. App. 1975). *See also* 37 Am. Jur. 2d *Fraud and Deceit* § 209 (1968).

6.10[2] Scope of Liability

6.10[2][a] Persons Who Receive Information

A defendant's liability is limited to the loss suffered

(1) by the person or one of a limited group of persons for whose guidance the defendant intended to supply the information or to whom the defendant knows that the plaintiff intended to supply the information; and

(2) through reliance upon the information in a transaction that the defendant intends the information to influence, or knows the plaintiff intends the information to influence, or in a substantially similar transaction.

Comment

This instruction is modeled on section 552 of the *Restatement (Second) of Torts* (1977) and subjects a supplier of negligent misrepresentations to liability only to those for whose benefit and guidance the information is supplied. As such, the defendant's liability is narrowed from that of a defendant of a fraudulent misrepresentation, who is liable to any person the defendant had reason to believe would act in reliance upon the fraudulent misrepresentation. *See Restatement (Second) of Torts* § 552 cmt. a (1977). *See also Granberg v. Turnham,* 333 P.2d 423 (Cal. Ct. App. 1958); *MacKowm v. Illinois Pub. & Printing Co.,* 6 N.E.2d 526 (Ill. App. Ct. 1937); *Doyle v. Chatham & Phenix Nat'l Bank,* 171 N.E. 574 (N.Y. 1930). *Cf.* 37 Am. Jur. 2d *Fraud and Deceit* § 194 (1968).

6.10[2][b] Public Duty to Provide Information

The defendant of a negligent misrepresentation who is under a public duty to give the information is liable to any members of the class for whose benefit the duty is created in any of the transactions in which the duty is intended to protect them.

Comment

This instruction is modeled on section 552 of the *Restatement (Second) of Torts* (1977). *See Mulroy v. Wright,* 240 N.W. 116 (Minn. 1931). *Cf.* 37 Am. Jur. 2d *Fraud and Deceit* § 194 (1968).

6.10[3] Damages

6.10[3][a] General Rule

If you find for plaintiff and against defendant, the next issue for your determination is the amount, if any, of plaintiff's damages. The damages recoverable for a negligent misrepresentation are those necessary to compensate the plaintiff for the monetary loss for which the misrepresentation is a legal cause, including

(1) the difference between the value of what plaintiff has received in the transaction and its purchase price or other value given for it; and

(2) monetary loss suffered otherwise as a consequence of the plaintiff's reliance upon the misrepresentation.

Comment

This instruction is modeled on section 552B of the *Restatement (Second) of Torts* (1977). *See Williams v. Spazier,* 21 P.2d 470 (Cal. Ct. App. 1933); *Doyle v. Chatham & Phenix Nat'l Bank,* 171 N.E. 574 (N.Y. 1930). *Cf.* 37 Am. Jur. 2d *Fraud and Deceit* §§ 220, 355 (1968).

6.10[3][b] Benefit of Bargain

In determining the amount, if any, of plaintiff's damages, you are instructed that plaintiff is not entitled to be awarded damages to compensate plaintiff for the benefit of plaintiff's contract or bargain with the defendant.

Comment

This instruction is modeled on section 552B of the *Restatement (Second) of Torts* (1977). *See Banker's Trust Co. v. Steenburn*, 409 N.Y.S.2d 51 (N.Y. 1978). However, some courts have allowed a plaintiff to recover for the benefit of its bargain. *Cf.* 37 Am. Jur. 2d *Fraud and Deceit* §§ 220, 353 (1968). In these jurisdictions, the following instructions should be given: "[T]o give the plaintiff the benefit of his contract or bargain with the defendant, you should award the difference in the value between what the plaintiff actually received and what he was fraudulently led to believe he would receive. Your award should put the plaintiff in the position he would have enjoyed if the misrepresentation relied upon had been true." Graham Douthwaite, *Jury Instructions on Damages in Tort Actions* 662 at § 15-2 (2d ed. 1988).

6.10[4] Plaintiff's Contributory Negligence

A plaintiff of a negligent misrepresentation cannot recover for any monetary loss suffered from relying on this misrepresentation if the plaintiff contributed to plaintiff's own loss by being negligent in relying on this misrepresentation.

Comment

This instruction is modeled on section 552A of the *Restatement (Second) of Torts* (1977). As set forth in § 6.07, a plaintiff's contributory negligence is not a defense to an action for fraudulent misrepresentation in most jurisdictions. (But see the exception contained in the comment to § 6.07.) However, the defense is available when the defendant is sued for negligence. *See Sedco Int'l S.A. v. Cory,* 552 F. Supp. 254 (S.D. Iowa 1981). *Cf.* 37 Am. Jur. 2d *Fraud and Deceit* § 209 (1968).

The instruction as drafted articulates the absolute ban to recovery caused by a plaintiff's contributory negligence. For those jurisdictions that have adopted comparative negligence standards, see the instruction in § 6.10[5].

6.10[5] Plaintiff's Comparative Negligence

If you find that the losses suffered by the plaintiff were the result of a combination of both the negligence of the defendant and the negligence of the plaintiff, then you must first determine the total amount of damages. You should decide the portion of these damages for which the plaintiff is responsible and the portion for which the defendant should be held responsible. Then you reduce the total amount of the plaintiff's damages by the portion attributable to the plaintiff, and award damages for the remaining total.

Comment

This instruction should be used for jurisdictions that have adopted comparative negligence standards and, for those jurisdictions, should be used in place of the instruction in § 6.10[4]. This instruction is modeled on Graham Douthwaite, *Jury Instructions on Damages in Tort Actions* 204 at § 5-8 (2d ed. 1988).

6.11 Innocent Misrepresentation

6.11[1] Elements of Liability

In this case, plaintiff seeks to recover money damages from the defendant for what plaintiff claims to be an innocent misrepresentation made by the defendant. To find liability for innocent misrepresentation, you, the jury, must find, by a preponderance of the evidence all of the following:

(1) that defendant, in a sale, rental, or exchange with plaintiff, made a misrepresentation of material fact that was not made fraudulently or negligently;

(2) that the misrepresentation of material fact was made for the purpose of causing or influencing the plaintiff to act or refrain from acting in reliance upon the misrepresentation;

(3) that plaintiff acted or refrained from acting in justifiable reliance on defendant's misrepresentation; and

(4) that plaintiff incurred a monetary loss.

Comment

This instruction is based on section 552C of the *Restatement (Second) of Torts* (1977). *See Lanning v. Sprague*, 227 P.2d 347 (Idaho 1951); *Wilson v. Jones*, 45 S.W.2d 572 (Tex. Comm. App. 1932). *Cf.* 37 Am. Jur. 2d *Fraud and Deceit* § 220 (1968). Materiality is defined in § 6.05, and justifiable reliance is defined in § 6.06[1].

6.11[2] Damages

If you find for plaintiff and against defendant, the next issue for your determination is the amount, if any, of plaintiff's damages. The damages recoverable for an innocent misrepresentation are the difference between the value of what plaintiff has parted with and the value of what plaintiff has received in the transaction.

Comment

This instruction is modeled on section 552C of the *Restatement (Second) of Torts* (1977). *See Anzalone v. Strand,* 436 N.E.2d 960 (Mass. App. Ct. 1982); *Aldrich v. Scribner,* 117 N.W. 581 (Mich. 1908). However, some courts have held that although innocent misrepresentations are sufficient for rescission, such misrepresentations cannot support an award of money damages. *Sheridan Drive-in, Inc. v. State,* 228 N.Y.S.2d 576 (N.Y. App. Div. 1962). *Cf. Union Bank v. Jones,* 411 A.2d 1338, 1342 (Vt. 1980); 37 Am. Jur. 2d *Fraud and Deceit* § 221 (1968).

6.12 Fraudulent Concealment

6.12[1] Elements of Liability

In this case, plaintiff seeks to recover money damages from the defendant because plaintiff claims defendant fraudulently concealed information from plaintiff. To find liability for fraudulent concealment, you, the jury, must find by a preponderance of the evidence

(1) that defendant, as a party to a transaction with plaintiff, intended to prevent plaintiff from acquiring material information;
(2) that defendant, by concealment or other action, intentionally prevented plaintiff from acquiring material information;
(3) that plaintiff was prevented from acquiring this material information by defendant's actions; and
(4) that as a result plaintiff suffered pecuniary loss.

Comment

This instruction is modeled on section 550 of the *Restatement (Second) of Torts* (1977). *See Ortho Pharmaceutical Corp. v. Sona Distribs., Inc.*, 663 F. Supp. 64 (S.D. Fla. 1987); *Russow v. Bobola,* 277 N.E.2d 769 (Ill. App. Ct. 1972). *Cf.* 37 Am. Jur. 2d *Fraud and Deceit* §§ 144, 216 (1968).

6.12[2] Damages

The plaintiff is entitled to recover as damages from the defendant the plaintiff's monetary loss caused by the defendant's fraudulent concealment. This amount includes the difference between the value of what has been received by plaintiff in the transaction and the value given for it by plaintiff. The plaintiff is also entitled to recover other monetary loss suffered as a result of plaintiff's reliance upon the fraudulent concealment.

Comment

The damages for fraudulent concealment are the same as those for fraudulent misrepresentation. *See King v. O'Reilly Motor Co.,* 494 P.2d 718 (Ariz. Ct. App. 1972); *Ollerman v. O'Rourke Co., Inc.,* 288 N.W.2d 95 (Wis. 1980). *Cf.* 37 Am. Jur. 2d *Fraud and Deceit* §§ 144, 216 (1968).

6.13 Fraudulent Nondisclosure

6.13[1] Elements of Liability

In this case, plaintiff seeks to recover money damages from the defendant because plaintiff claims defendant fraudulently failed to disclose information to plaintiff. To find liability for fraudulent nondisclosure, you, the jury, must find by a preponderance of the evidence

(1) that the defendant failed to disclose to plaintiff a fact the defendant knew might justifiably induce the plaintiff to act or refrain from acting in a business transaction;

(2) that the defendant was under a duty to plaintiff to exercise reasonable care to disclose the matter in question;

(3) that plaintiff relied on defendant's nondisclosure, which reliance influenced plaintiff's conduct concerning the business transaction;

(4) that plaintiff's reliance on defendant's nondisclosure was justifiable; and

(5) that defendant's nondisclosure caused plaintiff pecuniary loss.

Comment

This instruction is modeled on section 551 of the *Restatement (Second) of Torts* (1977). *See Chiarella v. United States,* 445 U.S. 222 (1980); *Everman Nat'l Bank v. United States,* 756 F.2d 865 (Fed. Cir. 1985); *Laventhall v. Gen. Dynamics Corp.,* 704 F.2d 407 (8th Cir. 1983); In re *Cifilia,* 124 B.R. 124 (Bankr. M.D. Fla. 1991). *Cf.* 37 Am. Jur. 2d *Fraud and Deceit* § 145 (1968).

6.13[2] Duty

In determining whether defendant was under a duty to plaintiff to exercise reasonable care to disclose the matter in question, you are instructed that the defendant, as one party to a business transaction, is under a duty to exercise reasonable care to disclose the following to plaintiff, before the transaction is consummated:

(1) matters known to defendant that plaintiff is entitled to know because of a fiduciary or other relationship of trust between them; and

(2) matters defendant knew to be necessary to prevent defendant's ambiguous statement from being misleading; and

(3) subsequently acquired information that defendant knew would make untrue or misleading a previous representation that when made was true or believed to be so; and

(4) the falsity of a representation not made with the expectation that plaintiff would act upon it if defendant subsequently learned that the plaintiff was to act in reliance upon it in a transaction with defendant; and

(5) facts (a) basic to the transaction that defendant knew plaintiff was about to enter into, under a mistake between them, and (b) that the plaintiff, because of the relationship between plaintiff and defendant, would have reasonably expected to be disclosed.

Comment

This instruction is modeled on section 551 of the *Restatement (Second) of Torts* (1977). *See Riggs Nat'l Bank of Washington, D.C. v. Freeman*, 682 F. Supp. 519 (S.D. Fla. 1988); *Wolf v. Brungardt*, 524 P.2d 726 (Kan. 1974); *Dennis v. Thomson*, 43 S.W.2d 18 (Ky. Ct. App. 1931). *Cf.* 37 Am. Jur. 2d *Fraud and Deceit* § 146 (1968).

6.13[3] Damages

The plaintiff is entitled to recover as damages from the defendant the plaintiff's monetary loss that was caused by defendant's fraudulent nondisclosure. This amount includes the difference between value of what has been received by plaintiff in the transaction and the value given for it by plaintiff. The plaintiff is also entitled to recover other monetary loss suffered as a result of plaintiff's reliance upon the fraudulent nondisclosure.

Comment

The damages for fraudulent nondisclosure are the same as those for fraudulent misrepresentation. *See Bruschi v. Brown,* 876 F.2d 1526 (11th Cir. 1989); *Newman v. Corn Exch. Nat'l Bank & Trust Co.,* 51 A.2d 759 (Pa. 1947). *Cf.* 37 Am. Jur. 2d *Fraud and Deceit* § 146 (1968).

Chapter Seven

Breach of Fiduciary Duties

7.01 Introduction

Robert E. Schaberg, Jack N. Sibley, and Edward Henderson, Jr.

The model jury charges in this chapter are for use in cases involving a breach of fiduciary duties. A cause of action for breach of fiduciary duty, like most commercial torts, requires a showing of duty, breach of duty, causation, and damage. For a comprehensive discussion of each of these elements (duty, breach, causation, damages), see Robert A. Kutcher & Benjamin W. Bronston, *Business Torts Litigation* ch. II (ABA, 1992).

Fiduciary relationships may arise as a matter of law by statute, contract, conduct, or confidential relationship. To determine whether a fiduciary duty exists, the trial court may need to make a factual inquiry regarding any proof of a confidential relationship. For example, section 23-2-58 of the Georgia Code defines confidential relations in the state of Georgia as follows:

> Any relationship shall be deemed confidential, whether arising from nature, created by law, or resulting from contracts, where one party is so situated as to exercise a controlling influence over the will, conduct, and interest of another or where, from a similar relationship of mutual confidence, the law requires the utmost good faith, such as the relationship between partners, principal and agent, etc.

Ga. Code Ann. § 23-2-58 (1982). Consequently, the factual circumstances of a particular case may indicate that any of a number of fiduciary duties has arisen. These duties include the duty of care, duty of loyalty, duty to account, duty of confidentiality, duty of full disclosure, duty to act fairly, and duty of good faith and fidelity.

The following model jury instructions deal with particular fiduciary duties that have been recognized in a commercial context. The model jury instructions that relate to corporate fiduciary duties may also apply, in certain circumstances, to the other fiduciary relationships.

7.02 Corporate Fiduciary Duties

You are instructed that corporate officers, directors, and controlling shareholders owe a fiduciary duty to the corporation and noncontrolling shareholders. As officers and directors of [corporation], defendants owed that corporation and its shareholders fiduciary duties. Defendants were required to discharge the duties of their respective positions in good faith and with that degree of diligence, care, loyalty, and skill that ordinarily prudent persons would exercise under similar circumstances in like positions. In this case, it is alleged that defendants breached their duty of care and duty of loyalty.

I shall now give you general instructions on the law concerning the duty of care, the duty of loyalty, and the business judgment rule.

Comment

It is settled law that corporate officers and directors occupy a fiduciary relationship with the corporation and its shareholders, and are held to the standard of utmost good faith and loyalty. *See* Marshall L. Small, "Transactions in Control and Tender Offers," 1 American Law Institute, *Principles of Corporate Governance: Analysis and Recommendations* pt. IV (1994); *Corporate Director's Guidebook,* 33 Bus. Law. 1591, 1599–1600 (1978); *Jones v. H.F. Ahmanson & Co.,* 460 P.2d 464 (Cal. 1969) (duty of majority shareholder to minority shareholder); *King Mfg. Co. v. Clay,* 118 S.E.2d 581 (Ga. 1961). *See also Quinn v. Cardiovascular Physicians, P.C.,* 326 S.E.2d 460 (Ga. 1985). For a discussion of the duties of care and loyalty and the business opportunity principle, see *Southeast Consultants, Inc. v. McCrary Engineering Corp.,* 273 S.E.2d 112 (Ga. 1980). *See also* Ga. Code Ann. § 14-2-851 (1989) (corporation may indemnify directors for actions taken in good faith).

7.03 The Business Judgment Rule

Officers and directors enjoy a presumption of sound business judgment. This presumption includes an assumption that the officers and directors acted on an informed basis.

You are instructed that a director or officer, to fulfill the requisite duty of care, must

(1) not have an undisclosed personal financial interest in the transaction that is the subject of the director's or officer's business judgment;
(2) be informed about the subject of the business judgment to the extent the director or officer believes to be appropriate under the circumstances, and such belief must be rational; and
(3) rationally believe that the director's or officer's business judgment is in the best interest of the corporation.

Plaintiffs, who are challenging the conduct of the officers or directors of [corporation], must prove that the officers or directors did not exercise the proper business judgment. Consequently, you must find that the defendants fulfilled their duty of care unless plaintiffs prove (a) that an officer or director had an undisclosed personal financial interest in the transaction that is the subject of the officer's or director's business judgment, or (b) that the officer or director was not informed about the subject of the business judgment to the extent the officer or director reasonably believed to be appropriate under the circumstances, or (c) that the officer or director did not rationally believe that such business judgment was in the best interest of the corporation, or (d) that no business judgment was in fact exercised.

If you find that defendant [corporation] exercised the proper business judgment, then you should find for the defendants and your inquiry is complete. If, however, you find that defendants did not exercise sound business judgment, then you should next consider whether defendants breached the duty of care.

Comment

Most courts agree that the business judgment rule extends only as far as the reasons that justify its existence, and that it does not apply when the corporate decision lacks a business purpose, involves a conflict of interest, or results from a prolonged failure to exercise oversight or judgment. Marshall L. Small, "Transaction in Control and Tender Offers," 1 American Law Institute, *Principles of Corporate Governance* pt. IV, § 4.01(c) (1994). *See Joy v. North,* 692 F.2d 880 (2d Cir. 1982), *cert. denied sub nom. Citytrust v. Joy,* 460 U.S. 1051 (1983); *but see Cramer v. Gen. Tel. & Elec. Corp.* 582 F.2d 259, 274 (3d Cir. 1978) (rationale for business judgment rule is that for corporation to be managed properly and efficiently, directors must be given wide latitude in handling of corporate affairs), *cert. denied,* 439 U.S. 1129 (1979); *Panter v. Marshall Field & Co.,* 646 F.2d 271, 294 (7th Cir.) (argument that directors have improper interest in alleged transactions because they would have to initiate suit against themselves raises no legally cognizable issue under Delaware corporate law), *cert. denied,* 454 U.S. 1092 (1981); *Tabas v. Mullane,* 608 F. Supp. 759, 766 (D.N.J. 1985) (Delaware law); *AC Acquisitions Corp. v. Anderson, Clayton & Co.,* 519 A.2d 103, 111 (Del. 1986). *See also* 1 American Law Institute, *Principles of Corporate Governance* pt. IV, § 4.01(d) cmt. f (1994); *Treadway Cos., Inc. v. Care Corp.,* 638 F.2d 357, 382 (2d Cir. 1980) (under New Jersey law, corporate director possesses same right as other shareholders to deal freely with personally owned shares of stock, provided director acts in good faith); *First Nat'l Bank of Lincolnwood v. Keller,* 318 F. Supp. 339, 347–49 (N.D. Ill. 1970); S. Samuel Arsnt, *The Business Judgment Rule Revisited,* 8 Hofstra L. Rev. 93, 130–33 (1979). A majority of states have adopted the Model Business Corporation Act (MBCA). Section 8.30 of the MBCA further defines a corporate director's or officer's duty of care and the business judgment rule.

7.04 Existence of Fiduciary Duty

7.04[1] Statutory Elements of Fiduciary Duty

You are instructed that a fiduciary relationship exists between two persons when one of them is under a duty to act for, or to give advice for, the benefit of the other upon matters within the scope of the relation. The duties that arise under such a relationship include the following: duty of care, duty of loyalty, duty to account, duty of confidentiality, duty of full disclosure, duty to act fairly, and duty of good faith and fidelity. A fiduciary who breaches any one of these duties as a fiduciary is guilty of tortious conduct to the person for whom the fiduciary should act.

When, as here, the plaintiff alleges a breach of fiduciary duty, you must answer the following four questions:

(1) Did a fiduciary relationship exist at the time of the alleged misconduct?
(2) If so, what was the scope of this fiduciary relationship?
(3) Are the duties within the scope of the relationship?
(4) Did defendants' acts constitute a breach of one or more of these duties?

It is for you to determine whether a fiduciary relationship existed between defendant [name] and plaintiff [name] at the time of the alleged misconduct. If you determine that such a relationship did exist, you must next determine the scope of this relationship. Then you must determine whether one or more of the duties listed above arose within the scope of the relationship, and whether defendant's conduct constituted a breach of one or more of these duties.

If you find that a fiduciary relationship existed between defendant [name] and plaintiff [name], and that defendant's conduct constituted a breach of one or more duties that arose within the scope of the relationship, then the plaintiff is entitled to a verdict for breach of fiduciary duty. You must then determine what damages, if any, were proximately caused by such acts or omissions that constituted the breach of duty.

However, if you should find that no fiduciary relationship existed at the time of the alleged misconduct, or that even in the presence of such relationship, the defendant's conduct did not constitute a breach of a duty arising within the scope of the relationship, then you must find for the defendant.

Comment

Local rules of procedure, the type of relation between the parties, and the intricacy of the transaction involved determine whether the beneficiary is entitled to redress at law or in equity. Section 874 of the *Restatement (Second) of Torts* (1979) provides a basic discussion of the existence of fiduciary duties and redress of breaches of such duties at law and in equity. *See also Restatement (Second) of Torts* § 2 (1959).

7.04[2] Nonstatutory Fiduciary Duties

You are instructed that although fiduciary duties often arise by statute (such as those between partner and partnership or administrator and heir), fiduciary duties also may arise under contractual relationships (such as those between principal and agent or lawyer and client).

A fiduciary duty of a contractual nature may be shown by the conduct of the parties or the existence of a confidential relationship between the parties. Indications of such a relationship include the following: the acting of one person for another, the having and the exercising of influence over one person by another, the reposing of confidence by one person in another, the dominance of one person by another, the inequality between the parties, or the dependence of one person upon another. Further considerations include weakness of age, mental strength, business intelligence, knowledge of the facts involved, or other conditions giving one party an advantage over the other.

You are instructed that in the absence of express contractual terms creating a fiduciary duty, such a duty may be inferred when one or more of the above-listed incidents of conduct is present. When one party places trust and confidence in a second party with that second party's knowledge, it is possible that a fiduciary relationship exists between the two parties.

I will now instruct you on the particular duty alleged by plaintiff to exist between plaintiff and defendant in this case.

Comment

For examples of nonstatutory fiduciary relationships created by conduct, see *Anderson v. Reynolds*, 588 F. Supp. 814 (D.C. Nev. 1984) (agreement to handle real estate transaction created fiduciary duty); *Matter of Vietri Homes, Inc.*, 58 B.R. 663 (Bankr. Del. 1986) (fiduciary confidence); and *Hofstetter v. Fletcher*, 905 F.2d 897 (6th Cir. 1988) (under Ohio law, de facto fiduciary relationship may result from confidential relationship, and existence of such relationship is question of fact to be determined by jury). *See also Riggs Nat'l Bank of Washington D.C. v. Freeman,* 682 F. Supp. 519 (S.D. Fla. 1988); *Craig v. First Am. Capital Resources, Inc.,* 740 F. Supp. 530 (N.D. Ill. 1990); *but see McClure v. Duggan,* 674 F. Supp. 211 (N.D. Tex. 1987); *Marriott Bros. v. Gage,* 704 F. Supp. 731 (N.D. Tex. 1988) ("subjective trust . . . cannot convert what would otherwise be arms-length dealing into a fiduciary relationship"), *aff'd,* 911 F.2d 1105 (5th Cir. 1990).

7.05 Duty of Due Care

7.05[1] Generally

Officers and directors of corporations have a duty to those corporations to perform their functions in good faith, in a manner they reasonably believe to be in the best interest of their corporations, and with the care that ordinarily prudent persons would reasonably be expected to exercise in a like position and under similar circumstances. This duty is the duty of care.

Plaintiffs have the burden of proving that defendants did not act with reasonable care in performing their functions and, unless you find plaintiffs have met that burden, no breach of the duty of care can be found.

Upon considering the instructions I have just given you on the duty of care, you must decide whether defendants, through their acts or omissions, breached their duty of care to one or more of the plaintiffs. If you do not find that defendants breached their duty of care, then they did not breach their fiduciary duty to plaintiffs, and are not liable for any losses that any of the plaintiffs may have suffered.

Comment

"Although the specific wording of court decisions has varied, they have long required a director or officer to be attentive to the functions and obligations of his position and to make inquiry when the circumstances would alert a reasonable director or officer to the need therefor." Marshall L. Small, "Transactions in Control and Offers," 1 American Law Institute, *Principles of Corporate Governance* pt. IV cmt., § 4.01 (a)(1)–(a)(2) (1994); *see also Briggs v. Spaulding,* 141 U.S. 132, 152 (1891); *Fitzpatrick v. Fed. Deposit Ins. Corp.,* 765 F.2d 569 (6th Cir. 1985). "Sound public policy dictates that directors and officers be given greater protection than courts and commentators using a 'reasonableness' test would afford." Marshall L. Small, "Transactions in Control and Offers," 1 American Law Institute, *Principles of Corporate Governance* pt. IV cmt. f, § 4.01(c) (1994); *First Nat'l Bank of Lincolnwood v. Keller,* 318

F. Supp. 339, 347–49 (N.D. Ill. 1970). For a detailed discussion of a corporate fiduciary's duty of good faith, see *Quinn v. Cardiovascular Physicians, P.C.*, 326 S.E.2d 460 (Ga. 1985). *See also Miller v. Miller*, 222 N.W.2d 71 (Minn. 1974) (discussion of business opportunity rule).

7.05[2] The Officer's Functions

Plaintiffs and defendants have submitted conflicting evidence concerning the functions of defendants.

An officer's or director's functions are those corporate tasks that the officer or director is responsible for performing.

In this case, to decide whether a defendant has performed the requisite functions in a manner consistent with defendant's duty of care, you must first decide, from the evidence submitted, what functions a particular defendant was responsible for performing.

Comment

The issue about whether an officer or director should have been alerted to peculiar circumstances necessarily revolves around the "functions" or duties that typically are ascribed to that officer or director. Marshall L. Small, "Transactions in Control and Tender Offers," 1 American Law Institute, *Principles of Corporate Governance* pt. IV cmt. b, § 4.01(a) (1)–(a)(2) (1994). *See Hoye v. Meek,* 795 F.2d 893, 896 (10th Cir. 1986) ("[D]irectors and officers are charged with knowledge of those things which it is their duty to know and ignorance is not a basis for escaping liability. Where suspicions are aroused, or should be aroused, it is the directors' duty to make necessary inquiries."); *see also Francis v. United Jersey Bank,* 432 A.2d 814, 822 (N.J. 1981) ("directors are under a continuing obligation to keep informed about the activities of the corporation").

7.05[3] "In a Like Position" Defined

For purposes of analyzing the duty of care, the phrase "in a like position" is intended to emphasize that the critical time for the assessment of the performance of an officer or director is the time of the alleged breach of duty. That is, you are to assess an officer's or director's performance as of the time of the alleged act, omission, or failure of oversight. You are not to use the benefit of hindsight in evaluating a director's or officer's performance.

Comment

"Among the factors that may have to be taken into account in judging a director's reasonable belief as to what was 'appropriate under the circumstances' are: (i) the importance of the business judgment to be made; (ii) the time available for obtaining information; (iii) the costs related to obtaining information; (iv) the director's confidence in those who explored a matter and those making presentations; and (v) the state of the corporation's business at the time and the nature of competing demands for the board's attention." Marshall L. Small, "Transactions in Control and Tender Offers," 1 American Law Institute, *Principles of Corporate Governance* pt. IV cmt., § 4.01 (a) (1994); *see also Harman v. Willbern*, 374 F. Supp. 1149, 1163 (D. Kan. 1974); *McRoberts v. Spaulding*, 32 F.2d 315, 317 (S.D. Iowa 1929); 3A William M. Fletcher, *Cyclopedia of Corporations* § 1030, at 18 (perm. ed. 1975).

7.05[4] "Under Similar Circumstances" Defined

As I stated earlier, an officer or director has a duty to perform requisite functions with the care that an ordinarily prudent person would reasonably be expected to exercise in a like position and under similar circumstances.

The phrase "under similar circumstances" recognizes that the nature and extent of the functions and obligations of an officer or director will vary depending upon such factors as the nature of the business, the urgency and magnitude of a problem, and the corporation's size and complexity. In deciding whether defendants have acted with the care that an ordinarily prudent person would reasonably be expected to exercise in a like position, you should take these circumstances into account.

Comment

A director or officer, once put on alert, will fail to make a reasonable inquiry if such director or officer does not believe that an adequate inquiry has been made or if the director or officer is unreasonable in believing such officer or director has made all the inquiry that is necessary. Marshall L. Small, "Transactions in Control and Tender Offers," 1 American Law Institute, *Principles of Corporate Governance* pt. IV cmt. b, § 4.01(a)(1)–(a)(2) (1994); *see also Briggs v. Spaulding,* 141 U.S. 132, 137 (1891); *McRoberts v. Spaulding,* 32 F.2d 315, 317 (D. Iowa 1929); *Fed. Deposit Ins. Corp. v. Boone,* 361 F. Supp. 133, 166 (W.D. Okla. 1972).

7.05[5] Sense of Balance and Fairness

The standards set forth in the duty of care should be applied with balance, fairness, and a realistic sense of what may reasonably be expected in given circumstances from a corporation's officers and directors. Your judgment about whether a given officer or director exercised the requisite care when the officer or director is charged with an act, an omission, or a failure of oversight should take into account all relevant circumstances. These may include

(1) whether the problem that allegedly developed because of the claimed act, omission, or failure of oversight was reasonably foreseeable at the time of the alleged act, omission, or failure of oversight;

(2) whether the magnitude of the problem that developed was reasonably foreseeable at the time of the alleged act, omission, or failure of oversight;

(3) the state of the corporation's business at the time of the alleged act, omission, or failure of oversight;

(4) the state of the economy or areas of the economy at the time of the alleged act, omission, or failure of oversight;

(5) the policies of regulatory authorities at the time of the alleged act, omission, or failure of oversight;

(6) the complexity and scale of the corporation at the time of the alleged act, omission, or failure of oversight;

(7) the policies of the board of directors and committees of the board at the time of the alleged act, omission, or failure of oversight;

(8) the reliability of, and confidence to be placed in, other directors, officers, employees, experts, and other persons and committees of the board; and

(9) the precise role the officer or director played within the corporation at the time of the alleged act, omission, or failure of oversight.

Comment

See § 7.06[1], cmt.; Marshall L. Small, "Transactions in Control and Tender Offers," 1 American Law Institute, *Principles of Corporate Governance* pt. IV cmt. h, § 4.01(a) (1994); *McRoberts v. Spaulding,* 32 F.2d 315, 316–17 (S.D. Iowa 1929).

7.06 Factors Determining Breach of Duty of Care

7.06[1] Custom, Practice, and Procedures

In determining whether an officer or director of a corporation breached the requisite duty of care, it is proper for you to consider the custom, practice, and procedures of similar corporations.

Comment

For example, under Oklahoma law, custom and usage of similar banks are properly considered by the trier of fact in determining duties of bank directors. *Fed. Deposit Ins. Corp. v. Boone,* 361 F. Supp. 133, 166 (W.D. Okla. 1972); *see also McRoberts v. Spaulding,* 32 F.2d 315 (S.D. Iowa 1928); *Wheeler v. Aiken County Loan & Sav. Bank,* 75 F. 781, 784 (D.S.C. 1896).

7.06[2] Duty to Supervise

An officer's or director's duty of care to the corporation includes the duty to use reasonable care in supervising other officers and employees over whom the officer or director has supervisory responsibility.

A director or officer is not an insurer of the fidelity and proper conduct of other directors, officers, and employees, and a director or officer is not liable for losses resulting from the wrongful acts or omissions of such persons, provided the director or officer has exercised ordinary care in discharging the director's or officer's own duties by exercising reasonable supervision over such persons and using reasonable care in their appointment.

Comment

See Fields v. Sax, 462 N.E.2d 983, 988 (Ill. App. Ct. 1989) (citing *Briggs v. Spaulding,* 141 U.S. 132 (1891)); *Francis v. United Jersey Bank,* 392 A.2d 1233 (N.J. Super. Ct. Law Div. 1978), *aff'd,* 432 A.2d 814 (N.J. 1981); 3A William M. Fletcher, *Cyclopedia of the Law of Private Corporations* §§ 1066, 1070 (1986).

7.06[3] Reliance on Subordinates and Delegation

Officers and directors are entitled to rely upon the honesty and integrity of their subordinates until something occurs to put them on notice that something is wrong.

It is also not a breach of duty for an officer or director to delegate responsibility to other officers or directors whose general business insight was confirmed by past service and reputation and when there was no reason to suspect them of mismanagement or wrongdoing.

Comment

See Harman v. Willbern, 374 F. Supp. 1149, 1164 (D. Kan. 1974), *aff'd,* 520 F.2d. 1333 (10th Cir. 1975); *Graham v. Allis-Chalmers Mfg. Co.,* 188 A.2d 125 (Del. 1963).

7.06[4] Reliance on Information Prepared by Others

In performing the required duty and functions, an officer or director who acts in good faith and reasonably believes that such reliance is warranted is entitled to rely on information, opinions, reports, and statements (including financial statements and other financial data), as well as decisions, judgments, or performance, prepared, presented, made, or performed by

(1) one or more directors, officers, or employees of the corporation, whom the director or officer reasonably believes merits confidence; or

(2) lawyers, public accountants, engineers, appraisers, or other persons whom the director or officer reasonably believes merit confidence.

Comment

"A right to rely is authorized by either legislative provisions or by court decisions in almost all jurisdictions." Marshall L. Small, "Transactions in Control and Tender Offers," 1 American Law Institute, *Principles of Corporate Governance* pt. IV cmt., § 4.02 (1994). *See also Graham v. Allis-Chalmers Mfg. Co.,* 188 A.2d 125 (Del. 1963); *Harman v. Willbern,* 374 F. Supp. 1149, 1164 (D. Kan. 1974), *aff'd,* 520 F.2d 1333 (10th Cir. 1975).

7.06[5] No Higher Standard of Care for Financial Institutions

Officers and directors of a financial institution do not owe a higher standard of care than do officers and directors of other corporations. Rather, the duty of care applicable to any officer or director must be determined individually in light of the position of the individual and the surrounding circumstances.

Comment

Marshall L. Small, "Transactions in Control and Tender Offers," 1 American Law Institute, *Principles of Corporate Governance* pt. IV cmt., § 4.01(a), n. 18 (citing *McDonnell v. Am. Leduc Petroleums Ltd.*, 491 F.2d 380, 383 (2d Cir. 1974)). The savings and loan crisis and the passage of the Financial Institution Reform, Recovery and Enforcement Act of 1989 (FIRREA) have resulted in a number of lawsuits by the Federal Deposit Insurance Corporation/Resolution Trust Corporation (FDIC/RTC) against officers and directors of failed savings and loans for breach of fiduciary duty. This instruction is important to establish that those officers and directors are not held to a higher standard than other corporate fiduciaries. The question is whether FIRREA claims for breach of fiduciary duty are controlled by a simple negligence or gross negligence standard. *Compare Fed. Deposit Ins. Corp. v. Canfield*, 967 F.2d 443 (10th Cir. 1992) (simple negligence standard), *cert. dismissed*, 113 S. Ct. 516 (1992) (en banc) *Fed. Deposit Ins. Corp. v. McSweeney*, 976 F.2d 532, 537–38 (9th Cir. 1992), *cert. denied*, 61 U.S. 3803 (1993); *Fed. Deposit Ins. Corp. v. Howse*, 892 F. Supp. 1554, 1568 (S.D. Tex. 1992). Other decisions support a gross negligence standard. *See Gaff v. Fed. Deposit Ins. Corp.*, 919 F.2d 384, 390–91 (6th Cir. 1990); *Fed. Deposit Ins. Corp. v. Swager*, 773 F. Supp. 1244, 1248 (D. Minn. 1991). For cases that find different standards for federal and state courts, see *Resolution Trust Corp. v. Gallagher*, 800 F. Supp. 595, 602 (N.D. Ill. 1992), and *Fed. Deposit Ins. Corp. v. Isham*, 777 F. Supp. 828, 832 (D. Colo. 1991).

7.06[6] Violation of Regulations of Governmental Agencies

A violation of the regulations of a governmental agency, does not, in and of itself, make a director or officer liable for any losses sustained by the corporation. Although conduct that violates a regulation may be considered, your decision about whether a defendant breached such duty must be based on all facts and the entire circumstances in the case as you shall find them.

Comment

See Lester v. John R. Jurgensen Co., 400 F.2d 393, 395–96 (6th Cir. 1968) (Ohio law); *Restatement (Second) of Torts* § 286 cmt. d, § 288 cmts. b, c (1965). Oftentimes officers and directors are charged with violating a rule or regulation of a governmental agency and the plaintiff argues that such a violation constitutes "negligence per se" and hence a breach of fiduciary duty. This instruction is meant to advise the jury that such conduct alone is not enough to find a breach of fiduciary duty.

7.06[7] Violation of Internal Policies

A violation of the corporation's internal rules and regulations with regard to policy and procedure does not, without more, make a director or officer liable for losses sustained by the corporation. The law imposes liability for lack of diligence in the conduct of the officer's or director's duties; however, it does not make him or her an insurer of the success of all ventures merely because corporate procedures are ignored.

Comment

First Nat'l Bank of Lincolnwood v. Keller, 318 F. Supp. 339, 347 (N.D. Ill. 1970) (citing *Hoehn v. Crews,* 144 F.2d 665, 673 (10th Cir. 1944), *aff'd. sub nom. Garber v. Crews,* 324 U.S. 200 (1945)). As with governmental rules and regulations, the FDIC/RTC often argues that the mere violation of an internal policy or procedure is sufficient to establish a breach of fiduciary duty. This instruction is meant to advise the jury that such conduct alone is not enough to find a breach of fiduciary duty. *See also Larimore v. Comptroller of Currency,* 789 F.2d 1244 (7th Cir. 1986); *but see Cache Nat'l Bank v. Hinman,* 626 F. Supp. 1341 (D. Colo. 1986) (directors who fail to investigate acceptance of loans may be held responsible for loss as having committed intentional violation of National Bank Act, 12 U.S.C. § 93).

7.06[8] Concluding Instruction on the Duty of Care

In light of the instructions I have just given you on the duty of care, you should decide whether a defendant, through actions or omissions, breached the duty of care to the corporation. Unless you find that a defendant breached the duty of care, the defendant did not breach such fiduciary duty to the plaintiff and is not liable for any losses that the plaintiff may have suffered.

Comment

About thirty-seven states have now enacted duty-of-care statutory provisions. Common law is the source of duty-of-care standards in about thirteen states. *See First Nat'l Bank of Lincolnwood v. Keller,* 318 F. Supp. 339 (N.D. Ill. 1970); *Hoyle v. Meek,* 795 F.2d 893 (10th Cir. 1986); *Hanson Trust PLC v. ML SCM Acquisition, Inc.,* 781 F.2d 264 (2d Cir. 1986).

7.07 Fiduciary Duty of Loyalty

The second fiduciary duty defendants owed [corporation] was the duty of loyalty. Defendants owed a duty of undivided and unqualified loyalty to [corporation]. The duty of loyalty means essentially that fiduciaries such as the defendants may not put their own personal interests ahead of those of [corporation]—neither in their dealings with [corporation] nor in their dealings with others. Those defendants were required as a result of this duty of loyalty to exercise the utmost good faith in furthering the interests of [corporation] and conserving its property.

Comment

Norlin Corp. v. Rooney, Pace, Inc., 744 F.2d 255, 264 (2d Cir. 1984); *Gearhart Indus. v. Smith Int'l, Inc.*, 741 F.2d 707, 719 (5th Cir. 1984); *Horwitz v. Southwest Forest Indus., Inc.*, 604 F. Supp. 1130, 1134 (D. Nev. 1985); *Jones v. H.F. Ahmanson & Co.*, 460 P.2d 464 (Cal. 1969); 3 William M. Fletcher, *Cyclopedia of the Law of Private Corporations* § 838 (rev. perm. ed. 1986).

7.08 Causation—Generally

If you find that any defendant breached a fiduciary duty to the plaintiff, you should then decide whether that breach proximately caused any losses claimed by the plaintiff.

I shall now instruct you on the law and burden of proof regarding proximate cause.

Comment

Restatement (Second) of Torts §§ 431, 432, 442B (1965); Marshall L. Small, "Transactions in Control and Tender Offers," 2 American Law Institute, *Principles of Corporate Governance* pt. VII, § 7.18 (1994); *see also Michelsen, et al. v. Penney, et al.,* 135 F.2d 409, 436 (2d Cir. 1943) (in suit against bank director for bank loss occasioned by director's negligence in violation of National Bank Act, act presented standard of care required, which was controlling test of negligence and provided for remuneration of those who suffered loss); *Pierce v. Lyman,* 3 Cal. Rptr. 2d 236 (Cal. Ct. App. 1991) (limiting elements of breach of fiduciary duty claim).

7.08[1] Elements of Causation and Burden of Proof

To find a defendant liable for breach of fiduciary duty, the breach must have caused plaintiff some damage. A defendant's breach is the cause of damage only when (1) the plaintiff has sustained or will sustain a loss of some type, (2) the defendant's act or omission was the cause-in-fact of the loss sustained, and (3) the defendant's act or omission was the legal cause of the loss sustained. Plaintiff bears the burden of proving all three of these elements.

Comment

See William L. Prosser, *Law of Torts* § 41, at 238 (4th ed. 1971); *Restatement (Second) of Torts* §§ 431, 432, 442B cmt. b; 1 Marshall L. Small, "Transactions in Control and Tender Offers," American Law Institute, *Principles of Corporate Governance* pt. VII cmt. d, § 7.18 (1994). *See also Anderson v. Akers,* 7 F. Supp. 924, 928 (W.D. Ky. 1934) (burden of proof rests on plaintiff). *See generally* Edward Brodsky & M. Patricia Adamski, *Law of Corporate Officers and Directors,* § 2.13 (1984). *See also Hanson Trust, PLC v. ML SCM Acquisition, Inc.,* 781 F.2d 264 (2d Cir. 1986).

7.08[2] Cause-in-Fact

You are instructed that cause-in-fact is the second element of proving causation in a breach of fiduciary duty case. This element requires plaintiffs to prove not only that they have suffered some loss, but also that such loss could have been avoided if the defendants had performed their duties as required by the duty of care.

You must weigh the evidence presented by both sides and decide whether plaintiffs have met their burden of proving that the loss could have been prevented if the defendants had performed their duties properly. If the defendants could not have prevented the losses, then they are not liable for those losses.

Comment

William L. Prosser, *Law of Torts* § 41, at 238 (4th ed. 1971); Marshall L. Small, "Transactions in Control and Tender Offers," 2 American Law Insitute, *Principles of Corporate Governance* pt. VII cmt. d, § 7.18 (1994), *see also Briggs v. Spaulding,* 141 U.S. 132 (1891); *Barnes v. Andrews,* 298 F. 614, 617 (D.N.Y. 1924); *Francis v. United Jersey Bank,* 432 A.2d 814, 826–29 (N.J. 1981).

7.08[3] Negligence—Defined

Negligence is the doing of some act that a reasonably prudent person would not do, or the failure to do something that a reasonably prudent person would do, when prompted by considerations that ordinarily regulate the conduct of human affairs. It is, in other words, the failure to use ordinary care, under the circumstances, in the management of one's person or property, or of agencies under one's control.

Comment

3 Devitt, Blackmar & Wolff, *Federal Jury Practice and Instructions* § 80.03 (1987); *Fane v. Zimmer, Inc.*, 927 F.2d 124 (2d Cir. 1991) (negligence is conduct that falls below standard of what reasonably prudent person would do under similar circumstances, judged at time of conduct at issue); *see also Needham v. White Lab., Inc.*, 847 F.2d 355 (7th Cir. 1988) (negligence is failure to take level of precautions commensurate with likelihood of magnitude of risk created by defendant's conduct; the greater the benefits of precaution, the more precautions must be taken).

7.08[4] Legal Cause

If you find that plaintiffs have proved the existence of damages and cause-in-fact, then you must decide whether plaintiffs have proved that defendants' acts or omissions were the "legal cause" of plaintiffs' injuries or losses. The issue you must decide under this element is whether the relationship between the defendants' acts or omissions and the losses sustained by plaintiffs is sufficiently close to attribute the losses to the defendants. Plaintiffs must prove two things to show legal cause: (1) that the defendants' acts or omissions were substantial factors in bringing about the loss, and (2) that the likelihood of injury would have been foreseeable to persons in the defendants' positions under similar circumstances.

You must weigh the evidence and decide whether defendants' acts or omissions were substantial factors in bringing about the losses and, if so, whether the losses sustained were reasonably foreseeable to persons in the defendants' positions. If you find that plaintiffs have not proven both elements, there can be no liability for any losses that may have been sustained by plaintiffs, and you must find for the defendants.

Comment

Marshall L. Small, "Transactions in Control and Tender Offers," 2 American Law Institute, *Principles of Corporate Governance* pt. VII cmt. d, § 7.18 (1994); *Restatement (Second) of Torts* §§ 431, 432 (1965); William L. Prosser, *Law of Torts* § 41, at 240 (4th ed. 1971); *see, e.g., E.F. Hutton Mortgage Corp. v. Pappas,* 690 F. Supp. 1465, 1473–75 (D. Md. 1988) (applying Maryland law); *Anderson v. Akers,* 7 F. Supp. 924, 946 (W.D. Ky. 1934); *Francis v. United Jersey Bank,* 432 A.2d 814, 826–29 (N.J. 1981) (applying New Jersey law).

7.08[5] "Foreseeable" Defined

Something is said to be foreseeable when it can be seen or known in advance; in other words, when it is reasonable to anticipate that something is a likely result of an act, omission, or failure of oversight. The law requires you to consider foreseeability because a person is not responsible for a consequence that is merely possible. A person is responsible only for a consequence that is probable according to ordinary and usual experience.

Comment

Black's Law Dictionary 332 (abridged 5th ed. 1983); William L. Prosser, *Law of Torts* § 41 (4th ed. 1971).

7.08[6] Unforeseeable Events

Unforeseen and unforeseeable events may include events beyond those attributable to the actions of a person or an entity. These may include

(1) the state of the economy or areas of the economy;
(2) changes in a particular industry;
(3) disruptions in a business that are attributable to causes outside the control of the defendant; and
(4) acts of nature.

Comment

See Raines v. Colt Indus., Inc., 757 F. Supp. 819 (E.D. Mich. 1991) (unforeseeable intervening cause breaks chain of causation and constitutes superseding cause that leaves alleged tortfeasor free of liability); *Restatement (Second) of Torts* §§ 440, 442 (1965). *But see T.M. Doyle Teaming Co., Inc. v. Freels,* 735 F. Supp. 777 (N.D. Ill. 1990) (intervening agency not sole proximate cause of injury if circumstances surrounding intervention were such as could reasonably have been expected to occur in ordinary course of events as indicated by common experience).

7.08[7] Plaintiffs' Negligence as a Superseding Cause

From the evidence presented, you must decide whether plaintiffs' conduct was negligent and, if so, whether that negligence was the immediate cause of any losses. If you so find, then defendants are relieved of liability unless

(1) at the time of the defendants' conduct defendants realized or should have realized that plaintiffs might act as they did; or that

(2) a reasonable person knowing the situation existing at the time of the conduct of the plaintiffs would not have regarded their conduct as highly extraordinary; or that

(3) the conduct of the plaintiffs was not extraordinarily negligent and was a normal consequence of the situation created by the defendants.

Comment

See Restatement (Second) of Torts §§ 442–53 (1977); *Fed. Deposit Ins. Corp. v. Blue Rock Shopping Ctr., Inc.*, 766 F.2d 744 (3d Cir. 1985); *E.F. Hutton Mortgage Corp. v. Pappas*, 690 F. Supp. 1465 (D. Md. 1988); *Fed. Deposit Ins. Corp. v. Carter*, 701 F. Supp. 730 (C.D. Cal. 1987); *but see Fed. Deposit Ins. Corp. v. Baker*, 739 F. Supp. 1401, 1406–07 (C.D. Cal. 1990) (criticizing *Carter* and dismissing defendants' affirmative defenses alleging contributory negligence by FDIC).

7.08[8] Third Party's Intentionally Tortious Act as a Superseding Cause

The act of a third person in committing an intentional tort or a crime can be a superseding cause that relieves a defendant of liability. This is true even when the defendant's conduct created a situation that afforded the third person an opportunity to commit such a tort or crime, unless the defendant realized or should have realized at the time of such conduct the likelihood that such a situation might be created and that a third person might avail himself or herself of the opportunity to commit such a tort or crime. From the instructions I will now give you on the elements of [crime or intentional tort alleged], you must decide whether any act of a third person relieves defendants of liability.

Comment

"For example, a defendant could allege that the fraud of certain borrowers and lead lenders was a superseding cause and thereby relieves the defendant of liability." This instruction is based on section 448 of the *Restatement (Second) of Torts* (1965). *See Fed. Deposit Ins. Corp. v. Imperial Bank,* 859 F.2d 101, 103 (9th Cir. 1988) (applying California law); *E.F. Hutton Mortgage Corp. v. Pappas,* 690 F. Supp. 1465 (D. Md. 1988).

7.08[9] Existence of Damage

An act, even if wrongful, may or may not cause an injury and if it causes no injury, there can be no liability. Consequently, plaintiffs must prove that they have suffered or will suffer such injury to recover damages. Otherwise there can be no liability for breach of a fiduciary duty, and you must find for the defendants.

Comment

See Marshall L. Small, "Transations in Control and Tender Offers," 2 American Law Insitute, *Principles of Corporate Governance* pt. VII cmts. a–e, § 7.18 (1994); *see also First Nat'l Bank of Lincolnwood v. Keller,* 318 F. Supp. 339, 348 (N.D. Ill. 1970); *Barnes v. Andrews,* 298 F. 614 (S.D.N.Y. 1924); *Francis v. United Jersey Bank,* 432 A.2d 814, 826 (N.J. 1981); *Kahle v. Mt. Vernon Trust Co.,* 22 N.Y.S.2d 454 (N.Y. Sup. Ct. 1940).

7.09 Damages—Generally

I will next instruct you on damages. You must not take these instructions as implying my view about which party is entitled to your verdict in this case. Instructions regarding the measure of damages are given for your guidance in the event you find in favor of plaintiffs from a preponderance of evidence in the case in accordance with the other instructions.

Comment

Bray v. Safeway Stores, Inc., 392 F. Supp. 851, 866 (N.D. Cal. 1975).

7.09[1] Compensatory Damages

If, under the Court's instructions, you find that the plaintiffs are entitled to a verdict against a defendant or defendants, then you may award plaintiffs damages in an amount that will reasonably compensate them for their losses, provided you find that such loss was or will be suffered by them and was proximately caused by the act or omission upon which you base the defendants' liability.

Comment

Marshall L. Small, "Transactions in Control and Tender Offers," 2 American Law Institute, *Principles of Corporate Governance* pt. VII cmts. a–e, § 7.18 (1994); 3 William M. Fletcher, *Cyclopedia of the Law of Private Corporations* § 838 (1994). *See, e.g., Lincoln Nat'l Life Ins. Co. v. NCR Corp.,* 603 F. Supp. 1393 (N.D. Ind. 1984), (to recover damages, plaintiffs have burden of proving they suffered damages), *aff'd,* 772 F.2d 315 (7th Cir. 1985); *Tom Shaw, Inc. v. Derektor,* 639 F. Supp. 1064 (D.R.I. 1986) (apart from issue of liability, to recover in negligence action plaintiff has burden of proving damages by fair preponderance of the evidence and damages are not to be presumed).

7.09[2] Reasonable Damages Not Speculative

Damages must be reasonable. If you find that the plaintiffs are entitled to a verdict, you may award them only the amount of damages necessary to compensate them reasonably for any losses caused by the defendants' alleged breach of duty. The plaintiffs must prove by a preponderance of the evidence that such losses were sustained as a proximate result of the alleged breach of duty.

You are not permitted to award speculative damages. This means that you may not include any compensation in the verdict for any prospective loss that, although possible, is not reasonably certain to happen in the future. From the evidence presented, you must decide what losses are reasonably certain to occur and you may award damages for those losses only.

Comment

See Johnson v. Miller, 596 F. Supp. 768 (D.C. Colo. 1984); *see also Far W. Fed. Bank, S.B. v. Director, Office of Thrift Supervision*, 787 F. Supp. 952 (D. Or. 1992).

7.09[3] Duty to Mitigate

Any person who claims damages as a result of an alleged wrongful act on the part of another has a duty under the law to "mitigate" those damages. This means that the person allegedly harmed must take advantage of any reasonable opportunity the person allegedly harmed may have had under the circumstances to reduce or minimize the loss or damage.

If you find that plaintiff, to minimize plaintiff's loss, failed to seek out or take advantage of opportunities that were reasonably available to plaintiff under the circumstances, then you must reduce the amount of plaintiff's damages by the amount the plaintiff could have reasonably gained if plaintiff had taken advantage of such opportunity. The defendant bears the burden of proving that plaintiff failed to mitigate plaintiff's damages.

Comment

See Bloomfield Fin. Co. v. Nat'l Home Life Assurance Co., 734 F.2d 1408 (10th Cir. 1984); *see also William Z. Salcer, Panfeld, Edelman v. Envicon Equities Corp.*, 744 F.2d 935 (2d Cir. 1984) (limited partners' recisionary damages reduced by tax benefits received from losses arising from general partners' alleged fraud); *but see Fed. Deposit Ins. Corp. v. Baker*, 739 F. Supp. 1401, 1407 (C.D. Cal. 1990) (holding regulators owed duty to public and not to defendant directors, officers, and outside appraisers of state-chartered, federally insured savings and loan).

7.09[4] Damages Not Apportioned

Even if you find that plaintiffs are entitled to recover damages against more than one defendant, you must return a verdict in a single sum against all defendants you find to be liable. That is, there is only one loss to plaintiffs and correspondingly only one damage award. Therefore, even if you find more than one defendant liable, you are not to divide the damages among the defendants. Rather, you must return one damage award against all those you find liable.

Comment

See 3 William M. Fletcher, *Cyclopedia of the Law of Private Corporations* § 1002, at 716 (perm. ed. 1994).

7.09[5] Punitive Damages

In addition to compensatory damages, you are allowed by law to award plaintiffs punitive damages. The purpose of such damages is to punish the wrongdoer for extraordinary misconduct, and to deter that wrongdoer or any wrongdoer from repeating similar conduct.

If you determine from a preponderance of the evidence that the plaintiffs are entitled to a verdict for actual or compensatory damages, and you further determine that the defendants' acts or omissions that proximately caused damage to the plaintiffs were malicious or wanton, you may add to the award of actual damages against the defendants such punitive or exemplary damages as you deem proper. Malicious or wanton acts or omissions are those that indicate a total disregard or indifference to the consequences.

Factors you may consider in awarding punitive damages include

(1) the character of the defendants' acts;
(2) the nature and extent of harm to the plaintiffs that the defendants caused or intended to cause; and
(3) the defendants' wealth.

Comment

See AMPAT/Midwest, Inc. v. Illinois Tool Works, Inc., 896 F.2d 1035 (7th Cir. 1990); *Fed. Deposit Ins. Corp. v. W.R. Grace & Co.*, 877 F.2d 614 (7th Cir. 1989), *cert. denied*, 110 S. Ct. 1524 (1990); *Aldrich v. Thomson McKinnon Sec., Inc.*, 756 F.2d 243 (2d Cir. 1985); *Bennett v. E.F. Hutton Co., Inc.*, 597 F. Supp. 1547 (D. Ohio 1984).

7.10 Partnerships

You are instructed that any partnership agreement includes, as a matter of law, an agreement for each partner to act in the utmost good faith toward the other partner or partners. This provision requires that partners deal fairly with each other, with the partnership and, if applicable, with limited partners, or else they are subject to liability for breach of fiduciary duty.

In this case, a partnership relationship existed between the defendant [name] and the plaintiff [name]. It is for you to determine whether the defendant violated defendant's fiduciary duty to deal fairly and honestly with defendant's partner [name], the plaintiff. If you find that the defendant breached such fiduciary duty as the plaintiff's partner, you must determine what damage, if any, was proximately caused by such acts or omissions that constituted the breach of partnership fiduciary duty.

If you find that the plaintiff is entitled to a verdict, you may award the plaintiff only such damages as will reasonably compensate for such injury and damage as you find, from a preponderance of the evidence in the case, that the plaintiff has sustained as a proximate result of the acts of the defendant.

Comment

For a discussion of partnership fiduciary duties, see *Allen v. Sanders,* 337 S.E.2d 428 (Ga. Ct. App. 1985); and *Crosby v. Rogers,* 30 S.E.2d 248 (Ga. 1944). *See also* Ga. Code Ann. § 23-2-58 (1982). For additional support see *Latta v. Kilbourn,* 150 U.S. 524, 541 (1893); *Meinhard v. Salmon,* 164 N.E. 545, 546 (N.Y. 1928); *Main v. Merrill, Lynch, Pierce, Fenner & Smith, Inc.,* 136 Cal. Rptr. 378 (Cal. Ct. App. 1977); *Yeomans v. Lysfjord,* 327 P.2d 957 (Cal. Ct. App. 1958).

7.10[1] General Partner, Limited Partners

You are instructed that partners, as a matter of law, stand in a fiduciary relationship to one another. Furthermore, in a limited partnership, a general partner, having exclusive power and authority to control and manage the partnership, owes the limited partners an even greater duty than is normally imposed.

You are instructed further that partners generally have a duty to render true and full information of all things affecting the partnership, and to account to the partnership for any benefit, derived by one partner without consent of the other partners, from any transactions connected with the conduct of the partnership.

In this case, the defendant [name] is a general partner in the [name of limited partnership], and plaintiff [name] is a limited partner in that partnership.

It is for you to determine, whether defendant [name], as general partner having exclusive power and authority to control and manage the partnership, breached defendant's duty to render true and full information of all things affecting the partnership or defendant's duty to account fully to the partnership for any benefits derived by defendant.

If you find that defendant as general partner breached defendant's duties to plaintiff as a limited partner, you must determine what damages, if any, were proximately caused by such acts or omissions that constituted the breach of duty.

If you should find that the plaintiff is entitled to a verdict, you may award the plaintiff only such damages as will reasonably compensate for such injury and damage as you find, from the preponderance of the evidence in the case, that plaintiff has sustained as a proximate result of the acts of the defendant.

Comment

For a detailed discussion of the fiduciary duty of a general partner to limited partners, see *Palmer v. Fuqua*, 641 F.2d 1146

(5th Cir. 1981); *Loft v. Lapidus*, 936 F.2d 633 (1st Cir. 1991); *Fleck v. Cablevision VII, Inc.*, 763 F. Supp. 622 (D.D.C. 1991); *Balabanos v. North American Investment Group, Ltd.*, 708 F. Supp. 1488 (N.D. Ill. 1988); and *Dymm v. Cahill*, 730 F. Supp. 1245 (S.D.N.Y. 1990).

7.11 Trustee

You are instructed that, as a matter of law, a trustee owes certain duties to the beneficiaries of a trust. In this case, the defendant was a trustee of a trust and plaintiff was a beneficiary of that trust. Among the duties owed by a trustee are the duty to administer the trust solely in the interests of the beneficiaries; the duty of full disclosure of material facts by the trustee when dealing on beneficiary's account; the duty to keep and render clear and accurate accounts of the administration of the trust; and the duty to take reasonable steps to take, to keep control of, and to preserve the trust property.

A trustee must discharge these duties in good faith and with that degree of diligence, care, and skill that ordinarily prudent persons would exercise under similar circumstances in a like position.

It is for you to determine whether the defendant, as trustee, violated its fiduciary duty to exercise that degree of diligence, care, and skill that ordinarily prudent persons would exercise in dealing with the beneficiaries' property held in trust.

If you find that the defendant breached its duties as trustee for the plaintiff, you must determine what damages, if any, were proximately caused by such acts or omissions that constituted the breach of fiduciary duty.

If you should find that the plaintiff is entitled to a verdict, you may award the plaintiff only such damages as will reasonably compensate for such injury and damage as you find, from a preponderance of the evidence in the case, that plaintiff has sustained as a proximate result of the acts of the defendant.

Comment

For a discussion of corporate trustee duties, see *Smith v. Hawks,* 355 S.E.2d 669 (Ga. Ct. App. 1987). *See also* Ga. Code Ann. § 7-1-310 (1989); *Himel v. Continental Illinois Nat'l Bank & Trust Co. of Chicago,* 596 F.2d 205 (7th Cir. 1979).

7.12 Estate Representatives

You are instructed that fiduciary duties are imposed on estate representatives upon appointment by the probate court. An estate representative has a fiduciary relationship with the heirs of the estate, and the representative must act fairly and make full disclosure of all actions taken in connection with estate assets. In this case, the defendant was the estate representative for the estate of [name], and owed a fiduciary duty to the plaintiff, a beneficiary.

This fiduciary relationship imposed a duty on the defendant, as estate representative, to discharge defendant's duties in good faith and with that degree of diligence, care, and skill that ordinarily prudent persons would exercise under similar circumstances in like positions. It is for you to determine whether the defendant, as estate representative, violated such fiduciary duty to act prudently.

If you find that the defendant breached such fiduciary duty as estate representative, you must determine what damages, if any, were proximately caused by such acts or omissions that constituted the breach of duty.

If you should find that the plaintiff is entitled to a verdict, you may award the plaintiff only such damages as will reasonably compensate for such injury or damage as you find, from a preponderance of the evidence in the case, that the plaintiff has sustained as a proximate result of the acts of the defendant.

Comment

For a discussion of fiduciary duties of estate representatives, see *In re Harrison,* 335 S.E.2d 564 (Ga. 1985).

7.13 Agency

You are instructed that a fiduciary relationship exists between a principal and an agent. In this case, the defendant was the agent of plaintiff, the principal.

The fiduciary relationship imposes a duty on an agent that the agent, within the limits of the agency, deal fairly and honestly with its principal and imposes the responsibility to disclose any conflicts between the principal's interest and the agent's interest that might make the agent act in its own best interest at the expense or to the detriment of the principal.

It is for you to determine whether the defendant, as agent, violated its fiduciary duties to deal fairly and honestly with the plaintiff, or to disclose to the plaintiff its relationship with [third party, with potential conflict of interest]. However, the defendant had no duty to disclose matters within the knowledge of the plaintiff.

If you find that the defendant, as a fiduciary, breached its duties as an agent for the plaintiff, you must determine what damages, if any, were proximately caused by such acts or omissions that constituted the breach of duty.

If you should find that the plaintiff is entitled to a verdict, you may award the plaintiff only such damages as will reasonably compensate for such injury or damage as you find, from a preponderance of the evidence in the case, that plaintiff has sustained as a proximate result of the acts of the defendant.

Comment

Agency relationships with their related fiduciary duties, can be created by contract, conduct, and confidential relationships. *See, e.g., Clyde Chester Realty Co. v. Stansell,* 259 S.E.2d 639 (Ga. Ct. App. 1979); *Youngblood v. Mock,* 238 S.E.2d 250 (Ga. Ct. App. 1977). *See also European Bakers, Ltd. v. Holman,* 338 S.E.2d 702 (Ga. Ct. App. 1985); *Scott v. Lumpkin,* 264 S.E.2d

514 (Ga. Ct. App. 1980); *L.A. Draper & Son, Inc. v. Wheelabrator-Frye, Inc.,* 813 F.2d 332 (11th Cir. 1987); *Gerdes v. Estate of Cush,* 953 F.2d 201 (5th Cir. 1992); *Apollo Technologies Corp. v. Centrosphere Indus. Corp.,* 805 F. Supp. 1157 (D.N.J. 1992); *Pierce v. Lyman,* 3 Cal. Rptr. 2d 236 (Cal. Ct. App. 1991).

7.14 Stockbrokers

You are instructed that a broker's duty to account to its customer is fiduciary in nature, resulting in an obligation to exercise the utmost good faith. This requirement of good faith demands that the broker make known to its customer all material facts that concern the transactions and subject matter of the broker-customer relationship.

It is for you to determine whether the defendant, as stockbroker, violated its fiduciary duty to deal fairly and honestly with the customer, or to act in the utmost good faith.

If you find that the defendant breached its duties as a stockbroker for the plaintiff customer, you must determine what damages, if any, were proximately caused by such acts or omissions that constituted the breach of duty.

If you should find that the plaintiff is entitled to a verdict, you may award the plaintiff only such damages as will reasonably compensate for such injury or damage as you find, from a preponderance of the evidence in the case, that plaintiff has sustained as a proximate result of the acts of the defendant.

Comment

For a full discussion of broker-customer relationships and fiduciary duties, see *Tigner v. Shearson-Lehman Hutton, Inc.*, 411 S.E.2d 800 (Ga. Ct. App. 1991); *Minor v. E.F. Hutton & Co., Inc.*, 409 S.E.2d 262 (Ga. Ct. App. 1991); *E.F. Hutton & Co., Inc. v. Weeks*, 304 S.E.2d 420 (Ga. Ct. App. 1983); *Aldrich v. Thomson McKinnon Securities, Inc.*, 756 F.2d 243 (2d Cir. 1985); and *Bennett v. E.F. Hutton Co., Inc.*, 597 F. Supp. 1547 (D. Ohio 1984).

7.15 Lawyer, Client

You are instructed that a fiduciary relationship exists, as a matter of law, between a lawyer and the lawyer's client. This relationship imposes a high standard of care and imposes a duty to provide competent legal representation. Such duty demands undivided loyalty and prohibits the lawyer from engaging in conflicts of interest. Furthermore, a lawyer's obligation not to misuse a client's confidence is even older than the duty to avoid conflicts of interest.

It is for you to determine whether defendant, as lawyer for plaintiff, violated the lawyer's fiduciary duties to provide competent legal representation and undivided loyalty, and to avoid conflicts of interest.

If you find that defendant breached the duties as lawyer for the plaintiff, you must determine what damages, if any, were proximately caused by such acts or omissions that constituted the breach of duty.

If you should find that the plaintiff is entitled to a verdict, you may award the plaintiff only those damages that will reasonably compensate for such injury and damage as you find, from a preponderance of the evidence in the case, that plaintiff has sustained as a proximate result of the acts of the defendant.

Comment

For a detailed discussion of the lawyer-client fiduciary duty, see *Maritrans GP, Inc. v. Pepper, Hamilton & Scheetz,* 602 A.2d 1277 (Pa. 1992); and *Mirabito v. Liccardo,* 5 Cal. Rptr. 2d 571 (Cal. Ct. App. 1992).

7.16 Lender, Borrower

You are instructed that a borrower-lender relationship does not create fiduciary duties in the absence of special circumstances. When such parties bargain at arms length, and each is looking out for its own interests, the lender may not be required to act primarily for the benefit of the borrower rather than itself. Such a requirement would convert ordinary day-to-day business transactions into fiduciary relationships when none were intended or anticipated.

However, a fiduciary relationship may be found between a lender and borrower when the lender is in a position to influence the borrower, or when there is a great disparity of bargaining power between the parties, or when a special relationship existed between the parties besides that of debtor-creditor, or when the lender actually assumes an advisory capacity regarding the borrower's business.

It is for you to determine whether any of the above-listed special relationships existed between the defendant [lender] and the plaintiff [borrower] in the case before you. You may also consider the facts and circumstances in this case to determine whether a confidential relationship exists between the parties on other terms.

If you find that such a fiduciary relationship was created between the parties by special facts or circumstances, you must then determine whether such duties were breached by the lender, and whether such breach was the proximate cause of any damages suffered by the plaintiff [borrower].

If you find that defendant [lender] breached its duties as a fiduciary for the plaintiff [borrower], you must determine what damages, if any, were proximately caused by such acts or omissions that constituted the breach of duty.

If you should find that plaintiff is entitled to a verdict, you may award the plaintiff only such damages as will reasonably compensate for such injury and damage as you find, from a preponderance of the evidence in the case, that

plaintiff has sustained as a proximate result of the acts of the defendant.

Comment

For a detailed analysis of the state of fiduciary duty between lenders and borrowers, see *Idaho First National Bank v. Bliss Valley Foods, Inc.*, 824 P.2d 841 (Idaho 1991); *Bloomfield v. Nebraska State Bank*, 465 N.W.2d 144 (Neb. 1991); *Richards v. Platte Valley Bank*, 866 F.2d 1576 (10th Cir. 1989); and *In re Horne*, 44 B.R. 796 (Bankr. Fla. 1984).

Chapter Eight

Misappropriation of Trade Secrets

8.01 Introduction

Daniel J. Gleason and Michelle J. Lipton

The model jury instructions in this chapter address the tort of misappropriation of trade secrets as governed by the common law (see *Restatement (First) of Torts* [hereinafter *Restatement*] § 757, cmts. (1939), or the Uniform Trade Secrets Act (14 U.L.A. 437 (1990 & Supp. 1992) [hereinafter UTSA]), as enacted with various modifications by thirty-eight states and the District of Columbia.

The following states have adopted a form of the UTSA: Alabama, Ala. Code § 8-27-1 *et seq.* (1993), effective Aug. 12, 1987; Alaska, Alaska Stat. § 45.50.910 *et seq.* (1995), effective Sept. 2, 1988; Arizona, Ariz. Rev. Stat. Ann. § 44-401 *et seq.* (1994), effective Apr. 11, 1990; Arkansas, Ark. Code Ann. § 4-75-701 *et seq.* (1994), effective Mar. 12, 1981; California, Cal. Civ. Code § 3426 *et seq.* (1970 supp. 1996), effective Jan. 1, 1985; Colorado, Colo. Rev. Stat. § 7-74-101 *et seq.* (1990 supp. 1995), effective July 1, 1986; Connecticut, Conn. Gen. Stat. § 35-50 *et seq.* (1987 supp. 1996), approved June 23, 1983; Delaware, Del. Code Ann. tit. 6, § 2001 *et seq.* (1993), effective Apr. 15, 1982; Florida, Fla. Stat. Ann. § 688.001 *et seq.* (1984), effective Oct. 1, 1988; Georgia, Ga. Code Ann. § 10-1-760 *et seq.* (1994 supp. 1995), effective July 1, 1990; Hawaii, Haw. Rev. Stat. § 482B-1 *et seq.* (1985 supp. 1992), effective July 1, 1989; Idaho, Idaho Code § 48-801 *et seq.* (1977 supp. 1995), effective July 1, 1993; Illinois, Ill. Rev. Stat. ch. 765, para. 1 *et seq.* (1993 supp. 1996), effective Jan. 1, 1988; Indiana, Ind. Code § 24-2-3-1 *et seq.* (1996), effective Sept. 1, 1982; Iowa, Iowa Code § 550.1 *et seq.* (1987 supp. 1996), effective Apr. 27, 1990; Kansas, Kan. Stat. Ann. § 60-3320 *et seq.* (1994), effective July 1, 1981; Kentucky, Ky. Rev. Stat. Ann. § 365.880 *et seq.* (1988), effective July 13, 1990; Louisiana, La. Rev. Stat. Ann. § 51:1431 *et seq.* (1987 supp. 1996), approved July 19, 1981; Maine, Me. Rev. Stat. Ann. tit. 10, § 1541 *et seq.* (1980 supp. 1995), effective May 22, 1987; Maryland, Md. Code Ann., Com. Law § 11-1201 *et seq.* (1990 supp. 1995), effective July 1, 1989; Minnesota, Minn. Stat. § 325C.01 *et seq.* (1995 supp.

1996), effective Aug. 1, 1980; Mississippi, Miss. Code Ann. § 75-26-1 *et seq.* (1972 supp. 1995), effective July 1, 1990; Montana, Mont. Code Ann. § 30-14-401 *et seq.* (1995), effective Oct. 1, 1985; Nebraska, Neb. Rev. Stat. § 87-501 *et seq.* (1994), effective July 9, 1988; Nevada, Nev. Rev. Stat. § 600A.010 *et seq.* (1986 supp. 1995), effective Mar. 5, 1987; New Hampshire, N.H. Rev. Stat. Ann. § 350-B:1 *et seq.* (1995 supp. 1995), effective Jan. 1, 1990; New Mexico, N.M. Stat. Ann. § 57-3A-1 *et seq.* (1995), effective Apr. 3, 1989; North Carolina, N.C. Gen. Stat. § 66-152 *et seq.* (1995); North Dakota, N.D. Cent. Code § 47-25.1-01 *et seq.* (1978 supp. 1995), effective July 1, 1983; Ohio, Ohio Rev. Code Ann. § 33.51 *et seq.* (1994), effective July 20, 1994; Oklahoma, Okla. Stat. tit. 78, § 85 *et seq.* (1995), effective Jan. 1, 1986; Oregon, Or. Rev. Stat. § 646.461 *et seq.* (1988), effective Jan. 1, 1988; Rhode Island, R.I. Gen. Laws § 6-41-1 *et seq.* (1992), effective July 1, 1986; South Carolina, S.C. Code Ann. § 39-8-1 *et seq.* (1976 supp. 1995), effective June 15, 1993; South Dakota, S.D. Codified Laws Ann. § 37-29-1 *et seq.* (1994), effective July 1, 1988; Utah, Utah Code Ann. § 13-24-1 *et seq.* (1996), effective May 1, 1989; Virginia, Va. Code Ann. § 59.1-336 *et seq.* (1992 supp. 1995), effective July 1, 1986; Washington, Wash. Rev. Code § 19.108.010 *et seq.* (1989 supp. 1996), effective Jan. 1, 1982; West Virginia, W. Va. Code § 47-22-1 *et seq.* (1995), effective July 1, 1986; Wisconsin, Wis. Stat. § 134.90 (1989 supp. 1995), effective Apr. 24, 1986; District of Columbia, D.C. Code Ann. § 48-501 (1990), effective Mar. 16, 1989.

The following states have not adopted the UTSA and instead look to the common law of trade secrets as embodied by section 757 of the *Restatement:* Massachusetts, Michigan, Missouri, New Jersey, New York, Pennsylvania, Tennessee, and Texas. *See, e.g., J.T. Healy & Son, Inc. v. James A. Murphy & Son, Inc.,* 260 N.E.2d 723 (Mass. 1970); Kublik, Inc. v. Hull, 224 N.W.2d 80 (Mich. Ct. App. 1974); *Nat'l Rejectors, Inc. v. Trieman,* 409 S.W.2d 1 (Mo. 1966); *Sun Dial Corp. v. Rideout,* 108 A.2d 442 (N.J. 1954); *Lehman v. Dow Jones & Co.,* 783 F.2d 285 (2d Cir. 1986) (citing *Eagle Comtronics, Inc. v. Pico, Inc.,* 453 N.Y.S.2d 470, 472 (N.Y. App. Div. 1982)); *Valco Cincinnati, Inc. v. N & D Machining Serv., Inc.,* 492 N.E.2d 814 (Ohio 1986);

Felmlee v. Lockett, 351 A.2d 273 (Pa. 1976); *Lowndes Prods., Inc. v. Brower,* 191 S.E.2d 761 (S.C. 1972); *Hickory Specialties, Inc. v. B & L Lab., Inc.,* 592 S.W. 2d 583 (Tenn. Ct. App. 1979); *Hyde Corp. v. Huffines,* 314 S.W.2d 763 (Tex.), *cert. denied,* 358 U.S. 898 (1958).

Vermont and Wyoming are the only states that have never explicitly followed section 757 of the *Restatement* nor adopted a version of the UTSA. However, Wyoming does protect trade secret information, and appears to follow the same definition of trade secret developed at common law as other states, which is embodied by the *Restatement. Ridley v. Krout,* 180 P.2d 124 (Wyo. 1947); *Campen v. Stone,* 635 P.2d 1121 (Wyo. 1981).

Although thirty-eight states and the District of Columbia have adopted a version of the UTSA, many of these states' courts continue to look to their common law trade secrets cases as "helpful guidance," even when the UTSA is faithfully applied. This practice is acceptable, and not necessarily contradictory, because the UTSA was intended to codify the common law and is based on the better reasoned *Restatement* cases. *See* UTSA, Prefatory Note.

The major public policies underlying the law governing trade secret misappropriation are the desire to maintain commercial standards of ethics among business competitors and the desire to allow for as much free competition and entrepreneurial activity in the marketplace as possible. The common law of trade secrets and the UTSA evince an attempt to accommodate these sometimes conflicting public policies by according trade secrets protection only when a wrongdoer has acquired a trade secret through improper means or has used or disclosed the information in violation of a confidential relationship (or a duty otherwise owed to plaintiff). *See, e.g., Restatement* § 757 cmt. a; UTSA § 1. Trade secrets law does not protect the owner of a trade secret from competitors who strive to, and acquire, the trade secret through proper means such as independent invention, reverse engineering, a gift or purchase from the owner, observation of an object on public display, or independent research of publicly available written information, such as trade directories and patent filings. *See, e.g., Restatement* § 757 cmt. a; UTSA § 1 cmt.

Although particular jurisdictions may emphasize one element of the tort over another, or define certain elements differently, all jurisdictions basically require that a plaintiff prove the following elements to prevail on a misappropriation of trade secrets claim:

(1) that a trade secret existed in which plaintiff had ownership rights when defendant committed the acts complained of by plaintiff;
(2) that defendant acquired the trade secret (a) through improper means, (b) through plaintiff's disclosure of the trade secret to defendant in a confidential relationship, or (c) under other circumstances in which defendant owed a duty not to use or disclose the trade secret;
(3) that defendant used or disclosed the trade secret without plaintiff's permission (note that under the UTSA, improper acquisition alone, without use or disclosure, is sufficient to establish liability); and
(4) that (a) plaintiff suffered harm as a direct and proximate result of defendant's use or disclosure of plaintiff's trade secret, or (b) defendant gained from such use or disclosure.

Proof of trade secret misappropriation is intensely fact specific. Courts, therefore, have had a difficult time formulating precise standards to define a trade secret and the tortious misappropriation of a trade secret. The practitioner should bear in mind that even if courts claim to apply objective standards and require minimum showings of proof, they will always "balance" and "weigh" a host of factors to determine whether a trade secret exists and whether a misappropriation has taken place. Most courts require that an alleged trade secret meet a rigorous definitional threshold establishing the owner's property interest in the information before considering whether the other elements of trade secret misappropriation are present. *See, e.g., Electro-Craft Corp. v. Controlled Motion, Inc.,* 332 N.W.2d. 890, 897 (Minn. 1983); *Colson Co. v.*

Wittel, 569 N.E.2d 1082, 1085, 1088 (Ill. App. Ct. 1991); *Koch Eng'g Co. v. Faulconer*, 610 P.2d 1094 (Kan. 1980); *Lowndes Prods., Inc. v. Brower*, 191 S.E.2d 761 (S.C. 1972); *Russell v. Wall Wire Prods. Co.*, 78 N.W.2d 1949 (Mich. 1956). A minority of states focus foremost on the relational history between the parties and whether a misappropriation can be found, often with little or no subsequent analysis of whether a trade secret exists. *See, e.g., E.I. DuPont de Nemours & Co. v. Christopher*, 431 F.2d 1012, 1016–17 (5th Cir. 1970); *Hyde Corp. v. Huffines*, 314 S.W.2d 763, 770 (Tex.), *cert. denied*, 358 U.S. 898 (1958); *Kamin v. Kuhnau*, 374 P.2d 912, 916, 919 (Or. 1962); *Henkle & Joyce Hardware Co. v. Maco, Inc.*, 239 N.W.2d 772, 777 (Neb. 1976).

The best reasoned cases, however, focus first on the threshold question: Does a trade secret exist that requires protection? *See* § 8.03 cmt., *infra*. This approach is logical, because regardless of whether the parties ever stood in a confidential relationship, there can be no liability for misappropriation absent the existence of a trade secret. *See generally* 2 R. Callmann, *The Law of Unfair Competition, Trademarks and Monopolies* § 14.02 (4th ed. 1992); R.M. Milgram, *Milgram on Trade Secrets* [hereinafter *Milgram*] § 1.09, at 1–61 (1990). The following jury instructions have been drafted with the above insights in mind.

One further note on these instructions is in order. As with any business case, there are many instructions relating to the manner in which a jury should proceed to evaluate the evidence that are generic to the jury process; for example, plaintiff's burden of proof, use of circumstantial evidence, and the standard of certainty required for prospective damages. These instructions do not attempt to cover such areas, as they are not peculiar to the trade secrets area.

8.02 Prima Facie Case

To recover on the trade secret claims plaintiff has made in this case, plaintiff must prove each of the following four elements by a preponderance of the evidence:

(1) that plaintiff possessed a trade secret;

(2) that defendant acquired the trade secret (a) through improper means, (b) through a confidential relationship with plaintiff, or (c) under other circumstances giving rise to a duty not to use or disclose the trade secret without plaintiff's permission;

(3) that defendant used or disclosed the trade secret without plaintiff's permission [note that under the UTSA, improper acquisition alone, without use or disclosure, is sufficient to establish liability]; and

(4) that (a) plaintiff suffered harm as a direct and proximate result of defendant's use or disclosure of plaintiff's trade secret, or (b) defendant obtained benefit from such use or disclosure.

I will go over each of these elements more specifically in the following instructions.

If after you consider all of the evidence you find that plaintiff has proven each of these elements in accordance with the legal requirements as I describe them to you, then you will consider the amount of money damages to be awarded to plaintiff, by following the instructions that I will give you relating to damages.

If, on the other hand, you find that plaintiff has not proven one or more of these elements, then defendant is not liable.

Comment

Restatement

Despite the varying degrees of detail with which courts establish the elements of a prima facie case for misappropriation of trade secrets, "the criteria are essentially the same in all instances." 1 Melvin F. *Jager, Trade Secrets Law* [hereinafter *Jager*] § 504[1] (1991) (and cases cited therein). *See also* 2 *Mil-*

gram, supra, § 7.07[1], at 7-213–25 (and cases cited therein). The above jury instruction was distilled from cases such as the following: *In re Certain Apparatus for Continuous Production of Copper Rod,* (ITC 1979); *Greenberg v. Croydon Plastics, Co.,* 378 F. Supp. 806, 811 (E.D. Pa.), *vacated on other grounds,* (E.D. Pa. 1974); *Rohm and Haas Co. v. Adco Chemical Co.,* 689 F.2d 424 (3d Cir. 1982); *Taco Cabana International, Inc. v. Two Pesos, Inc.,* 932 F.2d 1113, 1123 (5th Cir. 1991).

Uniform Act

One difference between the UTSA and the *Restatement* approach is that under the UTSA, improper acquisition alone is sufficient to establish liability for trade secret misappropriation. UTSA § 1(2). *See, e.g., Minuteman, Inc. v. Alexander,* 434 N.W.2d 773, 778 (Wis. 1989); *see also* Richard J. Cipolla Jr., "A Practitioner's Guide to Oklahoma Trade Secrets Law, Past, Present and Future: The Uniform Trade Secrets Act," 27 Tulsa L.J. 137 n.152 (damages available for improper acquisition alone, as acquisition may diminish indirect value of trade secret). *But see Ins. Assoc. Corp. v. Hansen,* 782 P.2d 1230, 1235 (Idaho 1989) (even if plaintiff possessed trade secret, claim fails without proof of use); Ala. Code § 8-27-3, 4 (1993) (improper disclosure or use in addition to acquisition required for liability under Alabama act).

8.03 Definition of Trade Secret

Before you consider defendant's actions, you must find that plaintiff possessed a trade secret. Broadly speaking, a trade secret may consist of any formula, pattern, device, program, method, technique, process, or compilation of information, including a customer list. However, to prove that particular information is entitled to special protection as a "trade secret," plaintiff must show

(1) that the information at issue is indeed secret;

(2) that plaintiff has taken reasonable measures to protect the secrecy of the information;

(3) that the information is sufficiently valuable so that it confers a competitive advantage on plaintiff over its business rivals; and

(4) that the information is continuously used in plaintiff's business [*Restatement* only].

I will explain each of these essential elements of a trade secret more specifically in the following instructions.

Comment

Restatement

According to the *Restatement,* an exact definition of a trade secret is not possible. *Restatement* § 757 cmt. b. Instead, the *Restatement* states that

> [a] trade secret may consist of any formula, pattern, device or compilation of information which is used in one's business, and which gives him an opportunity to obtain an advantage over competitors who do not know or use it. It may be a formula for a chemical compound, a process of manufacturing, treating or preserving materials, a pattern for a machine or other device, or a list of customers.

Id. The *Restatement* goes on to speak of "factors" to consider in evaluating whether a trade secret exists. The six traditional or core factors identified by the *Restatement* are the following:

(1) the extent to which the information is known outside of plaintiff's business;

(2) the extent to which it is known by employees and others involved in plaintiff's business;

(3) the extent of measures taken by the plaintiff to guard the secrecy of the information;
(4) the value of the information to plaintiff and plaintiff's competitors;
(5) the amount of effort or money expended by plaintiff in developing the information; and
(6) the ease or difficulty with which the information could be properly acquired or duplicated by others.

The above jury instruction's requirements of secrecy, reasonable measures to protect secrecy, and competitive advantage are distilled from these six oft-cited *Restatement* factors. An additional common law factor noted by the *Restatement*, but accorded less prominence in discussions by courts, is the requirement of continuous use in the operation of plaintiff's business. *See generally* 1 *Jager, supra* at § 5.04[2]; 1 *Milgram, supra*, § 2.02[1], at 2-30–34.

Uniform Act

Section 1[4] of the UTSA provides that

> "Trade Secret" means information, including a formula, pattern, compilation, program, device, method, techniques, or process, that:
>
> (i) derives independent economic value, actual or potential, from not being known to, and not being readily ascertainable by proper means by other persons who can obtain economic value from its disclosure or use, and
> (ii) is the subject of efforts that are reasonable under the circumstances to maintain its secrecy.

The language of some statutes will vary slightly from the UTSA, and changes in the jury instruction may be advisable to accommodate particular statutory language. *See, e.g.*, Ala. Code § 8-27-2 cmts. (1993 supp. 1995) (trade secret defined as information that (a) is used or intended for use in trade or business, (b) is included or embodied in a formula, pattern, compilation, computer software, drawings, device, method, technique, or process, (c) cannot be readily ascertained or derived from publicly available information, and (d) has significant economic value); Alaska Stat. § 45.50.940(3) (1995) (trade secret defined as "information" that has economic value, is not generally known or readily ascertainable, and is secret); Colo. Rev. Stat. § 7-74-102(4) (1990 supp. 1995) (trade secret definition differs from UTSA in that information *must* relate to plaintiff's business and there is no requirement that type of secrecy-preserving measures employed be reasonable; definition encompasses "the whole or any portion or phase of any scientific or technical information, design . . . procedure . . . improvement, confidential business or financial information, listing of names, addresses or telephone numbers, or other information relating to any business or profession which is secret and of value"); Conn. Gen. Stat. § 35-51(d) (1987 supp. 1996) ("formula, pattern and compilation" are deleted from UTSA's definition, and "drawing, cost data and customer list" are added); Ga. Code Ann. § 10-1-761(4) (1994 supp. 1995) and Ill. Rev. Stat. ch. 765, para. 2(d), cmts. (1993 supp. 1996) (in addition to types of information listed in UTSA, Georgia and Illinois acts add "information, including, but not limited to," technical or nontechnical data, a drawing, financial data, financial plans, product plans, or list of actual or potential customers or suppliers; also, under Illinois act, term "program" meant to cover computer programs and term "information" intended to include know-how and ideas used in computer science and biotechnology); Kan. Stat. Ann. § 60-3320(4) (1994) (includes "data" in definition of trade secret); Iowa Code § 550.2(4) (1987 supp. 1996), Me. Rev. Stat. Ann. tit. 10, § 1542(4) (1980 supp. 1995), Neb. Rev. Stat. § 87-502(4) (1994), Va. Code Ann. § 59-1-336 (1992 supp. 1995), and W. Va. Code § 47-22-1(d) (1995) (these statutes broaden trade secret definition by explicitly making list of types of information nonexclusive; in addition, Nebraska statute adds "drawing" and "code" to list of information that may constitute trade secret); Minn. Stat. § 325c.01(5) (1995 supp. 1996) (adds words "information or computer software, including a formula . . ." to definition of trade secret); N.C. Gen. Stat. § 66-152(3) (1995) (North Carolina act specifies that trade secret is business or technical information, and also adds "compilation of information to the UTSA definition"); Or. Rev. Stat. § 646.461(4) (1988) (Oregon act adds drawing, cost data, and customer list to UTSA definition of trade secret).

8.03[1] Secrecy

To determine that a trade secret exists you must first decide whether the information was indeed secret when defendant's allegedly wrongful conduct occurred. Matters that are generally known to the public at large or to people in a trade or business are not trade secrets. Nor can information be considered a trade secret if it would be ascertainable with reasonable ease from publicly available information. In addition, a trade secret must possess enough originality so that it can be distinguished from everyday knowledge.

The secrecy requirement for information to qualify as a trade secret, however, does not mean that absolute secrecy must be maintained—in the sense that no one else in the world possesses the information. Rather, a plaintiff must demonstrate that the information was known only to it or to a few others who have also treated the information as a trade secret.

Comment

Although neither the *Restatement* nor the UTSA specifically require a finding of "novelty," courts routinely require some degree of novelty or originality for information to be accorded trade secret status. Although information need not evince the same degree of novelty required for patent protection, it must possess sufficient originality to separate it from everyday knowledge or knowledge commonly used by people in a trade or business. *See, e.g., Northup v. Reish,* 200 F.2d 924 (7th Cir. 1953) (Restatement case); *Corroon & Black-Rutters & Roberts, Inc. v. Hosch,* 325 N.W.2d 883, 893 (Wis. 1982) (dissenting opinion); *Technicon Data Sys. Corp. v. Curtis 1000, Inc.,* 7644 1984 WL 8268 (Del. Ch. Aug. 21, 1984) (Delaware Trade Secret Act case); *Electro-Craft Corp. v. Controlled Motion, Inc.,* 332 N.W.2d 890, 899 (Minn. 1983) (Minnesota Trade Secret Act case); *Dionne v. Southeast Foam Converting & Packaging, Inc.,* 397 S.E.2d 110, 113–14 (Va. 1990) (Virginia Trade Secret Act).

Restatement

The case law is replete with references to the requirement that information be secret to be accorded trade secret protection. *See, e.g., J.T. Healy & Son, Inc. v. James A. Murphy & Son, Inc.*, 260 N.E.2d 723, 730 (Mass. 1970); *Zoecon Indus., Div. of Zoecon Corp. v. Am. Stockman Tag Co.*, 713 F.2d 1174, 1179 (5th Cir. 1983); *K-2 Ski Co. v. Head Ski Co.*, 506 F.2d 471, 473–74 (9th Cir. 1974); *Speedry Chem. Prods., Inc. v. Carter's Ink Co.*, 306 F.2d 328, 331 (2d Cir. 1962); *Kubik, Inc. v. Hull*, 224 N.W.2d 80, 91–93 (Mich. Ct. App. 1974).

Uniform Act

To determine whether information is secret, the courts in UTSA states generally focus on whether the information is generally known or readily ascertainable using proper means. *See Pub. Sys., Inc. v. Towry*, 587 So. 2d 969, 973, (Ala. 1991) (information that is readily available or derived from publicly available information without investment of substantial time, effort, and research is not protectable); *Allen v. Johar, Inc.*, 823 S.W.2d 824 (Ark. 1992) (information accorded trade secret status when it contained personnel information not generally known and developed through expenditure of much time and money); *Electro-Craft Corp. v. Controlled Motion, Inc.*, 332 N.W.2d 890, 899, (Minn. Ct. App. 1985); *Fleming Sales, Co. v. Bailey*, 611 F. Supp. 507, 513 (N.D. Ill. 1985) (holding that when information known throughout an industry such information not protectable regardless of secrecy measures employed); *Kozuch v. CRA-MAR Video Ctr., Inc.*, 478 N.E.2d 110, 113 (Ind. Ct. App. 1985) (holding trade secret does not exist when information reasonably discoverable from other sources); *see also Scott v. Snelling & Snelling, Inc.*, 732 F. Supp. 1034, 1044 (N.D. Cal. 1990); *Colorado Supply Co. v. Stewart*, 797 P.2d 1303, 1306 (Colo. Ct. App. 1990), *cert. denied*, 91SC171 1991 Colo. LEXIS 708 (Colo. Feb. 1991); *Kavanaugh v. Stump*, 592 So. 2d 1231 (Fla. Dist. Ct. App. 1992); *Xpert Automation Sys., Corp. v. Vibromatic Co.*, 569 N.E.2d 351, 356 (Ind. Ct. App. 1991); *Steenhoven v. College Life Ins. Co.*, 458 N.E.2d 661, 666–67 (Ind. Ct. App.), *reh'g denied*, 460 N.E.2d

973 (Ind. Ct. App. 1984); *Mid-America Nat'l Agency, Inc. v. Albert H. Wohlers & Co.,* (D. Kan. 1988).

The California and Illinois statutes do not include the requirement that trade secret information "not be readily ascertainable by proper means." Under these statutes, therefore, a trade secret may consist of information that could have been legally obtained. The "readily ascertainable" standard is, however, available as a defense in both states. *See* Cal. Civ. Code § 3426 *et seq.,* cmts. (1970); Ill. Rev. Stat. ch. 765 para. 2(a), cmts. (1996); *Gillis Associated Indus., Inc. v. Cari-All, Inc.,* 564 N.E.2d 881, 886 (Ill. App. Ct. 1990); *Rockwell Graphic Sys. v. Dev. Indus.,* 730 F. Supp. 171, 176–77 (N.D. Ill. 1990), *rev'd on other grounds,* 925 F.2d 174 (7th Cir. 1991).

8.03[2] Reasonable Measures to Protect Secrecy

Plaintiff must prove that it took reasonable measures to protect the secrecy of information for the information to be accorded trade secret protection. There are no absolute requirements that define what measures are "reasonable" in a given situation. That depends on the circumstances of each case, but factors you may wish to consider in evaluating whether "reasonable" measures were taken here could include the following:

(1) whether plaintiff made it a practice to apprise its employees or others involved with its business that the information is a trade secret and/or is to be kept confidential;

(2) whether plaintiff required employees or others involved in its business or with its business to sign confidentiality agreements or covenants not to compete regarding the information;

(3) whether plaintiff restricted access to the information on a "need to know basis"; or

(4) whether plaintiff generally maintained tight security to protect the alleged trade secret, and did not voluntarily disclose it to others, except in confidence.

Comment

This instruction lists four of the most commonly discussed measures for protecting the secrecy of trade secret information, but ultimately the test is not readily defensible in terms of whether any one (or even any group) of specific factors is present or absent and to what degree. Relevant factors will most often depend on the facts of a particular case; some of the factors listed here may not be relevant at all. In fact, factors not listed here may, in some circumstances, be enough to establish reasonable secrecy measures. This list then, is not meant to be, and cannot be, comprehensive.

Restatement

See CVD, Inc. v. Raytheon Co., 769 F.2d 842, 851–52 (1st Cir. 1985) ("Heroic measures to ensure secrecy are not essential, but reasonable precautions must be taken."), *cert. denied,* 475 U.S. 1016 (1986); *J.T. Healy & Son, Inc. v. James A. Murphy & Son, Inc.,* 260 N.E.2d 723, 731 (Mass. 1970) (reasonable security precautions include "constant warnings to all persons to whom the trade secret has become known and obtaining from each an agreement, preferably in writing, acknowledging its secrecy and promising to respect it"); *Ecolab, Inc. v. Paolo,* 753 F. Supp. 1100, 1112 (E.D.N.Y. 1991) (reasonable security measures to protect trade secrets include employee confidentiality agreements and need-to-know disclosure to employees); *Anaconda Co. v. Metric Tool & Die Co.,* 485 F. Supp. 410, 422 (E.D. Pa. 1980) ("Although the secrecy maintained was by no means absolute, it was such that except by the use of improper means, defendant would have had difficulty in acquiring the information."); *Jostens, Inc. v. Nat'l Computer Sys., Inc.,* 318 N.W.2d 691, 700–01, (Minn. 1982) (inadequate security measures found when no confidentiality policy, and information plaintiff sought to protect published in article not marked "secret" or "confidential"); *E.I. DuPont de Nemours & Co. v. Christopher,* 431 F.2d 1012, 1016–17 (5th Cir. 1970) (holding reasonable security measures do not require plaintiff build impenetrable fortress around its construction site to shield secrets from competitor's aerial photography).

Uniform Act

See Allied Supply Co. v. Brown, 585 So. 2d 33, 36 (Ala. 1991) (holding adequate security measures not taken when employees had free access to customer lists, lists not marked "confidential," and many copies available within company); *United Centrifugal Pumps v. Cusimano,* 708 F. Supp. 1038 (W.D. Ark. 1988) (adequate measures to maintain secrecy include disclosure only upon execution of confidentiality agreement, limited access to location where trade secret used, surveillance of files containing information, and computer information accessible only by special password); *Allen v. Johar, Inc.,* 823 S.W.2d 824 (Ark. 1992) (adequate secrecy measures found when information not allowed out of plaintiff's building and old information destroyed); *Vacco Indus., Inc. v. Van Den Berg,* 6 Cal. Rptr. 602 (Cal. Ct. App. 1992), (secrecy measures adequate when employer kept visitor logs, required sign-out sheets for confidential documents, maintained document destruction policy, and required that confidential information be kept in locked cabinets); *Network Telecommunications, Inc. v. Boor-Crepeau*, 790 P.2d 901, 902 (Colo. Ct. App. 1990) (trade secret found to exist when information given to employees only on need-to-know basis, employees advised that information was trade secret, and access to company plant controlled and limited); *Colorado Supply Co. v. Stewart*, 797 P.2d 1303, 1306 (Colo. Ct. App. 1990) (same holding), *cert. denied*, No. 89CA0989 1991 Colo. LEXIS 708 (Colo. Feb. 1991); *Sheets v. Yamaha Motors Corp.*, 849 F.2d 179, 183–84, (5th Cir. 1988) (holding reasonable security measures not taken when plaintiff publicly displayed product containing alleged trade secret, installed alleged trade secret in other products without instructing customers not to disclose it, and allowed others to take pictures and examine product without requiring confidentiality agreements), *aff'd in part and rev'd in part*, 891 F.2d 533 (2d Cir. 1990), *reh'g denied*, 897 F.2d 528 (5th Cir. 1990); *Electro-Craft Corp. v. Controlled Motion, Inc.*, 332 N.W.2d 890 (Minn. Ct. App. 1983) (reasonable efforts to keep information secret include combination of physical security, confidentiality procedures, and policies that put employees and others on notice of information's secrecy), *appeal after remand*, 370 N.W.2d 465 (Minn. Ct. App. 1985); *Surgidev Corp. v. Eye Technology, Inc.*, 828 F.2d 452, 455 (8th Cir. 1987) (secrecy measures found adequate when information shared with employees only on need-to-know basis, employees on notice that information secret and signed nondisclosure agreements, and visitor access restricted in areas containing information); *Aries Info. Sys., Inc. v. Pacific Management Sys. Corp.*, 366 N.W.2d 366, 368–69, 440 (Minn. Ct. App. 1985) (secrecy measures adequate when information had proprietary notices attached and employees signed confidentiality agreements); *Dionne v. Southeast Foam Converting & Packaging, Inc.*, 397 S.E.2d 110, 113–14 (Va. 1990) (secrecy measures adequate when information never disclosed to anyone other than plaintiff's lawyer, unauthorized people excluded from building where trade secret kept, and all people, including family members, who had only information regarding trade secret required to sign confidentiality agreements); *Boeing Co. v. Sierracin Corp.*, 738 P.2d 665, 676 (Wash. 1987) (secrecy measures adequate even though information disclosed to Federal Aviation Administration, as such information not available to public on demand); *Machen, Inc. v. Aircraft Design, Inc.*, 828 P.2d 73, 78–79 (Wash. Ct. App.) (adequate secrecy measures include advising employees that information is trade secret, limiting access to information to need-to-know basis, limiting and controlling access to location where trade secret kept, and advising others outside business of information's secrecy), *review denied*, 841 P.2d 47 (Wash. 1992).

8.03[3] Competitive Advantage

A trade secret must be valuable either to plaintiff or to its business rivals in the sense that, as long as it is secret, the information provides plaintiff with an actual or potential competitive business advantage over its rivals. To help you determine whether plaintiff enjoyed, or was likely to enjoy, such a competitive advantage, you may consider such things as

(1) the degree to which the information was generally known or readily ascertainable by others;
(2) the extent to which plaintiff used or uses the information in its business;
(3) whether profits or increased efficiency enjoyed by plaintiff's business are due to the information;
(4) what gain or benefits defendant's business obtained from the information;
(5) what money, effort, and time plaintiff expended to develop the information; and
(6) the ease or difficulty of acquiring or duplicating the information through independent development, research of publicly available information, or taking apart and analyzing a product properly acquired to learn its secrets (a process called "reverse engineering").

Comment

The list of factors set forth in this instruction includes those factors most commonly referred to by the courts. Again, the inquiry is so fact specific that depending upon the circumstances of a particular case, some of these factors may not be relevant at all, while others, not listed, may establish the requirement of competitive advantage.

Restatement

In defining a trade secret, the *Restatement* requires that the information "give [the holder of it] an opportunity to obtain an advantage over competitors who do not know or use it." *Restatement* § 757 cmt. b. *See also Salsbury Lab., Inc. v. Merieux Lab., Inc.*, 735 F. Supp. 1555 (M.D. Ga. 1989) (element of competitive advantage significant in determining whether information deserves trade secret protection); *Jet Spray Cooler, Inc. v. Crampton,* 385 N.E.2d 1349 (Mass. 1979) (citing competitive advantage as element of trade secret); *Rohm and Haas Co. v. Avco Chem. Co.,* 689 F.2d 424, 430–31 (3d Cir. 1982) (evidence of plaintiff's competitive advantage included fact that plaintiff derived four highly successful products from information in dispute and that defendant tried for years to duplicate plaintiff's manufacturing process without success); *Sheridan v. Mallinckrodt, Inc.,* 568 F. Supp. 1347, 1352 n.7 (N.D.N.Y. 1983) (plaintiff's manufacturing process conferred competitive advantage on plaintiff because it required less attention from machine operators and made it easier to detect defects in plaintiff's products, thus helping to control production costs); *FMC Corp. v. Spurlin,* 596 F. Supp. 609 (W.D. Pa. 1984) (holding that showing of competitive advantage necessary for trade secret protection); *Thermotics, Inc. v. Bat Jac Tool Co.,* 541 S.W.2d 255 (Tex. Civ. App. 1976) (plaintiff's profits before and after alleged misappropriation by defendant constitutes evidence of competitive advantage).

Uniform Act

In defining a trade secret, the UTSA requires that the information "derive independent economic value, actual or potential, from not being known to, and not being readily ascertainable by proper means by other persons who can obtain economic value from its disclosure or use." UTSA § 1[4]. To determine whether information has "independent economic value" under the UTSA, most courts look to whether the information confers a "competitive advantage" upon the plaintiff. Thus, although the language of the UTSA differs on its face from that of the *Restatement,* both, in practice, require the same proof. *See, e.g., Religious Technology Ctr. v. Wollersheim,* 796 F.2d 1076, 1090 (9th Cir. 1986); *Secure Serv. Technology, Inc. v. Time & Space Processing, Inc.,* 722 F. Supp. 1354, 1360 n.14, (E.D. Va. 1989); *Electro-Craft Corp. v. Controlled Motion, Inc.,* 332 N.W.2d 890, 900–01, (Minn. Ct. App. 1983), *appeal after remand,* 370 N.W.2d 465 (Minn. Ct. App. 1985); *New England Ins. Agency, Inc. v. Miller,* No. CV-89-0285030-5 1991 WL

65766, 65767 (Conn. Super. Apr. 16, 1991). *See also United Centrifugal Pumps v. Cusimano,* (W.D. Ark. 1988) (information has independent economic value when competitor would have to spend at least as much time, effort, and money as plaintiff had expended to obtain information using proper means); *ABBA Rubber Co. v. Seaquist,* 286 Cal. Rptr. 518 (Cal. Ct. App. 1991) (customer list has economic value to competitors if information on list will allow competitor to direct its efforts to specific group of customers who use its product, and if competitor did not otherwise know, or could not otherwise economically ascertain, prospective clients); In re *R & R Assoc., Inc.,* 119 B.R. 302, 304 (Bankr. M.D. Fla. 1990) (information has independent economic value when plaintiff spent considerable time, effort, knowledge, and expense compiling information and when information secret and not available from other sources); *Aries Info. Sys., Inc. v. Pacific Management Sys. Corp.,* 366 N.W.2d 366, 368, (Minn. Ct. App. 1985) (computer program had independent economic value because not generally known, available only through plaintiff, and plaintiff generated extensive revenues from sale of program); *Surgidev Corp. v. Eye Technology, Inc.,* 828 F.2d 452, 456 (8th Cir. 1987) (defendant's intention to use plaintiff's information is circumstantial proof of economic value).

8.03[4] Continuous Use in Business [*Restatement* Only]

For the information to be a trade secret, it must be put to continuous use in plaintiff's business. "Continuous use" means regular use in the business, including at the time of defendant's alleged wrongful conduct. Stated another way, information that is never used or used only for single or passing events in the operation of plaintiff's business is not continuous use. If the information at issue was not in continuous use in the operation of plaintiff's business at the time that defendant's alleged wrongful conduct occurred, then it is not a trade secret.

Comment

Restatement

According to the *Restatement,* purported trade secrets that are never used in the operation of the business, or used only for single or ephemeral events, may not be accorded trade secret protection. *See, e.g., Lehman v. Dow Jones & Co.,* 783 F.2d 285, 298 (2d Cir. 1986); *Victor Chem. Works v. Iliff,* 132 N.E. 806 (Ill. 1921). One justification postulated for the continuous use requirement is that unless a plaintiff can show continuous use, it is uncertain whether plaintiff would be able to protect the secrecy of such information and that such information would actually confer a competitive advantage. 1 *Milgram, supra,* § 2.02[1], at 2-29.

Many courts, however, either ignore or liberally construe the continuous use requirement set forth in the *Restatement. See, e.g., Syntex Ophthalmics, Inc. v. Tsuetaki,* 701 F.2d 677, 683 (7th Cir. 1983); *Sikes v. McGraw-Edison Co.,* 671 F.2d 150, 157 (5th Cir. 1982); *see generally* 1 *Jager, supra* at § 5.04[2]; 1 *Milgram, supra,* § 2.02[1], at 2-30–34. For example, many states hold that when an inventor negotiates with a manufacturer to produce a device the inventor has developed, even when the information is not currently part of a production process bringing in sales for the inventor, the information may still be accorded trade secret status. *See, e.g., Ferroline Corp. v. Gen. Aniline & Film Corp.,* 207 F.2d 912 (7th Cir. 1953) (applying New Jersey law); *Jet Spray Cooler, Inc. v. Crampton,* 282 N.E.2d 921 (Mass. 1972) (trade secret protection granted to information never actually used in plaintiff's business). "Negative" information, or information about the sorts of products or processes that will not work, is also often accorded trade secret protection without being in continuous use. *See generally* 1 *Milgram, supra,* § 2.02[1], at 2-36–38 (and cases cited therein). Given that such information confers a competitive advantage on the discoverer in the form of a potential head start into more fruitful research or production possibilities, and that a rival may yet waste time and money repeating another business's mistakes, courts in some *Restatement* states hold that such "negative" information may constitute a trade secret even though such information will never be put to continuous use in the operation of a business.

Uniform Act

The UTSA does not include a "continuous use" requirement. Accordingly, information that was not in use at the time of defendant's actions, as well as information that has never been put to use, including "negative" information, may constitute a trade secret. *See, e.g., Courtesy Temporary Serv., Inc. v. Camacho,* 272 Cal. Rptr. 352, 357–58 (Cal. Ct. App. 1990) (customer list held protectable even when part of extensive research in compilation of list included finding entities that would not subscribe to plaintiff's services); *Morton v. Rank Am., Inc.,* 812 F. Supp. 1062 (C.D. Cal. 1993).

8.04 Acquisition by Defendant

You must determine whether defendant acquired the trade secret under circumstances that impose a duty defendant owed to plaintiff. Defendant would have a duty to plaintiff if defendant acquired the information (a) by using improper means, (b) through a confidential relationship with plaintiff, or (c) under other circumstances in which the law imposes a duty on defendant regarding use of the information. Let me discuss each of these with you in detail.

8.04[1] Improper Means

If plaintiff proves that defendant acquired the trade secret by theft, bribery, trespass, misrepresentation, or through corporate espionage, such as wiretapping, defendant has used "improper means." It would also be improper if defendant learned the trade secret from a third party who used improper means to acquire the information or who breached a duty of confidentiality in disclosing the information, when the defendant knows or should know that it is acquiring a trade secret belonging to another. Improper means also includes inducing another either to use improper means to acquire the information or to breach a duty of confidentiality that person owed to plaintiff.

It is not improper, on the other hand, to acquire information through independent development, research of public resources (such as, for example, trade directories, patent filings, or even the telephone book), or purchase of a product that contains trade secrets and then disassembling it to analyze those secrets (a process called "reverse engineering"). Similarly, a party who obtains information by mistake, or without knowledge or reason to know that the information is a trade secret, has not acquired the trade secret through improper means.

Comment

Restatement

The above instruction deals with acquisition through improper means, such as corporate espionage and theft. *See E.I. DuPont de Nemours & Co. v. Christopher,* 431 F.2d 1012, 1016–17 (5th Cir. 1970) (holding competitor who attempted to discover DuPont's trade secrets through aerial photography of DuPont plant under construction liable for wrongful acquisition of trade secrets). In reality, these situations are far less common than acquiring the information through lawful means, such as in the context of a confidential relationship, and then misusing the information. An example would be a former employee competing or sharing information with a new employer. *See, e.g., Milgram, supra,* § 5.05, at 5.18 n.2 (stating that "[i]ndustrial espionage is rarely described in civil actions" and that "[t]he type of case civil actions frequently depict involves an errant employee or former employee together with a culpable or too 'relaxed' next employer"). The classic example of a confidential relationship that is often implied-at-law is that of employee to employer. *See also* § 8.04[2] cmt., *infra.*

Uniform Act

This definition of "improper means" might be considered somewhat less comprehensive than the definition used by UTSA, in that the instruction excludes "breach . . . of duty to maintain secrecy," which is included in the UTSA. *See* UTSA § 1[1]. Because these instructions cover the concept of acquisition of the secret first and then wrongful disclosure or use, a breach of duty to maintain secrecy is not treated as acquisition by "improper means." Subsequent instructions on wrongful use and disclosure cover this concept.

Note also that the UTSA's definition of "improper means" ("[t]heft, bribery, misrepresentation, breach or inducement of a breach of duty to maintain secrecy, or espionage through electronic or other means") is subject to some variation in state statutes that are based on the UTSA. *See, e.g.,* Ala. Code § 8-27-2(2) (1993) ("improper means" also includes trespass and other deliberate acts committed for purpose of gaining access to information by means of "electronic, photographic, telescopic or other aids to enhance normal human perception" when owner has reasonable expectation of privacy); Ill. Rev. Stat. ch. 765, para. 2(a), cmts. (1996) ("improper means" also includes "breach of a confidential relationship or other duty to maintain secrecy" and any conduct improper under circumstances); N.C. Gen. Stat. § 66-152 (1995) (term "improper means" not used; rather, violation of statute includes only acquisition, use, or disclosure of plaintiff's trade secret without plaintiff's express or implied authority). The practitioner should consider these variations when formulating this instruction.

Unlike the *Restatement*, the UTSA imposes liability for mere acquisition of a trade secret using improper means; neither disclosure nor use of the trade secret is required for liability to attach. *See* § 8.05, *infra*. Thus, if the misappropriation claim is based on improper acquisition alone, the misappropriation instruction should end here, to be followed by the damages instructions. *But see* Ala. Code § 8-27-3 (1993) (holding that requirements for proof of misappropriation codify common law, and no liability for improper acquisition alone).

8.04[2] Confidential Relationship

You must determine whether defendant acquired the information through a confidential relationship with plaintiff.

To determine whether the trade secret was disclosed to defendant through a confidential relationship you may consider whether, based on the dealings between the parties, defendant knew or should have known that plaintiff expected the information to be kept secret and whether plaintiff's expectation was reasonable.

At times an agreement about confidentiality will be express, as when there is a written agreement between the parties specifying that defendants will not disclose or use the information unless authorized to do so. At other times an agreement about confidentiality will be implicit from the circumstances of the parties' dealings. You may find a confidential relationship existed between the parties based either on an express agreement between the parties or one implied from the circumstances of their dealings.

Comment

The above instruction, or portions of it, would be used if there is an issue about whether an express or implied-in-fact confidential relationship exists (often not disputed by the parties). In such cases, the relevant inquiry would involve classic jury issues, such as what the parties subjectively believed about the nature of their relationship and what a reasonable person would have believed under the circumstances.

However, some confidential relationships are commonly implied as a matter of law (except when the parties expressly contract otherwise), including employer-employee relationships, joint venture or partnership relationships, or prospective licensee-licensor relationships. *See generally* 1 *Milgrim, supra,* at §§ 5.00–.03. Whether a confidential relationship is to be implied as a matter of law is typically a question of law for the court and not the jury.

Uniform Act

See Surgidev Corp. v. Eye Technology, Inc., 648 F. Supp. 661, 694–95 (D. Minn. 1986), *aff'd*, 828 F.2d 452 (8th Cir. 1987) (plaintiff can prove confidential relationship by presenting proof of express contract or continuous trusting relationship that gives rise to duty not to disclose); *United Centrifugal Pumps v. Cusimano*, 708 F. Supp. 1038 (W.D. Ark. 1988); *Vacco Indus., Inc. v. Van Den Berg*, 6 Cal. Rptr. 2d 602 (Cal. Ct. App. 1992) (1992) (essence of misappropriation claim is breach of faith or confidence).

8.04[3] Other Circumstances Giving Rise to Duty

A person may come into possession of a trade secret in a manner that does not, at that time, impose an obligation running to the owner but if circumstances change, a duty not to use or disclose the information would arise. One such situation occurs when a person acquires the trade secret by mistake or accident, not having reason to believe it belongs to another. Another occurs when a person innocently buys the information from another, not having reason to know that it is stolen information. In such situations, defendant is not liable for its use or disclosure of the trade secret as long as defendant does not know or has not been put on notice of facts that would otherwise make its use or disclosure wrongful.

Nonetheless, a duty may later arise regarding use or disclosure of another's trade secret that was first acquired in good faith and without knowledge of plaintiff's rights in the information; that is, once the innocent party is put on notice of the mistake or theft.

Thus, you must decide whether defendant acquired plaintiff's trade secret by mistake, accident, or in good faith without knowledge that the information came from a third person who had obtained the information through improper means or through a confidential relationship. If you determine that defendant initially acquired plaintiff's trade secret through one of these innocent means, you must next decide whether defendant ever learned or was put on notice that its acquisition of the trade secret occurred through mistake, accident, or through a third party's use of improper means or breach of a confidential relationship. If you determine that defendant later acquired such actual or constructive notice, then defendant's duty to plaintiff would begin only on the date when defendant first acquired such knowledge.

Comment

Restatement

Note that this instruction does not address one situation recognized in the *Restatement;* that is, when a defendant has, in good faith, paid fair value for the secret, or has so changed its position before receiving notice that to subject it to liability would be unfair. In that circumstance, a defendant is not liable for past or future use of the information. *See Restatement* § 758.

A defendant who acquires trade secret information by mistake, accident, or in good faith, without notice that its acquisition derived from a third person who was in breach of a duty to plaintiff, is not liable for using or disclosing the trade secret, as long as defendant does not know and is not on notice of circumstances that otherwise would have made its acquisition of the information improper.

The *Restatement* differs from the UTSA in that the latter explicitly allows for plaintiff to recover for defendant's future use of plaintiff's trade secret, even when the defendant has already materially changed defendant's position in reliance on such information. *See* UTSA § 3 cmt.

Uniform Act

The UTSA codifies the common law rule that one who acquires a trade secret by accident, mistake, or from a third party without knowledge that such person was under a duty not to use or disclose the information in dispute owes no duty to plaintiff until put on actual or constructive notice of plaintiff's rights.

The following state statutes differ slightly from the UTSA: Va. Code. Ann. § 59.1-336 (1995), and Wis. Stat. § 134.90 (1995) (these acts impose liability if when defendant used or disclosed trade secret, defendant knew, or had reason to know, that it acquired its knowledge of trade secret by accident or mistake; irrelevant whether defendant's disclosure or use was before or after defendant materially changed defendant's position); Or. Rev. Stat. § 646.461(2) (1988) (Oregon statute does not discuss liability for disclosure or use of trade secret acquired by accident or mistake).

8.05 Wrongful Use or Disclosure

You must determine whether defendant wrongfully used or wrongfully disclosed the trade secret in question.

A defendant who has acquired trade secret information by improper means has no right to use or to disclose the information in any way whatever. Thus, any use or disclosure by a defendant who has acquired a trade secret by improper means is wrongful.

A defendant who originally acquired information through a confidential relationship may not disclose such information in any way that goes beyond the scope of authorization it received from plaintiff regarding use and disclosure. That is, a person receiving trade secret information in confidence may use or disclose the information only in strict accordance with the understanding under which the information was given to the person. Any other use or disclosure is wrongful.

A person who comes into possession of trade secret information without realizing that it has been, for example, acquired through improper means, or who acquires the information by mistake or accident not having reason to believe that it belongs to another, is authorized to use that information only as long as the person does not know, and does not have reason to know, that the information in fact belongs to another. Hence a defendant who has acquired trade secret information in a manner that does not give rise to liability initially is nonetheless liable for the use or disclosure of that information *after* defendant is informed or is put on notice by other facts that it has acquired trade secret information that rightfully belongs to plaintiff.

Comment

A defendant who has acquired plaintiff's trade secret information by mistake or accident, or without knowledge of a third party's use of improper means or breach of a confidential relationship, is not liable for any use or disclosure of a trade secret before receiving actual or constructive notice of plaintiff's rights in the information. As noted in comments to the preceding instruction, when defendant has already materially changed defendant's position in detrimental reliance before receiving such notice, to the extent that to subject defendant to liability would be inequitable, then defendant is also immune to liability for defendant's future use or disclosure. *See Restatement* § 758. *See also* § 8.04[3] cmt., *supra.* Because the questions of whether defendant changes its position in material reliance before receiving notice, and whether it would be inequitable to hold defendant liable for future use and disclosure under such circumstances are more appropriate for a judge than a jury, they have been excluded from these jury instructions.

Restatement

In contrast to the UTSA, under which mere acquisition of a trade secret is actionable, the *Restatement* requires a finding of use or disclosure by defendant, or that defendant will likely use or disclose plaintiff's trade secret in the future, to impose liability on defendant. *See Hunter v. Fisons Corp.,* 776 F.2d 1 (5th Cir. 1985) (holding existence of trade secret or confidential relationship immaterial if defendant did not use information); *Abraham Zion Corp. v. Lebow,* 593 F. Supp. 551 (S.D.N.Y. 1984) (holding plaintiff must prove commercial use by defendant to establish liability), *aff'd,* 761 F.2d 93 (2d Cir. 1985); 2 *Milgrim, supra,* § 7.07[1], at 7-225 (noting that "even disclosure to defendant in a legally protectable relationship of an established trade secret, without more, is not grounds for relief," because plaintiff must still prove use or disclosure).

8.06 Compensatory Damages

If you find that defendant is liable to plaintiff for its conduct, then you should consider whether plaintiff has suffered monetary damages as a result. You should address the issue of damages, however, only if you first determine that defendant is liable to plaintiff on any of the bases we have discussed previously.

As with issues of liability, the plaintiff has the burden to prove to you that it has suffered harm due to the wrongful conduct of defendant. I will discuss with you three potential ways to approach such damages: (1) profits lost by plaintiff, (2) benefits gained by defendant, or (3) a reasonable royalty.

Let me now go over each of these alternatives.

8.06[1] Plaintiff's Lost Profits

Plaintiff claims that it has lost profits from misuse of trade secrets. If you find that plaintiff would have realized profits from employing trade secrets in its business that it has lost due to the wrongful conduct of defendant, then you may measure damages by the amount of such lost profits for the particular periods of time that I will cover with you in a moment.

Comment

See comments following instructions relating to all damages instructions.

8.06[2] Defendant's Benefit

You may also consider what benefit defendant has gained from misuse of plaintiff's trade secrets. Regardless of whether you find that plaintiff itself suffered losses, if you find that defendant benefited from using a trade secret belonging to plaintiff, then you may award the monetary value that you attribute to those benefits as the measure of plaintiff's damage.

[*Restatement* Only]

Plaintiff is entitled to recover the greater of (1) plaintiff's own lost profits, or (2) defendant's gained profits.

These are, however, alternative approaches to damages, not cumulative measures of damages. Therefore, you may award damages, if you were to find damages, based on only one of these alternative approaches; that is, plaintiff's lost profits *or* defendant's gained benefits, but you may not award *both* types of damages.

[Uniform Act Only]

These two approaches to damages are different in some respects but may also overlap. That is, it may be that defendant profited from particular sales that plaintiff would have made had defendant not competed using the trade secrets.

In that situation, the two ways of approaching damages that I have just described would measure the identical damages—whether viewed as plaintiff's loss or defendant's gain. The law does not permit a plaintiff to recover twice for the same damages. Thus you may include as damages *both* plaintiff's lost profits *and* defendant's gain *only* if and to the extent that they do not overlap in this way. Stated in other words, if you were to include lost sales in calculating plaintiff's lost profits because defendant made the sales, then the value of those same sales should be excluded from any calculation of defendant's gains that you may make.

Comment

See comments following instructions relating to all damages instructions.

8.06[3] Royalties

[*Restatement* Only]

There is a third way to measure damages, which you may use if you find that plaintiff has been or will likely be damaged but when you cannot fairly determine plaintiff's losses or defendant's gains. In that event, you may measure damages by assessing a reasonable royalty.

[Uniform Act Only]

Plaintiff is claiming damages in the form of a royalty.

You may measure damages in terms of a royalty, but only if you find that plaintiff has presented evidence of what a reasonable royalty would be. Furthermore, a royalty can be awarded only to cover the time period during which damages would accrue, which I will discuss with you in a moment.

Some of the factors you may consider in determining the amount of a reasonable royalty include such things as

(1) the price that past purchasers or licensees have paid for use of the trade secret;
(2) the total value of the secret to plaintiff, including its development costs, if any;
(3) the uses for the information that the defendant had in mind; and
(4) the time and effort that would have been required before the defendant or another competitor could have acquired or likely acquired the same or equivalent information through proper means.

Comment

See comments following instructions relating to all damages instructions.

8.06[4] Time Period for Damages

Plaintiff would be entitled to damages running only for as long as (1) you find that its trade secret would be entitled to protection, plus (2) an additional period, if any, that you find that the trade secret afforded defendant a competitive advantage, such as providing defendant a head start in its business.

Comment Regarding Damage Instructions Generally

It is important to keep in mind that unlike the UTSA, the *Restatement* takes an either/or approach to measuring damages—either plaintiff's lost profits, or defendant's gains. The *Restatement* treats royalty damages as an alternative to both measures, available only if neither plaintiff's lost profits nor defendant's gain can be shown. By contrast, the UTSA allows the plaintiff to choose royalty damages regardless of what else can be proved. Hence the actual types of proof offered at trial may well dictate modifications to these instructions.

Many cases refer to damages suffered by plaintiff in terms of lost profits, and that phrase is used in these instructions. However, in some jurisdictions, plaintiff's damages might better be described in terms of "losses," to calculate not only lost profits but also detriments such as loss of direct overhead and general and administrative expenses resulting from defendant's misappropriation. 2 *Milgrim, supra,* § 7.08[3], at 7-386 (citations omitted). Likewise, as for defendant's illicit gains, many cases speak in terms of "unjust enrichment," and some speak of "profits." The model instructions describe these concepts as "gains" or "benefits," terms more likely to be meaningful to a juror.

Similarly, the measure of a reasonable royalty will vary from jurisdiction to jurisdiction, and practitioners are advised to review the standards adopted by their jurisdictions. The list of factors cited in the instruction on a reasonable royalty is not meant to be comprehensive; rather, it is a collection of the more common measures of a reasonable royalty that courts have approved.

Of course, lost profits, unjust enrichment, gains, or other benefits are not consistently applied concepts from jurisdiction to jurisdiction, and may be subject to differing standards under various state laws. For example: What costs should be deducted from gross revenues to calculate lost profit damages? Who has the burden of proving the deductions from gross revenues that are appropriate to calculate defendants' gains? Care should be given to use terms that are accepted in the particular jurisdiction.

The generally less stringent burden imposed on a plaintiff when proving damages, as opposed to proving liability, will also vary by jurisdiction and has accordingly not been covered.

Restatement

For examples of cases discussing the *Restatement* approach, see the following: *Curtiss-Wright Corp. v. Edel-Brown Tool & Die Co.*, 407 N.E.2d 319 (Mass. 1980) (holding that higher amount of plaintiff's profits or defendant's unjust enrichment is proper measure of damages); *Jet Spray Cooler, Inc. v. Crampton*, 385 N.E.2d 1349 (Mass. 1979) (plaintiff not entitled to both profits made by defendant and plaintiff's own profits); *Telex Corp. v. Int'l Business Mach. Corp.*, 510 F.2d 894, 893 (10th Cir.) (plaintiff entitled to its own lost profits or defendant's unjust enrichment), *cert. dismissed*, 423 U.S. 802 (1975); *Sperry Rand Corp. v. A-T-O, Inc.*, 447 F.2d 1387, 1392–93 (4th Cir. 1971) (plaintiff may recover either from lost profits or accounting of defendant's unjust enrichment); *Hayes-Albion v. Kuberski*, 311 N.W.2d 122 (Mich. Ct. App. 1981) (holding damages for misappropriation may be measured by profits lost by plaintiff or profits gained by defendant); *Wiebold Studio, Inc. v. Old World Restorations, Inc.*, 484 N.E.2d 280 (Ohio Ct. App. 1985) (either plaintiff's lost profits or defendant's unjust enrichment appropriate measure of damages); *Molex, Inc. v. Nolen*, 759 F.2d 474 (5th Cir. 1985) (reasonable royalty measure of damages remedy applied); *Univ. Computing Co. v. Lykes-Youngstown Corp.*, 504 F.2d 518, 538–39 (5th Cir. 1974) (listing factors to be considered to determine reasonable royalty measure of damages); *see also* William F. Johnson, *Remedies in Trade Secret Litigation,* 72 Nw. U. L. Rev. 1004, 1023 (1978); 2 *Milgrim, supra,* § 7.08[3], at 7-155; 2 R. Callman, *Unfair Competition, Trademarks and Monopolies* § 59.3, at 496 (3d ed. 1968); M.A. Rosenhouse, *Proper Measure and Elements of Damages for Misappropriation of Trade Secret,* 11 A.L.R. 4th 12 (1982).

As mentioned in earlier comments, under section 758 of the *Restatement,* damages are not awardable when someone, acting in good faith, pays value for the information without knowledge of a misappropriation, or materially changes his or her position before receiving notice—an exception to the common law rule. When imposing liability under such circumstances would be inequitable, both past and future use of the trade secret is permitted, as no tortious misappropriation has taken place.

Uniform Act

The following states' statutes vary slightly from the UTSA or contain greater detail: Ala. Code § 8-27-4(1)(b), (c) (1993) provides for monetary damages equal to defendant's profits and any other benefits to defendant attributable to misappropriation *and* plaintiff's actual damages resulting from misappropriation, if actual damages not duplicative of defendant's profits; to prove defendant's profits, plaintiff must present proof of defendant's gross revenues; defendant then has burden of proving its deductible expenses and other elements of profit not attributable to misappropriation); *see also Alabama G.S.R. Co. v. Morrison,* 202 So. 2d 155 (Ala. 1967); *Telex Corp. v. Int'l Business Mach. Corp.,* 510 F.2d 894, (10th Cir.), *cert. dismissed,* 423 U.S. 802 (1975) (Alabama act follows common law precedent in these cases); Or. Rev. Stat. § 646.465(2) (1988) (provides for actual loss and unjust enrichment; however, total amount of damages shall not be less than amount of reasonable royalty); Wis. Stat. § 134.90(4) (1989 Supp. 1995) (court may award damages).

The *Restatement* instruction should be used for North Carolina. N.C. Gen. Stat. § 66-154(b), 66-154(a)(2) (1995) (damages either plaintiff's losses or defendant's unjust enrichment, whichever is greater; if defendant acquired trade secret mistakenly but in good faith, these damages cannot be awarded for period of defendant's innocent disclosure or use, although injunction may be granted).

Under the UTSA, a good faith acquirer who did not know or have reason to know that it had acquired another's misappropriated trade secret, and who changed its position in material reliance on the "secret" information it received, may not be liable for monetary damages if the imposition of money damages would be inequitable. However, if the acquirer receives notice that the information was misappropriated and continues to misappropriate the information, the acquirer may be liable to the owner for damages occurring after notice was received. *But see* N.C. Gen. Stat. § 66-154(a)(2) (1995) (reasonable royalty may be awarded by court if defendant acquired trade secret in good faith or by mistake and used trade secret to defendant's benefit).

Under some statutes, reasonable royalty damages are awarded by the court and are available only if neither plaintiff's lost profits nor defendant's unjust enrichment can be proven. *See.* Cal. Civ. Code § 3426.3(b) (1996); Ga. Code Ann. § 10-1-763(a)(1995); Ill. Rev. Stat. ch. 765, para. 4(a) (1996); Ind. Code § 24-2-3-4(b) (1996). *See also* Va. Code Ann. § 59.1-338 (1995) (allows for award of reasonable royalty if such amount greater than any other provable measure of damages); Wis. Stat. § 134.90(4) (1995) (provides for reasonable royalty award to be awarded by court, if this sum is greatest provable amount of damages).

The Alabama, Alaska, Arkansas, Connecticut, Delaware, Idaho, Louisiana, Minnesota, Montana, North Dakota, and Washington acts *do not* provide for a reasonable royalty measure of damages.

8.07 Exemplary Damages [No model instructions provided.]

Comment

Depending on whether plaintiff is pursuing a trade secrets claim based on a contract or tort theory of recovery, plaintiff may be able to recover exemplary or punitive damages. Although generally not awarded in contract actions, punitive damages are available in many states under tort theories. Often the standard for punitive damages under a tort theory of trade secret misappropriation will be whether the defendant acted willfully and maliciously in misappropriating plaintiff's trade secret. The measure of punitive damages available to plaintiff varies from state to state, and practitioners are advised to review the standard for the particular state involved. *See, e.g., Reinforced Molding Corp. v. Gen. Elec. Co.,* 592 F. Supp. 1083 (W.D. Pa. 1984) (holding outrageous or egregious conduct required for punitive damages); *Molex, Inc. v. Nolen,* 759 F.2d 474 (5th Cir. 1985) (exemplary damages appropriate when defendant's misappropriations maliciously, wantonly, or oppressively done); *Gen. Aniline & Film Corp. v. Frantz,* 272 N.Y.S.2d 600 (N.Y. App. Div. 1966) (holding punitive damages justified for misappropriation of trade secrets when individual defendants committed willful and intentional breaches of confidence and acted in wanton disregard of plaintiff's property rights), *modification denied,* 274 N.Y.S.2d 634 (N.Y. App. Div. 1966); *W. R. Grace & Co. v. Hargadine,* 392 F.2d 9 (6th Cir. 1968) (holding exemplary damages appropriate under Ohio law for sufficiently malicious misappropriation of trade secrets); *Hayes-Albion v. Kuberski,* 311 N.W.2d 122 (Mich. Ct. App. 1981). *See generally* M.A. Rosenhouse, *Proper Measure and Elements of Damages for Misappropriation of Trade Secret,* 11 A.L.R.4th 12 § 36 (1982); 2 *Milgrim, supra,* § 7.08[3][c], at 7.401–05).

Uniform Act

Under the UTSA, the *court* may grant exemplary damages, not exceeding double the compensatory damages. UTSA § (b). Hence, there would be no jury instruction given. Nonetheless, some state statutes allow the jury to grant such damages. *See, e.g.,* Colo. Rev. Stat. § 7-74-104(2) (1995) (court or *jury* may award exemplary damages, not to exceed monetary damages awarded); N.C. Gen. Stat. § 66-154(c) (1995) ("trier of fact" has discretion to award punitive damages). Two states, Alabama and Oregon, do not specify whether the court or the jury may award damages. Ala. Code § 8-27-4 (1993); Or. Rev. Stat. § 646.465(3) (1988). All state statutes provide for exemplary damages, except for Arkansas, Louisiana, and Nebraska.

The amount of exemplary damages that may be awarded may vary. *See, e.g.,* Ala. Code § 8-27-4 (1993) (exemplary damages cannot exceed amount awarded for lost profits or other monetary damages, but shall not be less than $5,000); Minn. Stat. § 325C.04 (1996) (court may award exemplary damages in amount it deems just and equitable); Miss. Code Ann. § 75-36-7(2) (1995) and Mont. Code Ann. § 30-14-404 (1995) (no limit on exemplary damages specified); N.C. Gen. Stat. § 66-153(c) (1995) (trier of fact has discretion to award exemplary damages).

Jury Instructions Resource Bibliography

Amy Pavlik*

Most states have jury instructions that are generally accepted by the state courts. The form of title and the status of these instructions—whether that be official or unofficial approval by a judicial body, or even just widespread recognition—varies substantially. A few federal courts have also compiled jury instructions, and several compilations of specialty jury instructions exist as well. The following list includes the most recent editions of published jury instructions.

A. States

Alabama

Alabama Pattern Jury Instructions, Civil—Second Edition. Alabama Pattern Jury Instructions Committee, Civil. Rochester, N.Y.: Lawyers Cooperative Publishing Co., 1993.

Pattern Jury Instructions—Criminal—Third Edition. Alabama Law Institute, edited by Judge Joseph A. Colquitt. Tuscaloosa: University of Alabama, Alabama Bar Institute for Continuing Legal Education, and Administrative Office of Courts, 1994 (supplemented).

Alaska

Alaska Pattern Civil Jury Instructions. Harvey S. Perlman. Anchorage: Alaska Bar Association, 1984 (supplemented).

Alaska Pattern Jury Instructions, Criminal—1987 Revisions. Criminal Pattern Jury Instruction Committee. Anchorage: Alaska Bar Association, 1987.

Arizona

Recommended Arizona Jury Instructions, Civil—Second Edition. Civil Jury Instructions Committee, Hon. E. G. Noyes Jr., chairman. Phoenix: State Bar of Arizona, 1991.

---

*Amy Pavlik is a librarian at the Chicago-Kent College of Law in Chicago, Illinois.

Recommended Arizona Jury Instructions, Criminal. Criminal Jury Instruction Committee, Rudolph J. Gerber, chairman. Phoenix: State Bar of Arizona, 1989.

Arkansas

Arkansas Model Jury Instructions, Civil. Arkansas Supreme Court Committee on Jury Instructions, Civil, Winslow Drummond, chairman. St. Paul: West Publishing Co., 1989.

Arkansas Model Jury Instructions, Criminal—Second Edition. Arkansas Supreme Court Committee on Jury Instructions. Charlottesville, Va.: Michie Co., 1994.

California

BAJI Forms—California Jury Instructions, Civil—Eighth Edition. Committee on Standard Jury Instructions, Civil, of the Superior Court of Los Angeles County, California. Paul G. Breckenridge Jr. St. Paul: West Publishing Co., 1995 (supplemented).

CALJIC Forms—California Jury Instructions, Criminal—Fifth Edition. Committee on Standard Jury Instructions, Criminal, of the Superior Court of Los Angeles County, California. St. Paul: West Publishing Co., 1989 (supplemented).

California Jury Instructions—Misdemeanor (CALJIC). Committee on Misdemeanor Jury Instructions of the Superior Court of Los Angeles County, California. Philip H. Richards. St. Paul: West Publishing Co., 1971 (supplemented).

Colorado

Colorado Jury Instructions, Civil—Third Edition. Colorado Supreme Court Committee on Civil Jury Instructions. San Francisco: Bancroft-Whitney Co., 1989 (supplemented).

Colorado Jury Instructions, Criminal—Revised as of January 1, 1983. Colorado Supreme Court Committee on Criminal Jury Instructions. St. Paul: West Publishing Co., 1983 (supplemented).

Connecticut

Connecticut Jury Instructions (Civil)—Fourth Edition. Douglass B. Wright and William L. Ankerman. West Hartford: Atlantic Law Book Co., 1993.

Connecticut Criminal Jury Instructions. David M. Borden and Leonard Orland. St. Paul: West Publishing Co., 1986.

Delaware

Delaware Criminal Code: Pattern Jury Instructions. Committee on Pattern Jury Instructions, Joseph T. Walsh, Associate Judge, Superior Court, chairman. Wilmington: Committee on Pattern Jury Instructions, 1974.

District of Columbia

Standardized Jury Instructions for the District of Columbia—Revised Edition. District of Columbia Bar Association, Young Lawyers Section. Washington, D.C.: Bar Association of the District of Columbia: 1985.

Criminal Jury Instructions, District of Columbia—Fourth Edition. Young Lawyers Section, Bar Association of the District of Columbia. Washington, D.C.: Young Lawyers Section, Bar Association of the District of Columbia, 1993.

Florida

Florida Standard Jury Instructions in Civil Cases. Supreme Court Committee on Standard Jury Instructions in Civil Cases. Tallahassee: Florida Bar Association, 1986 (supplemented).

Florida Standard Jury Instructions in Criminal Cases. Supreme Court Committee on Standard Jury Instructions in Criminal Cases. Tallahassee: Florida Bar Association, 1981 (supplemented).

Standard Jury Instructions in Misdemeanor Cases. Conference of County Court Judges, Criminal Law Reform and Rules Committee. Orlando: Conference of County Court Judges, Criminal Law Reform and Rules Committee, 1991.

Georgia

Suggested Pattern Jury Instructions—Third Edition. Council of Superior Court Judges of Georgia. Athens: Carl Vinson Institute of Government, University of Georgia, 1991 (supplemented).

Hawaii

Hawaii Standard Jury Instructions, Criminal. Hawaii Supreme Court. Honolulu: Hawaii Supreme Court, 1991.

Idaho

Idaho Jury Instructions—1988 Edition. Idaho Pattern Jury Instruction Committee, Robert C. Huntley, chairman. Boise: Idaho Law Foundation, 1988.

Illinois

Illinois Pattern Jury Instructions, Civil—Third Edition. Illinois Supreme Court Committee on Jury Instructions in Civil Cases. St. Paul: West Publishing Co., 1990 (supplemented).

Illinois Pattern Jury Instructions, Criminal—Third Edition. Illinois Supreme Court Committee on Jury Instructions in Criminal Cases, James B. Haddad, former chairman, Robert J. Steigmann, chairman. St. Paul: West Publishing Co., 1992.

Illinois Non-Pattern Jury Instructions—Second Edition. Carl L. Rowley and John M. Moyers. Rochester, N.Y.: Lawyers Cooperative Publishing, 1991 (supplemented).

Indiana

Indiana Pattern Jury Instructions, Civil—Second Edition. Indiana Judges Association. Charlottesville, Va.: Michie Co., 1989 (supplemented).

Indiana Pattern Jury Instructions, Criminal—Second Edition. Indiana Judges Association. Charlottesville, Va.: Michie Co., 1991 (supplemented).

Iowa

Iowa Civil Jury Instructions. Iowa State Bar Association, Special Committee on Uniform Court Instructions. Des Moines: Iowa State Bar Association, 1987 (supplemented).

Iowa Criminal Jury Instructions. Iowa State Bar Association, Special Committee on Uniform Court Instructions. Des Moines: Iowa State Bar Association, 1988 (supplemented).

Kansas

Pattern Instructions for Kansas, Criminal (3d). Kansas Judicial Council Advisory Committee on Criminal Jury Instructions. Topeka: Kansas Judicial Council Advisory Committee on Criminal Jury Instructions, 1993.

Kentucky

Kentucky Instructions to Juries: A text on the Law Relating to Instructions to Juries in Civil and Criminal Cases, with Forms of Instruction and Notes of Cases Bearing on Such Instructions—Fourth Revised Edition. William S. Cooper. Cincinnati: Anderson Publishing Co., 1993 (supplemented).

Louisiana

Louisiana Jury Instructions—Third Edition. Louisiana Association of Defense Counsel. Baton Rouge: Louisiana Association of Defense Counsel, 1989.

Criminal Jury Instructions. Cheyney C. Joseph Jr. and P. Raymond Lamonica. St. Paul: West Publishing Co., 1994.

Maine

Maine Jury Instruction Manual—Second Edition. Donald G. Alexander. Portland: Tower Publishing Co., 1990 (supplemented).

Maryland

Maryland Civil Pattern Jury Instructions—Third Edition. Maryland State Bar Association, Inc., Standing Committee on Civil Pattern Jury Instructions. Baltimore: Maryland Institute for Continuing Professional Education of Lawyers, 1993.

Maryland Civil Jury Instructions and Commentary. Rosalyn B. Bell. Charlottesville, Va.: Michie Co., 1993.

Maryland Criminal Pattern Jury Instructions. Maryland State Bar Association, Inc., Committee on Criminal Pattern Jury

Instructions. Baltimore: Maryland Institute for Continuing Professional Education of Lawyers, 1991 (supplemented).

Maryland Criminal Jury Instructions and Commentary—Second Edition. David E. Aaronson. Charlottesville, Va.: Michie Co., 1988.

Massachusetts

Model Jury Instructions for Use in the District Court—1995 Edition. Commonwealth of Massachusetts, District Court Department of the Trial Court. Salem, MA: Administrative Office of the District Court, 1995 (supplemented).

Jury Instructions for Civil Trials: What to Tell the Jury. John O. Mirick, chair, et al. Boston: MCLE, 1995.

Michigan

Michigan Standard Jury Instructions, Civil—Second Edition. Michigan Supreme Court Committee on Standard Jury Instructions. Ann Arbor: Institute for Continuing Legal Education, 1981 (supplemented).

Michigan Criminal Jury Instructions—Second Edition. Michigan State Bar Standing Committee on Standard Criminal Jury Instructions, Timothy K. McMorrow, reporter 1987–89, Judge Randy L. Tahvonen, reporter 1989–90. Ann Arbor: Institute of Continuing Legal Education, 1989 (supplemented).

Minnesota

Minnesota Practice includes jury instructions in volumes 4 and 10.

Mississippi

Mississippi Model Jury Instructions, Civil—Second Edition. Mississippi Judicial College, a Division of the Mississippi Law Center. St. Paul: West Publishing Co., 1992 (supplemented).

Mississippi Model Jury Instructions, Criminal—Second Edition. Mississippi Judicial College, a Division of the University of Mississippi Law Center. St. Paul: West Publishing Co., 1992 (supplemented).

Missouri

Missouri Approved Jury Instructions—Fourth Edition. Missouri Supreme Court Committee on Jury Instructions. St. Paul: West Publishing Co., 1991.

Montana

Montana Pattern Jury Instructions, Civil. Montana Supreme Court Commission on Civil Jury Instructions. Helena: State Bar of Montana, 1987.

Montana Criminal Jury Instructions (MCJI). Montana Supreme Court Commission on Criminal Jury Instructions. Helena: State Bar of Montana, 1990.

Nebraska

Nebraska Jury Instructions, Civil—Second Edition. Nebraska Supreme Court Committee on Civil Practice and Procedure. St. Paul: West Publishing Co., 1992 (supplemented).

Nebraska Jury Instructions, Criminal—Second Edition. Nebraska Supreme Court Committee on Criminal Practice and Procedure. St. Paul: West Publishing Co., 1992 (supplemented).

Nevada

Nevada Pattern Jury Instructions, Civil. Jerry Carr Whitehead and Richard Edward Thornley. Charlottesville, Va.: Michie Co., 1986.

New Hampshire

New Hampshire Civil Jury Instructions—Revised Edition. Walter L. Murphy and Danel C. Pope. Orford, N.H.: Equity Publishing Co., 1992.

New Hampshire Criminal Jury Instructions. New Hampshire Bar Association, Criminal Justice Section. Concord: New Hampshire Bar Association, 1985.

New Jersey

Model Jury Charges, Civil—Fourth Edition. New Jersey Supreme Court Committee on Model Jury Charges, Civil. New

Brunswick, N.J.: New Jersey Institute for Continuing Legal Education, 1992.

Model Jury Charges, Criminal—Third Edition. New Jersey Institute for Continuing Legal Education. New Brunswick, N.J.: New Jersey Institute for Continuing Legal Education, 1990 (supplemented).

New Mexico

Uniform Jury Instructions, Civil. New Mexico Supreme Court. Charlottesville, Va.: Michie Co., 1991 (supplemented).

Uniform Jury Instructions, Criminal.. New Mexico Supreme Court. Charlottesville, Va.: Michie Co., 1978 (supplemented).

New Mexico Statutes, Judicial Volumes contain jury instructions for civil and criminal cases.

New York

New York Pattern Jury Instructions, Civil—Second Edition. Committee on Pattern Jury Instructions, Association of Supreme Court Justices, Bernard S. Mayer, chairman. Rochester: Lawyers Cooperative Publishing Co., 1974 (supplemented).

Criminal Jury Instructions, New York (CJI)—Second Edition. Committee on Criminal Jury Instructions of the Office of Court Administration of the State of New York. New York: Office of Court Administration, 1995 (supplemented).

Criminal Jury Instructions, New York (CJI Misdemeanors)—First Edition. Committee on Criminal Jury Instructions of the Office of Court Administration, the Supreme Court Justices Association, and the County Judges Association of the State of New York. New York: Office of Court Administration, 1981 (supplemented).

North Carolina

North Carolina Pattern Jury Instructions for Civil Cases. North Carolina Conference of Superior Court Judges, Committee on Pattern Jury Instructions. Raleigh: North Carolina Conference of Superior Court Judges, 1975 (supplemented).

North Carolina Pattern Jury Instructions for Criminal Cases. North Carolina Conference of Superior Court Judges, Committee on Pattern Jury Instructions. Raleigh: The Conference, 1982 (supplemented).

North Carolina Pattern Jury Instructions for Motor Vehicle Negligence. North Carolina Conference of Superior Court Judges, Committee on Pattern Jury Instructions. Raleigh: The North Carolina Conference of Superior Court Judges, 1978.

North Dakota

North Dakota Pattern Jury Instructions, Civil. State Bar Association of North Dakota. Bismarck: State Bar Association of North Dakota, 1986 (supplemented).

North Dakota Pattern Jury Instructions, Criminal. State Bar Association of North Dakota. Bismarck: State Bar Association of North Dakota, 1985.

Ohio

Ohio Jury Instructions: A Collection of Standard Jury Instructions in Civil and Criminal Cases. Jury Instructions Committee of the Ohio Judicial Conference. Cincinnati: Anderson Publishing Co., 1993 (supplemented).

Jury Instructions for the Penalty Phase. Ohio Public Defender Commission and the Ohio Death Penalty Task Force of the Ohio Criminal Defense Lawyers Association. Columbus: Ohio Death Penalty Task Force, 1983.

Oklahoma

Oklahoma Uniform Jury Instructions, Civil—Second Edition. Oklahoma Supreme Court Committee for Uniform Civil Jury Instructions. Oklahoma City: Oklahoma Bar Association, 1993.

Oklahoma Uniform Jury Instructions, Criminal. Commission on Oklahoma Uniform Jury Instructions, Criminal. Norman: Oklahoma Center for Criminal Justice, 1981.

Oregon

Oregon Jury Instructions for Civil Cases—1993 Revision. Oregon State Bar, Committee on Uniform Civil Jury Instructions. Lake Oswego: Oregon State Bar, 1993 (supplemented).

Oregon Jury Instructions for Criminal Cases—1994 Revision. Oregon State Bar, Committee on Uniform Criminal Jury Instructions. Lake Oswego: Oregon State Bar, Continuing Legal Education, 1994 (supplemented).

Pennsylvania

Pennsylvania Suggested Standard Jury Instructions, Civil. Civil Instructions Subcommittee of the Pennsylvania Supreme Court Committee for Proposed Standard Jury Instructions. Harrisburg: Pennsylvania Bar Institute, 1981 (supplemented).

Pennsylvania Suggested Standard Jury Instructions, Criminal. Criminal Instructions Subcommittee of the Pennsylvania Supreme Court Committee for Proposed Standard Jury Instructions. Harrisburg: Pennsylvania Bar Institute, 1979 (supplemented).

Rhode Island.

None.

South Carolina

Jury Instructions for Criminal Cases in South Carolina. F. Patrick Hubbard. Columbia, S.C.: South Carolina Bar Continuing Legal Education, 1994 (supplemented).

South Dakota

South Dakota Pattern Jury Instructions, Civil. Committee on Pattern Jury Instructions, State Bar of South Dakota. Pierre: State Bar of South Dakota, 1988 (supplemented).

South Dakota Pattern Jury Instructions, Criminal. State Bar of South Dakota. Pierre: State Bar of South Dakota, 1987 (supplemented).

Tennessee

Tennessee Pattern Jury Instructions, Civil—Second Edition. Committee on Pattern Jury Instructions, Civil, of the Tennessee Judicial Conference, June F. Entman, reporter. St. Paul: West Publishing Co., 1988.

Tennessee Pattern Jury Instructions, Criminal—Third Edition. Committee on Pattern Jury Instructions, Criminal, of the Tennessee Judicial Conference, Jean A. Stone, reporter. St. Paul: West Publishing Co., 1992.

Texas

Texas Pattern Jury Charges—Second Edition. Committee on Pattern Jury Charges of the State Bar of Texas. Austin: The State Bar of Texas, 1987 (supplemented).

Texas Criminal Pattern Jury Charges. Committee on Criminal Pattern Jury Charges of the State Bar of Texas. Austin: State Bar of Texas, 1975.

Texas Court Charges, Banking and Debtor/Creditor. Will G. Barber, editor. Austin: Butterworth Legal Publishers, 1992.

Texas Court Charges, Commercial Contracts. Will G. Barber, editor. Austin: Butterworth Legal Publishers, 1992.

Texas Court Charges, Commercial Torts and DTPA. Will G. Barber, editor. Austin: Butterworth Legal Publishers, 1992.

Texas Court Charges, Insurance. Will G. Barber, editor. Austin: Butterworth Legal Publishers, 1992.

Texas Court Charges, Labor and Employment. Will G. Barber, editor. Austin: Butterworth Legal Publishers, 1992.

Texas Court Charges, Negligence Actions. Will G. Barber, editor. Austin: Butterworth Legal Publishers, 1992.

Texas Court Charges, Probate and Family Law. Will G. Barber, editor. Austin: Butterworth Legal Publishers, 1992.

Texas Court Charges, Real Property and Landlord-Tenant. Will G. Barber, editor. Austin: Butterworth Legal Publishers, 1992.

Utah

Model Utah Jury Instructions, Civil—1993 Edition. Utah State Bar. Charlottesville, Va.: Michie Co., 1993.

Vermont

Standard Jury Instructions. Vermont Trial Lawyers Association. Montpelier: Vermont Trial Lawyers Association, 1992.

Virginia

Model Jury Instructions in Virginia, Civil—1988 Replacement Edition. Model Jury Instructions Committee, J. Aubrey Matthews, chairman, Kenneth R. Redden, reporter. Charlottesville, Va: Michie Co., 1988 (supplemented).

Virginia Model Jury Instructions, Criminal—1989 Replacement Edition. Model Jury Instructions Committee, J. Aubrey Matthews, chairman, Kenneth R. Redden, reporter. Charlottesville, Va.: Michie Co., 1989 (supplemented).

Virginia Jury Instructions—Second Edition. Emanual Emroch, L. Paul Byrne, and Michael J. Herbert. St. Paul: West Publishing Co., 1990.

Washington

Washington Pattern Jury Instructions, Civil—Third Edition. Washington Supreme Court Committee on Jury Instructions, Hon. George T. Shields, chairman. St. Paul: West Publishing Co., 1989.

Washington Pattern Jury Instructions, Criminal—Second Edition. Washington Supreme Court Committee on Jury Instructions. St. Paul: West Publishing Co., 1994.

West Virginia

West Virginia Criminal Jury Instructions—Third Edition. Elizabeth Zuccari Murphy. Charleston: Criminal Law Research Center, West Virginia Public Defender Services, 1994.

Wisconsin

Wisconsin Jury Instructions, Civil. Wisconsin Civil Jury Instructions Committee for the Wisconsin Judicial Conference. Madison: University of Wisconsin—Extension, Department of Law, 1981 (supplemented).

Wisconsin Jury Instructions, Criminal. Wisconsin Criminal Jury Instructions Committee. Madison: University of Wisconsin Law School, 1988 (supplemented).

Wyoming

Wyoming Civil Pattern Jury Instructions—Revised April 1994. Civil Jury Instructions Committee of the Wyoming State Bar. Cheyenne: Wyoming State Bar, 1994.

Wyoming Pattern Jury Instructions, Criminal (WPJIC). Wyoming Pattern Jury Instructions Committee. Laramie: Wyoming Pattern Jury Instructions Committee, 1978.

B. Federal Courts

5th Circuit

Pattern Jury Instructions, Civil Cases—1995 Edition. Committee on Pattern Jury Instructions, District Judges Association, Fifth Circuit. St. Paul: West Publishing Co., 1995.

Pattern Jury Instructions, Criminal Cases, with Case Annotations. Committee on Pattern Jury Instructions, District Judges Association, Fifth Circuit. St. Paul: West Publishing Co., 1990.

6th Circuit

Pattern Jury Instructions, Criminal Cases, with Case Annotations, Committee on Pattern Jury Instructions, District Judges Association, Sixth Circuit. St. Paul: West Publishing Co., 1991.

8th Circuit

Manual of Model Civil Jury Instructions for the District Courts of the Eighth Circuit—1995 Edition. Committee on Model Jury Instructions Within the Eighth Circuit. St. Paul: West Publishing Co., 1995.

Manual of Model Criminal Jury Instructions for the District Courts of the Eighth Circuit—1994 Edition. Committee on

Model Criminal Jury Instructions Within the Eighth Circuit. St. Paul: West Publishing Co., 1994.

9th Circuit

Manual of Model Civil Jury Instructions for the Ninth Circuit—1993 Edition. Committee on Model Jury Instructions, Ninth Circuit. St. Paul: West Publishing Co., 1993.

Manual of Model Criminal Jury Instructions for the District Courts of the Ninth Circuit—1995 Edition. Committee on Model Criminal Jury Instructions Within the Ninth Circuit. St. Paul: West Publishing Co., 1995.

11th Circuit

Pattern Jury Instructions, Civil Cases, with Annotations and Comments. Committee on Pattern Jury Instructions, District Judges Association, Eleventh Circuit. St. Paul: West Publishing Co., 1990.

Pattern Jury Instructions, Criminal Cases, with Annotations and Comments—1990 Edition. Committee on Pattern Jury Instructions, District Judges Association, Eleventh Circuit. St. Paul: West Publishing Co., 1990.

General

Federal Criminal Jury Instructions—Second Edition. Josephine R. Potuto, Stephen A. Saltzburg, and Harvey S. Perlman. Charlottesville, Va.: Michie Co., 1991.

Federal Jury Practice and Instructions. Edward J. Devitt, Charles B. Blackmar, and Michael A. Wolff. St. Paul: West Publishing Co., 1987.

Modern Federal Jury Instructions, Civil. Leonard B. Sand, John S. Siffert, Walter P. Laughlin, and Steven A. Reiss. New York: Matthew Bender, 1993.

Modern Federal Jury Instructions, Criminal. Federal Judicial Center, Fifth Circuit, Sixth Circuit, Seventh Circuit, Eighth Circuit, Ninth Circuit, Eleventh Circuit. New York: Matthew Bender, 1991.

C. Subject

Jury Instructions for Civil and Criminal RICO Cases, with Commentary. American Bar Association, Criminal Justice Section, RICO Cases Committee. Provo, Utah: Brigham Young University, 1987.

Jury Instructions for Contract Cases. Robert E. Kehoe. Chicago: Comerford and Boyd, 1995.

Jury Instructions in Automobile Negligence Actions–Second Edition. Graham Douthwaite and Ronald W. Eades. Charlottesville, Va.: Michie Co., 1991.

Jury Instructions in Criminal Antitrust Cases—1964–1976. American Bar Association, Section of Antitrust Law. Chicago: American Bar Association, 1978.

Jury Instructions in Criminal Antitrust Cases—1976–1980. American Bar Association, Section of Antitrust Law. Chicago: American Bar Association, 1982.

Jury Instructions in FELA Cases—1990 Revised Edition. Palisades, Calif.: National Association of Railroad Trial Counsel, 1990.

Jury Instructions in Intellectual Property Cases. Duane Burton. Denver: Big Foot Press, 1980 (supplemented).

Jury Instructions in Real Estate Litigation. Graham Douthwaite. Charlottesville, Va.: Michie Co., 1991.

Jury Instructions on Damages in Tort Actions—Third Edition. Ronald W. Eades. Charlottesville, Va.: Michie Co. 1993.

Jury Instructions on Medical Issues—4th Edition. Graham Douthwaite. Charlottesville, Va.: Michie Co., 1992.

Jury Instructions on Products Liability. Graham Douthwaite. Charlottesville, Va.: Michie Co., 1987.

Jury Instructions on Products Liability—Second Edition. Ronald W. Eades. Charlottesville, Va.: Michie Co., 1993.

Model Jury Instructions: Business Torts Litigation—Third Edition. Business Torts Litigation Committee, Subcommittee on Jury Instructions, Section of Litigation, American Bar Association. Chicago: American Bar Association, 1996.

Model Jury Instructions—Public Offering Litigation. Christopher P. Hall. Chicago: American Bar Association, 1986.

Model Jury Instructions: Securities Litigation. American Bar Association, Section of Litigation, Securities Litigation Committee, Subcommittee on Accounting Issues. Chicago: American Bar Association, 1996.

Sample Civil RICO Jury Instructions. American Bar Association, Section of Antitrust Law, Private Antitrust Litigation Committee. Chicago: American Bar Association, 1994.

Sample Jury Instructions in Civil Antitrust Cases—1991 Edition. American Bar Association, Section of Antitrust Law. Chicago: American Bar Association, 1991.

Sample Jury Instructions in Criminal Antitrust Cases. American Bar Association, Section of Antitrust Law. Chicago: American Bar Association, 1984.